The Pursuit Of Freedom
An Inspiring, Two-Volume, Memoir Series

By
Mark Cass

Copyright 2020 © by Mark W. Cass
All Rights Reserved

Published by Up Your Averages Publishing
First Print Edition 2020
ISBN: # 978-1-64059-137-0

No part of this publication may be reproduced or distributed in print or electronic formats without permission by the author. Please respect the hard work of the author and do not participate in or encourage the piracy of copyrighted materials. Though these events did really occur, some of the names and locations have been changed to protect the author from legal liability.

Written by Mark Cass | MarkWCass.com
Front Cover Photo Kelly Howell
Back Cover Photo Anisity Rowe
Book Cover Design by, Tom Messina | TotalConcept.com
Thanks to Andrew Carlson for the ISBN's

Illustrations hand-drawn by Louis Civale an incredibly talented artist. Who remains trapped inside the 'Jungle'.
Expected release date 2023.

Other than when not, every word of this book is true.

Most of my life has been spent relentlessly pursuing Freedom. This is much of my story.

*- **Mark***

What People Are Saying

I found this book to be an incredibly fast read. Once I picked it up, I could not put it down. - **Louis C.**

I have known Mark for several years and am always amazed at his lively stories. I'm so glad he compiled them into one book. - **Clark B.**

A fun and informative read. At least one lesson learned per chapter. - **Fernando V.**

I knew Mark while he was living out the stories he tells in this book. Every word is true. Great read, better dude. – **Brock H.**

So much inspiration is packed inside these pages. Cannot believe this is not a movie already. - **Tony D.**

Never have I ever enjoyed reading a book as much as I have this one – It has everything. Thrilling and emotional stories, poetry, illustrations, photos. Like I said, Everything. – **Gary L.**

Do you know someone struggling in life to get a job, get clean, or just get ahead – Have them read this book. - **Linda W.**

I was sad to see this book end. Can not wait for his next one. – **Shobha P.**

Loved reading this book. I found myself crying, laughing, and cheering the whole way through. - **Lisa S.**

Book One: The Jungle
Dedications

Many people have helped me throughout my life and this book is presented together in two different volumes because my life has been lived out on two different planets. I am speaking figuratively, of course. But not really.

Book One: The Jungle, is dedicated to my many friends who have passed through the Correctional system, as well as the many who are still trapped there.

The Jungle is further dedicated to my family. Without whose unwavering support, I may not have even survived long enough to tell this tale. Further, book one is dedicated to anyone struggling to overcome a bad set of circumstances and anyone who may be wondering if there is a God; and to those who desire intimacy with Him.

Last but not least, I personally dedicate this book to Jeremy, Nick, Turtle, Jay, Cotton, Wendy, Uncle Tony, my Mom, my Dad, and to Chas Wilson who encouraged me to 'make my mess, my message.'

Book One: The Jungle

The Lesser of Two Evils   **12**
Jungle Stories   **26**
- This Too Shall Pass   27
- The Jungle   32
- The First Guy I Ever Seen Get Stabbed   38
- Heart Check   41
- Surprise Attack   45
- My Greatest Pain   48
- Learning to Be Appreciate   54
- Addict in The Box   60
- Hanging Out the Window   64
- The Night The Cops Gave My Weed Back   66
- Turning 21 In Confinement   72
- Son Of A Preacher   79
- Unanswered Prayers   85

Some of The Greatest People That I Ever Met   **93**
- Jeremy Spoken   96
- Reverend Nick   102
- Turtle   117
- Jay   124
- Cotton   129
- Wendy   136

The Rest of The Story   **140**
- Baker CI   141
- Baker Work Camp   159
- Washington CI   184
- Cross City CI   190
- Pompano Work Release   195
- Miami North Work Release   207

The Day I Got Out   **213**
Honorable Mentions   **223**
Six for The Road   **228**
End Book One   **237**

Book Two: Serial Entrepreneur

Book Two: Serial Entrepreneur	238
Dedications	239
Waking Up Free	240
The Next Few Days, Months, and A Year or Two or So	249
Dating, Relapse, & Marriage	263
Mr. Smith	271
Married to The System	275
Self-Employed	278
My Darkest Days	286
Building A Business	289
Mya	305
Top of The Page	311
Reinventing Myself	335
Marley	340
Changing Careers	348
Effective Marketing Solutions	351
Doing Things Differently	356
Back to Scrapping	366
Anisity	371
Blue Grey Marketing	373
Networking	378
Trusted with Leadership	381
Meeting Chas Wilson	387
Moving to Texas	392
Up Your Averages	393
Clemency Hearing 2019	397
A Hundred Thousand Dollar Yes or A Million Dollar No	415
Afterward	419
Other Books by Author	420

Illustrations
Drawn by Louis Civale

Welcome to The Jungle	25
This Too Shall Pass	30
Lonely Guy	32
Shower Fight	44
Choking Each Other	46
My Picture of You	49
Fry Guy	56
Mustard Packet	58
Shakedown	65
My Reflection	77
Divine Protection	82
3 Meal Trays	86
Light at The End of The Tunnel	89
Chapter 33	131
Where Do I Fit in The Picture	151
Smackdown	165
6 to Go	230

Poems
Original Poetry Written by Mark Cass

My Wish Came True	31
As Bad As I	34
Blue Christmas	35
I Miss My Life	36
Welcome to The Jungle	40
My Picture of You	50
That Must Be You	51
Where Are You Now	52
I Think About You	53
Addict in The Box	63
Going Over The Rails	70
Nowhere Bound	71
My Reflection	76
When He Was on The Cross	83
Right There with Me	84
Outside	88
Light at The End of The Tunnel	90
One Friend (For Leah)	231
No News Is Good News	232
Tool in The Masters Hand	233
Desperate Need of a Coat of Paint	234
Hello Me	235
What's A Visitor to Think?	236
(The First Poem I Ever Wrote)	
The Last Poem I Ever Wrote	262

Book One: The Jungle
July 31, 1992 – June 5, 2003

Capricorn

"In 752 AD, the Japanese Empress Koken wrote a lyrical poem in praise of the Eupatorium plant, whose leaves turn a vivid shade of yellow in summer. Recently, scientists punctured the illusion she was under, demonstrating that the lovely foliage of the Eupatorium is caused by a disease virus. In my view, though this should not diminish our appreciation of the poem or the plant.
I have noticed that a lot of the world's beauty forms in response to a wound. In fact, I expect that you are in the midst of that very process right now."

- **June 5th, 2003 -** *New Times Magazine*

The Lesser of Two Evils

The biggest mistake of my life happened on July 31, 1992. There were days that came before it. 6,790 of them to be exact, but none before or since have been quite so impactful as this day. This was the day that my life changed forever. The day my destiny began. Every day prior had just been preparation, for what this day would bring.

 I remember it well. The Homicide detective, Agent Harry, and his partner Agent Cooper had both agreed to give me a heads up when they were coming to get me. They were even nice enough to let me finish out the week at a new job that I had started. So that when I went to jail, I would have at least one paycheck and would not have to go in broke.

When they arrived, Agent Harry allowed me to step into the back bedroom with another brother and have a word of prayer with a concerned member of my church.

I then said goodbye to everyone and told them all I would be back. The detectives agreed not to handcuff me as I walked out of the house and into their waiting car. Being as I had been so cooperative; they had no reason to think I would run.

The ride to the jail was even somewhat of an enjoyable one. As both homicide detectives granted my request to run through a Burger King drive-thru before taking me on to the jail. As long as I agreed not to tell anyone that they did so when we arrived downtown. I agreed, and even remember telling them both this joke from the back seat.

"This dude was driving along a deserted back road when he stopped and picked up a hitchhiker walking towards town. As the two are riding along – there just so happen to be a Stoplight at a dirt road crossing and the driver just blew right through it – did not stop, slow down, or even look around.

The hitchhiker looked around kind of nervous and said, "Hey dude, you just ran a Stop sign" and the driver replied, "Don't worry about it – My brother does it all the time".

They go on a little further and start to get into the outskirts of town, and they are now passing traffic on the road when the light turns from yellow to red really quickly and the driver just blows right past it again. He never stopped, slowed down, or even took a look around; and the hitchhiker said "Hey dude them deserted country roads were one thing, but we are on asphalt now, in traffic. You have to stop at these red lights" and the driver replied "I told you don't worry about it – my brother does this all the time" and then he drove on a little further and got into the heart of the city when the light turned red again and stopped a long line of traffic so that another long line could go and the driver just blew right past the red light once again never even stopped, slowed down, or looked around; and the hitchhiker said "That's it! Just let me out at the next corner" and the driver replied once more "Don't worry about it – my brother does it all the time." And they drove on.

Pretty soon they came to a red light that suddenly turned green and the driver locked up his brakes, squealed his tires, and stopped on a dime. The hitchhiker hits his head on the windshield and exclaims "Man what's wrong with you? It is green, why are you stopping? GO!!!!" and the driver looks back at proclaims "Are you crazy? My brother might be coming".

They laughed, I laughed, and you probably are too. It is a funny joke. Especially when I get all into it and tell it with sound effects and use my hands for animations. This lets you know I had no idea, what was about to happen to me.

I had not an inkling of a clue at that moment, the amount of trouble that I was in. The cops told me I had done the right thing and I believed them. As It turns out, I had not!

No sooner, had I swallowed the last bite of my Whopper Junior w/ cheese, they were walking me out of the Sheriff's Dept. in handcuffs, parading me in front of news cameras, and charging me with First Degree Felony Murder!

"Wait a minute?" "What?" "What are you talking about?" "I told you I wasn't even there when it happened, I didn't do this." "You had me take a lie detector test and I passed." "What's going on?" "This is a mistake."

And it was a mistake – on many different levels. I was the one who made the mistake. I made the mistake of choosing the wrong influences. I had been somewhere I should not have been, and I had information about a crime. I went to see an attorney who advised me to keep my mouth shut, but the Police seemed so friendly and like they wanted to help me. I cooperated with them. Fully! *Against my attorney's advice.*

I believed them when they said, "if you weren't the one who committed this crime, then you won't be in any trouble." But the attorney had warned me not to talk to them. I had a real dilemma and did not know what to do. The cops told me that "guilty people keep quiet, lawyer up, and plead the 5th". I was not guilty! I did not do it. So what advantage was there to be gained by me acting as if I was guilty? They asked me. I could not see one. I had no reply to that question. But I did have a lot of questions and I felt a need to explain my side of things. This was all a grave misunderstanding. This guy robbed me; I did not rob him.

I needed to say something about this. Or this was going to get out of hand very quickly. I sought the counsel and advice of family, friends, and church leaders. I explained that they were talking about giving me the electric chair if I did this. But If I did not do it, I would get probation. However, I needed to tell them that I did not do it and explain to them what did happen in order for them to help me; but my attorney said to keep quiet. What do I do? I did not know.

The guy robbed me; I did not rob him. I was just going to get back what he took from me. We went unarmed, without malicious intent. I was the only one who knew that though. I was the only one that could stop this talk of First-degree Murder. It was important that I cooperate. The rest of my life was at stake. Many hours and many prayers were spent making that decision. Without any clear direction, but with only good intentions and a desire to do what was right, I gave a full statement to the police about the events in question on the night of July 6th, 1992. Took them out there, walked them around, and answered every question they had.

I had never been in any kind of serious trouble before. I was a preacher's kid. I smoked a little weed and had skipped school on occasion to hang out with girls, but nothing major, nothing felonious, and certainly nothing violent. Ever! I have always been very truthful and transparent. To a fault!

I was under immense pressure. I had just turned 18. I had very little experience running afoul of the law. Police, lawyers, and courtrooms, and the way that the system works were all unfamiliar to me. I had always been taught to tell the truth. So, I did.

Turns out, one should never talk to the police at all. Under any circumstances, if they have been suspected or accused of a crime. I did not know that then! Life taught me that later.

I had always thought the police were good guys. I did not know they could lie to you. Promise you things that were not true. I should have suspected something wasn't right when during my recorded statement the detective asked me if I had been promised anything in exchange for cooperation and I said *"Yes. You said you'd help me get probation since I didn't commit this crime and had already left before the fight ever even happened."* and they shut the recording off, rewound the tape just a touch, and said, "You can't say that." "If you say that we promised you anything on tape, while we are recording, then we can't help you. We are going to ask you again and you have to say No. Ok?" I naively agreed, and we rerecorded the segment again. My attorney was disgusted with me. They had had nothing on me at all until I opened my mouth.

I was still hung up and confused about, the term 'Felony Murder' and what in the heck that meant. Is there such a thing as a 'Misdemeanor Murder' I wondered out loud? My attorney laughed at my naivete and said "No, all murders are Felonies". That is what I thought. "So why the special annotation of the word 'Felony' in the term?" I still did not understand.

He explained Florida law and the Felony Murder Rule which states *if a death occurs as a result of a felony being committed. Then all parties involved in the felony are guilty of murder.* That is a paraphrase, but an accurate one.

I explained to my attorney that I did not go over there to commit a crime. "The guy owed me money. I was going to get back what he took from me". That is not theft, I reasoned. My attorney then replied, "But when you used a house key that you no longer had the authorization to use, your entry into the house, technically became classified as a 'burglary'; and the guy inside the house died as a result of an altercation he had with your co-defendant during said burglary".

"But I left before anything happened, meaning I disengaged from what you are defining as a burglary" I argued. "And that's what we will have to argue at trial" he replied.

"Trial? What are you talking about? The detective said he was going to talk to the Prosecutor and get me probation because I cooperated. I passed a lie detector test they had me take and everything" were all my replies.

Then he informed me that the results from polygraph tests are not admissible in court and that I should "never believe the cops. They are legally allowed to lie to you to obtain a confession. That is why we told you not to say anything. You are not getting probation. They just indicted you for 1st Degree Murder. I can probably keep you out of the electric chair because you're so young and the fact that you were not present when the altercation occurred is undisputed, but your codefendant is on the run and is a wanted fugitive, probably on his way out of the Country. Who knows if they will ever catch him or not; But they have you sitting right here in the Lee County Jail. They are not letting you go anywhere. You can consider yourself lucky if you end up with anything less than Life in prison!"

That was just one of many conversations I would have with my attorney. I really could not believe it. I had no idea how my life had been brought to this. One night hanging out with a chick and her friend had led to a conversation about past wrongs done to me and $40 that was still owed to me by someone else, and this dude, whom I hardly even knew, went and hit the guy, killed him, and was now on the run, and because they couldn't find him they were going to prosecute me. This could not be real – **but it was!**

I would spend an entire year in the Lee County Jail, carrying this unbearable weight. I woke up each morning facing either the electric chair or life in prison as the only two options for my future. All because of an act of violence that I neither committed nor witnessed.

These were the most horrifying days of my life. 365 days without sunlight. 365 days of slowly going insane. 365 days of fighting for survival literally. 365 days of despair. Consecutively, all in a row. 365 days.

It wore me down, and once I was worn down, I was willing to confess to the JFK Assassination, and any other crime they needed to clear off their books. *If they would just let me out of this cell*. It was then that the State Attorney offered me a plea agreement of 40 years in exchange for a Guilty plea of Second-Degree Murder.

Still, I refused and did not think that they understood the facts of the case very well and asked my attorney for a court hearing and an opportunity to plead my case to the Judge. Certainly, he could make these people understand that I did not do this. The cops promised me probation. Why was that not happening?

The judge was very fair. He heard me out and in open court he explained that during the pretrial process, there was not a lot that he could do. The ball was really in the court of the States Attorney's office and then he turned and addressed them and said something to the effect of, "I would hope that after hearing Mr. Cass speak today that you would reconsider your stance and offer him a plea deal with an amount of time more commensurate with his participation level in the offense." He then turned back and informed me, that if the State Attorney did not offer me something lower, that I was willing to accept, that he would advise me to take my case to trial where he would have a lot more say in the procedures. Man was that ever a hint. He knew it was not right to send me to prison on these charges.

The State sensed I might receive favor from the judge too if we proceeded to trial and came back the next week and offered me 22 years in prison instead of 40, in exchange for a plea of 'No contest' (meaning an admission of guilt was not required) to a charge of Second Degree Murder and First Degree Burglary.

My attorney explained that I could take my chances at trial, but I'd be going to trial on 1st Degree Murder charges and if they

found me guilty, then I'd only be eligible for one of two possible sentences. Life or Death.
No other option would exist.

Or he told me, I could accept these 22 years and the peace of mind knowing that I would at least one day get out before I turned 30. The sooner I started, the sooner it would all be over *or so I thought*.

I have spent many long hours wondering if I should have gone to trial. It seemed as if the Judge was on my side. I probably would have beat this entire case. If I had had anything better than an overworked Public Defender that I felt was already biased against me for not heeding his advice earlier.

Accepting their 'deal' and 22 years was the much preferable choice at the time. As it meant, I could be out in 7 years. Considering credit for County jail time already served and the amount of gain time that was being awarded by the Florida Department of Corrections (aka the D.O.C) at the time. I was presented with two evils.

I chose the lesser of the two.

On July 6th, 1993 I stood in a court of law and plead 'No Contest' to a crime that I did not commit.

The courtroom was full of people. Almost everyone I knew was there. No one could believe this was happening to me. They had all written letters to the Judge, asking for leniency, asking for boot camp, or probation. There were almost a hundred letters presented to the Judge, at the time of my sentencing. All speaking of my good character, and my <u>not</u> being present when the crime occurred.

My little sisters needing their big brother. My parents needing their son. My community needing me back in it. Everyone rallied.

None of it mattered, as the Judge was moved with compassion but was powerless to do anything since this was a plea agreement and all he could do was approve it or deny it. He had no authority to change it.

They sent me to prison a week later. I was classified as a violent offender and would go on to serve a total of 10 years, 10 months, 4 days, 10 hours, and 32 minutes.

This book serves as the first of a series of memoirs I am going to write about my life. A record of my time, the poems I wrote, the lessons I learned, and the sharing of personal experiences that I had while 'growing up inside the Chain Gang'. As well as a history of the lessons that I have continued to learn after my release and subsequent return to society. This part of my life would serve to prepare me for a life that was yet to come.

I needed to go through this experience to be able to share it with you. We do not get the advantage of seeing our life as a whole, we only get to live it each moment at a time but as we go on, we can begin to see it as a beautiful mosaic.

On July 31, 1992, I felt like the Universe shook up my world. Like a pair of dice, I was tossed and tumbled. When I stopped rolling. I had landed with my back against the wall and I was somewhere else. It seemed like I had been transported to an uncivilized section of another planet.

A place dominated by racism and violence. The rules of this new society that I was thrust into, were different than the free and civilized world that I had just left. I had never been anywhere like this before.

It was a journey into darkness. A place where every 'friend' had an agenda. Where all the rules of normalcy and civil society were turned upside down. Evil was good and kindness was despised. Then taken advantage of.
Weakness was an invitation to brutality.

Some days, I was not sure if I would ever make it out alive. Other days, I just prayed. Then there were a few other days I just acted stupidly. Those days grew less and less as time wore on though. Being stupid never has done much good for anyone. I was no exception.

The first part of this book deals very heavily with my first two years in the Florida Department of Corrections. When I acted out, did not care about the rules, I smoked a lot of weed, got into a lot of fights, spent a lot of time in confinement, and I wrote a lot of poetry.

In the section after, I will introduce you to some of the greatest people that I have ever met, and I will share with you how and why each was significant to me, as well as what it was that I learned from them.

We will finish the book with a chronological telling of the rest of my story with many details shared along the way.

The experiences are very much the reason why I am who I am today though. My grit and tenacity, the appreciation I have for little things around me, my knowledge of the law, and my Entrepreneurial hustle all came from this training ground.

I shared a dorm with a guy named Maurice Young, who is otherwise known as 'Trick Daddy'. Some of you may have heard of him. If you have not, then feel free to Google him. We were both in B- Dorm at Desoto Correctional Institution and that was referred to as the 'Jitterbug' dorm. An informal term used by the D.O.C to describe inmates that were under 21 years of age. We were all housed together in the same dorm.

Imagine the ruthlessness of a wide-open dormitory with more than eighty teenage boys living in it and almost every one of them has Life sentences and knows that they are never going home. Ever!

Now imagine that these same guys are so full of bitterness, hate, and rage because of the heavy weight of the time they carry. Coupled with the fact that they do not want anyone else to ever go home either. This environment is further pressurized by large groups of peers, separated by color and hometowns all hyping each other up and encouraging each other to increase the cruelty and violence that they bestowed upon anyone they determined to be weaker than them. I lived in this environment, and life was tough for anyone in this dorm that was either new, or White, and I was both. So, there were a lot of fights.
Thus, its nickname, the "Gladiator Dorm".

I was under 21, so that is where they put me. It was my initiation to prison. I called it the Jungle and wrote a poem about it. I wrote a lot of poems. That is how I survived.
I hung out on my bunk, listened to my headphones, and wrote. I wrote letters, and I wrote poetry.

Writing provided me a way to escape it all, and to travel somewhere else in my mind. My wildest and craziest days incarcerated were spent here. It is where I grew up, meaning I was not yet grown upon my arrival but was much more so upon my leaving. When I arrived, my attitude needed some adjusting.

It was early September 1993 when I arrived at Desoto. My release date at that time was 2014. I was angry. I was resentful. I was in a dorm where fighting was a prerequisite to staying alive and I did not care about a single one of them people's rules.

This attitude of mine wouldn't change until I woke up in a confinement cell on the morning of my 21st birthday, and decided to change who I was, how I thought about myself, and how I did time, but I'm getting way ahead of myself here. We will get there. For now, though let me describe in a little more detail for you the kind of environment it was that they sent me to. The environment that was Desoto Correctional Institution. One of the best, and one of the worst, places that I have ever been to.

I am not going to dwell on violence and wrongdoing much, but I do need to explain what my first year and a half was like. It's imperative to understand what the environment was like that I came from, and had to overcome.

To do that, I have selected a variety of short stories to share with you. I call them 'Jungle Stories' and they make up the first section of this book. After reading those, I will introduce you to some of the greatest people that I have ever met. Are you ready? Let's go way down in the Jungle deep.

Jungle Stories

The most intimidating part of any prison experience is your arrival. The Reception centers deliver busloads of new inmates to their newly assigned institutions every week. Each Institution has a scheduled day each week for the shipping and receiving of inmates. Everyone housed there knows when it is, and where the bus pulls up at.

Once a week, all the Predators, all the Vultures, all the Con-Men, and the Hustlers, as well as anyone else that is curious about who's coming and going from the Institution that week, will line up near the sally port gate to watch all the new guys get off the Blue Bird bus. They are looking for anyone that looks weak. Anyone that they can terrorize, intimidate, or otherwise take advantage of. They are seeking out anyone that looks like they are new. They all targeted me.
It was not an enviable position to be in.

Two days before though, the Lord had provided me with the strength that I would need to walk through this Jungle and He would go on to provide me with future lessons as well that would teach me what it meant to rely on Him for strength, for protection, and sustenance. Here is what happened just before I arrived at Desoto Correctional Institution in September 1993.

This Too, Shall Pass

I was sound asleep in my bunk one morning about 3:00 am at the Central Florida Reception Center when I heard the steel door of my cell open with a clang and an officer yell "Cass, get up – pack your stuff – you're being transferred" "Where to?" I replied, hoping for an answer. "I can't tell you" – "Security!" was the officer's reply.

I packed my meager assortment of belongings at the bottom of a pillowcase specifically, a *toothbrush, toothpaste, a Bible, a pad of paper, 2 envelopes, a pen, and a Styrofoam cup soup.* I then lined up at the door with about 20 other people all transferring out on the same day. We were escorted outside and joined a line of about 70 other people coming from different dorms on our way to the chow hall to pick up a bag lunch and wait for our bus.

Once inside the chow hall, we joined several hundred other inmates all waiting to be transferred as well. We sat on backless wooden benches, eating sandwiches that consisted of one piece of bologna, smashed between two pieces of bread, a single pack of mustard, a warm carton of milk, and a discolored, soft, brown apple. *I passed on the food and just drank the lukewarm milk.*

After they passed out all the bag lunches. We continued to sit in stony silence for several hours until the busses began to pull up, and one by one they'd call people's last names, and they'd line up, officers would outfit them with leg shackles and handcuffs and shuffling on to the bus, they would go.

One by one they would call names and fill up busses. I remained silent and still on that same hard, wooden bench and was beginning to wish that I would have at least ate the sandwich.

The clock ticked very slowly, and the day dragged on. Finally, somewhere about 3:00 or 4:00 in the afternoon, after every other bus had left, they called my name, shackled me, and I shuffled my feet along and boarded this Bluebird bus that had been outfitted for prison transport. Three men for every two-man seat. Expanded metal over the windows and a 5-gallon bucket in the very back should the need arise for one of us to use the restroom while enroute.

We rode for hours headed South. The bus was hot, and it began to stink after one or two had used the bucket in the back. It was highly uncomfortable, and none of us knew where we were going, and what should have been a three-and-a-half-hour drive from Orlando to Miami seemed to take at least six. When we arrived, it was after dinner and I had not eaten breakfast, or lunch and the officers went to the kitchen and brought us out these same bag lunches that were offered to us in Orlando that morning. This time, I scarfed down every bite.

We rolled into South Florida Reception Center in Miami, Florida sometime around 8:00 pm and had to be strip-searched, and all our property inventoried before anyone on the bus could be assigned a dormitory or a bunk.

By the time, all the processing was done, and a bunk was assigned to me, it was well after 2:00 am and I had been up for nearly 24 hours. I was hungry, I was scared, and I was exhausted as I walked into my dormitory and was given a bunk assignment. It was a bottom bunk, in a two-man cell, on the second floor, next to a shower stall.

So up the stairs I went, the officer opened the door, and it was dark but I could tell a large black guy was on the top bunk as one of the security lights from outside was shining in through the window and as I laid down on my bottom bunk having completed my first day in transit, headed to my first Major

Institution. I contemplated the 22 years that I had just received, and how had I ever gotten myself into this mess and wondering if I would even survive to tell the tale.

It was then, right at that moment, that I looked up and on the bottom of the bunk above me, someone before me had written: "This Too, Shall Pass!"

Out of all the prisons, out of all the dormitories, and out of all the bunks, this is the one I got. I took it as a message from God. I drew strength from it and fell asleep comforted, and with Peace in my heart.

Little did I know then, how much I was going to need it. Or how much that saying would come to mean to me in the days to come.

Nothing is forever. Not the good times, not the bad. Appreciate each moment for what it is worth because each one of them is fleeting. No matter what you are going through – It Shall Pass. *You just have to keep waking up in the morning*!

My Wish Came True

I wanted to be famous

Live in a big house, made of stone

Picture in all the papers

I wanted to be known

Live for free

And never have work to do

Unfortunately,

My Wish Came True

The Jungle

There was never a movie I had seen, or a tv show that I had watched, or a conversation that I ever had that could have prepared me for the reality that was waiting on me once I arrived at Desoto Correctional Institution. The horrors that existed behind those razor wire fences, or for how heavy the loneliness weighs on your chest at night, when you have been removed from everything you have ever known.

After a while, you do get used to it, but it never goes away. You just learn to carry it everywhere you go. Like a baby on your hip that never grows legs and walks.

Nothing you've ever experienced can prepare you for having your entire life snatched away and exchanged for a world filled with people that hate you just because you're White, or Black, or Mexican, or Puerto Rican, or Asian, or Muslim, or Jewish. People inside, just hate you because that is what everyone inside is full of, Hate.

Hate, Violence, and Perversion are the culture. Agenda driven friendships and acts of violent intimidation are the codes by which the people inside live by. There is no other 'normal'. The guards hate the inmates, and the inmates hate the guards. Blacks do not like Whites. Whites do not like Blacks, and the Spanish guys most always, only dealt with each other.

When I laid down at night, I would pray for God to take it all away, but *He never did*! I had to walk this journey all by myself. It was scary, it was dark, I cried, I prayed, I grew strong, I overcame, and only then did I come to realize that I was never alone at all. *God walked with me the entire way.*

In the beginning, I wrote every day just to keep it all from bottling up inside of me. It is how I stayed sane.

As Bad As I

Lonely man on a deserted island

                      Screaming out to an empty sea

Hanging on to a thread of hope, praying for a miracle,

                      Praying desperately

Little girl lost, alone, deep in the woods

                      Crying into the night

Scared, confused, blinded by her tears

                      And overcome with fright

Innocent man, staring out day after day

                      From a lonely prison cell

The cruel hand of fate has reduced his life

                      To a living hell

For just one granted wish, there is not anything

                      These people would not try

For they all are sick and just want to go home,

                      But none as bad as I

Blue Christmas

The county decorates the street, families decorate their home
But there is nothing to decorate for those that are alone
Yuletide carolers sing, hoping to spread Christmas cheer
But to me, December is the loneliest time of year
I used to love this 'Winter season' with open arms I would welcome December
But now it brings back memories too painful to remember
Most people are wearing green and red. I've no choice but to wear blue
And the people I am forced to live with are adorned in that color too
But blue seems appropriate, considering our atmosphere and mood
We've nothing to look forward to except the thought of some decent food
There are no lights or decorations, no presents, not even a tree No warmth, love, or joy – not even friends or family
Some wish for a Christmas that's white, others want to receive something new
All that is immaterial to me, I just want a Christmas that is not blue

I Miss My Life

I miss my mom and daddy
    I miss my little sisters too
        I miss my friends and family
            And all the things we used to do
I miss church on Sunday mornings
    I miss the parties on Friday night
        Lord, I miss the good times
        I am even thankful for a few of the fights
I miss hanging out with the fellas
    I even miss my ex-best friend
        I sit and think about them
            And wonder how they have all been
I miss the winters cold
    I miss the summer's heat
        I miss going to the movies
            Then making out in my back seat
I miss the smell of Grandmas kitchen
    I miss the sound of Grandpas radio
        I remember how the family would all
            come together
        And one by one we would all go
I've missed the chance for children
    I have missed the chance for a pretty little wife
        Come to think of it,
            I miss my life!

Christmas Eve '91 | 4 days before I turned 18

The First Guy I Ever Seen Get Stabbed

Desoto CI | September 1993

Lest you think my poetry is filled with hyperbole and 'No way it can be that bad' I will start by telling you about the first time I saw a guy get stabbed.

Most prisons have phones inside the dormitories. This was not the case at Desoto. Instead, they had two phone shacks located in the middle of the compound. Each one was a chain-link fenced-in area that held ten phones apiece, and at certain times of the day, they were open for inmate use. All calls home being 'collect' of course.

I had just dialed up my grandmother, and she was asking me how I was, and I was telling her that I was ok. When suddenly, a White guy came running from off in the distance barreling towards me at full speed. Three Black guys were running behind him just as fast. He got all the way to right in front of me when he slipped and fell, and the three Black guys descended on him and each one pulled out a homemade knife *aka as a 'shank',* and proceeded to stab this guy repeatedly.

To this day, I do not know who he was, who they were, or what happened to any of them, or why any of that occurred. I had just gotten there.

I do remember saying to my grandmother though, "Oh My God Grandma" and she said, "what's wrong honey?"

I replied, " some Black dudes were chasing this White guy and he fell and now they are stabbing him RIGHT IN FRONT OF ME" and she said, "well you just stay right here on the phone with me, don't you go over and get involved in it".

I said, "I'm not, but Wow! I can't believe it". It was a fantastic introduction to prison and they way disputes were often handled.

I have seen more fights than I can count. I have seen other people stabbed and hit upside their heads with metal pipes. There are many stories that I could still tell. It is not a place I would ever want to go again but if nothing else; You learn manners. You learn not to steal. You learn not to reach across someone's plate at the table, and you learn not to be disrespectful. All these things will get you hurt very badly, possibly killed.

However, if someone brings a fight to you, you must be able to stand up and defend yourself. Winning or losing does not matter, but your willingness to defend yourself, the things that belong to you, and your 'rear-end' most certainly does. If not, there will be someone who tries to take all three. I borrowed a song title from my favorite band and wrote a poem to describe it for the folks back home.

Welcome to The Jungle

Welcome to the Jungle
The jungle made of concrete and steel
Where people act like Gorillas
To hide the way that they feel
Welcome to the Jungle, it gets worse here every day
We're caged like animals in this Jungle where we play
'Boys' think they're girls, and men think so too
And the only colors you will ever see are brown, grey, and blue
Welcome to the jungle
Yes, that's what it is indeed
For when new prey comes along
Everyone gathers round to feed
Staking their claim on that one or this one over here
Trying so hard to disguise their own intimate fear
Welcome to the Jungle
Where to simply live is a struggle to survive
You ask Gods protection each morning
and thank him at night that you are still alive
You're in the Jungle
Where sex and violence rule
In the name of selfishness and greed
And it's become no big deal
To get to watch someone bleed
Here in the Jungle, Racism is King
And one slip of the tongue can cost you everything
That's how it is way down in the jungle deep
You keep one eye open, cause it's not even safe to sleep
Welcome to the Jungle.

I do not want to dwell too much on violence, and I did not get myself involved in many things that resulted in violence. However, no one goes through prison without having to engage in at least a few skirmishes. I will tell you about two that I was involved in. Both fights were brought to me while in the shower coincidentally. The first at Desoto and the last, four years later at Marion CI.

Here is the first. I call it **Heart Check.**

I had only been at Desoto for about three weeks when this fight took place. It had to happen eventually; someone was bound to try me. I was the new white boy in the dorm, and they call it a 'Heart check'. They want to see where your 'Heart' is, or if you have any. Will you fight? Are you a coward? Will you back down? Or will you stand up? Someone is always going to step up and try you. They want to find out what you are made of. I was no different. Let me set the scene for you.

In prison, most everyone has a hustle. *Meaning they have devised some way to support themselves and their habits.*
I just so happened to run a lotto board. Meaning I would take a sheet of paper and draw 100 squares on it. 10 squares horizontal and 10 squares vertical.
Then I would go sell each square for $1.00. Meaning if I sold the entire board, I would have $100. Being as we were not allowed to carry cash, money was paid in the form of food items and cigarettes. Two packs of cookies were $1.00, one pack of Top 'roll your own' tobacco was $1.00. A pack of Marlboro's went for $5.00; two Styrofoam cup soups were $1.00 and so on.

As I sold squares, people would mark their initials on the individual square and we would all wait till that night when the local news drew the daily lotto numbers, and whatever the lotto numbers were, I would use the last two. For example, if the winning number on the tv was 362, then whoever had number 62 on my square board was the winner. I would pay out $75 and keep $25.

I did this nearly every day and had developed regulars. If the winner was in my dorm then they got paid immediately. If the winner was in another dorm then they got paid first thing the next morning. It was one of these evenings when I had a locker full of food that I happen to be getting ready for a shower when a Black dude from Miami, whose friends had hyped him up to try and come over and try to take my stuff, approached fully dressed, wearing boots and said: "I'm hungry."

I was wearing my state-issued boxer shorts and a pair of flip flops that I used for shower slides and replied "yeah, me too, but this stuff in my locker is for my lotto board – It's not mine" and I shut my footlocker and locked the lock.

I attempted to walk off but he stood in my way, blocked my path, and said "Cracker, I told you I was hungry. I want a pack of cookies" and I replied "and I told you, nothing in that locker belongs to me, you're going to have to get a hustle or write home and ask for some money. I don't have anything for you." I then stepped around him and continued to the shower.

The dormitory shower area was wide open with about ten showerheads on the back wall and a little half wall in front that served as a shelf for your toiletries.

When I stepped into the shower stall area and set my soap, shampoo, and towel on the wall, I couldn't help but notice ten or twelve of his buddies all standing around waiting for me to strip down and get underneath the water and launch some sort of attack. So, I turned on the water and just stepped underneath it while remaining in my flip flops and boxers. Not long after I turned the water on that same guy stepped into the open area showers with me and was holding a razor blade melted onto the end of a toothbrush, in his hand, and asked "You're still not going to give me any cookies?"

I looked down at his attempt to intimidate me, chuckled, and replied "You're correct, I'm still not going to give you anything, but you can hand me my shampoo if you'd like." His buddy's snickered and replied, "Ooh he thinks he's a funny White boy too."

Clearly, this had not gone the way he had imagined it would go and now all his friends were gathered around amping him up to do something. So, he stuck out his index finger and poked me right in my face, and when he did, I hit him! Right then! Right there. Bam!

When I did, it was like dynamite went off. He swung, I swung, and it was on. All his homeboys circled around us, chanting Fight, Fight, Fight, and the rest of the dorm came running just as quick and formed a circle around us that was three or four layers of people thick.

This was a tradition in the Gladiator dorm. They did it to make it more difficult for the officers to get through the crowd to break us up. So, the fight would last longer. As would their entertainment.

We threw punches, we wrestled, I slammed him against the sink and kicked him between his legs, he kneed me in between mine, and then we wrestled some more. Both of us were relieved when the officer's backup finally came, and the officers broke up the crowd enough to make their way through to put us both in handcuffs. I had shown no fear, I did not give up anything that belonged to me, I stood my ground, even though I was outnumbered and disadvantaged. I fought for what was mine. I had won Respect! Which is all it was ever about anyway - just seeing if I had any 'Heart'.

Surprise Attack

1996 | Marion Cl

This incident occurred a few years later in 1997, while at Marion. I was in a dorm known as a T Dorm. *A two-story building with three wings going out in each direction shaped like the letter T. Right in the middle is the officer's control station.*

These types of dorms are all two-man cells and there is very little that the officers can see. Right in the middle of the wing is a bathroom, consisting of two single man shower stalls *with a shower curtain*, two toilet stools with a half wall between them, two urinals, and two sinks. They offer a fair amount of privacy, which is a rare commodity when incarcerated.

The 7:00 pm count had just cleared, and I took my towel and toiletries to the shower, hung my towel up, stepped in the shower, closed the curtain behind me, and began to enjoy my privacy. When suddenly I was attacked.

The shower curtain tore open and this completely naked Black dude jumped inside the one-man shower stall with me and grabbed me by my throat. I grabbed him by his throat in return and squeezed his neck just as tight as he was squeezing mine. After a few moments of us choking each other, I pushed him backward,. This caused him to trip backward over the three-inch retainer wall that outlined the shower. He fell onto the floor in front of the toilet. I pounced like a Lion and began to rain down blows all about his head, body, and shoulders. *Bam, Bam, Bam.*

I had my fists balled up and was dropping straight missiles down on him. Or attempting to anyway. He managed to roll around enough to make it out and run down the hallway naked to his room. I grabbed my towel and ran down the hall the other way towards my room. It was on! We were going to War!

We both ran back to our cells to get dressed and then one of us was going to kill the other one, right then and there. When the dude came back down my hallway, *to obstruct the officer's view or to prevent an easily obtained escape by either one of*

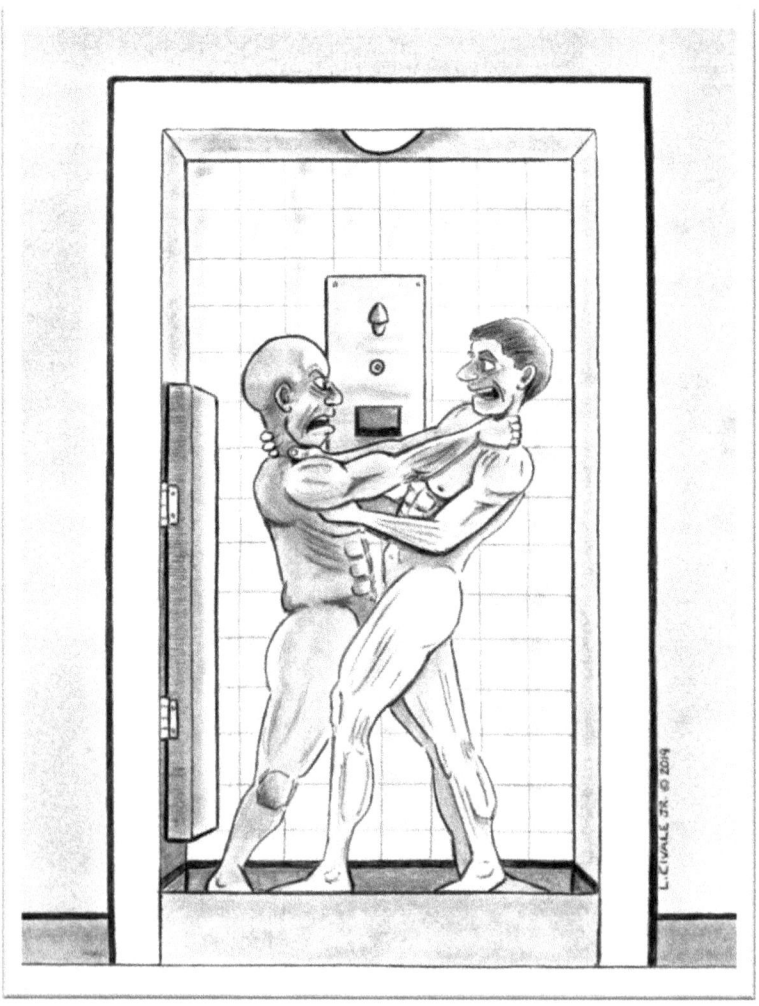

us, people began to open each of their doors out into the hallway. Blocking off the hallway behind him as he passed. When he approached my door, I kicked it open, knocking him backward, then jumped on him again as he stumbled.

Bam, Bam, Bam – I rained more blows down. Eventually, he made it back up to his feet, his head was bleeding, and he was wobbly, but we squared off again and he had his back to the South wall which housed a great big industrial fan with 4-foot blades, encased in a giant steel cage. It was on and providing circulation for the wing.

Every single person had come out of their room to watch and were now cheering me on. This was important because it meant the fight had been called a 'one on one' and no one could jump in. The fight was between me and him and everyone on the wing was supporting me.

Blacks, Whites, Hispanics, even the one Asian guy on the wing. They were all cheering me on and yelling encouraging words to me. I felt like I was in the Octagon, with a million screaming fans. I lowered my shoulder, ran straight for him, hit him with my shoulder, and just kept driving him backwards until I slammed him, and specifically his back, into the corner of the steel cage housing the fan at the end of the hall.

The impact had knocked the wind out of him, and he slid to the floor. Then someone yelled Pōlice. We all scattered back to our cells, as the Pōlice made their way through all the doors that had been opened and obstructing their view. When the officers asked what happened, no one knew anything. No one saw anything. The other dude told them he could not remember how he ended up there. *Which may or may not have been true.* Never again did I get into another fight in prison!

My Greatest Pain

I ended the last chapter by saying that never again did I get into another fight in prison. That is true in the literal sense, but in the figurative sense, I fought a battle with my heart daily. I had a girlfriend at the time of my arrest. We had grown close after the news broke of my pending incarceration. She wrote to me twice when I first went to jail and then she went ghost. The last words she ever wrote to me were "I love you" and "My View Needs You." Never did I ever get a goodbye, I am sorry, I met someone, Don't ever write me again, nothing.

I was so homesick and had already lost so much, and now my girlfriend would not answer the phone, return a letter, or even provide an explanation. That hurt me worse than any other pain I had ever felt. I slowly went mad. A little more each day.

Shortly after I heard her proclaim to me that she loved me for the first time, Fate dictated that another word would never pass between us. The anguish of not knowing what had happened, or why she would so militantly block me out of her life was the inspiration for many legal pads full of poetry. I will share only a few.

'My Picture of You' was the first. It was my favorite. It was written in 1993 while I was still in the County Jail.

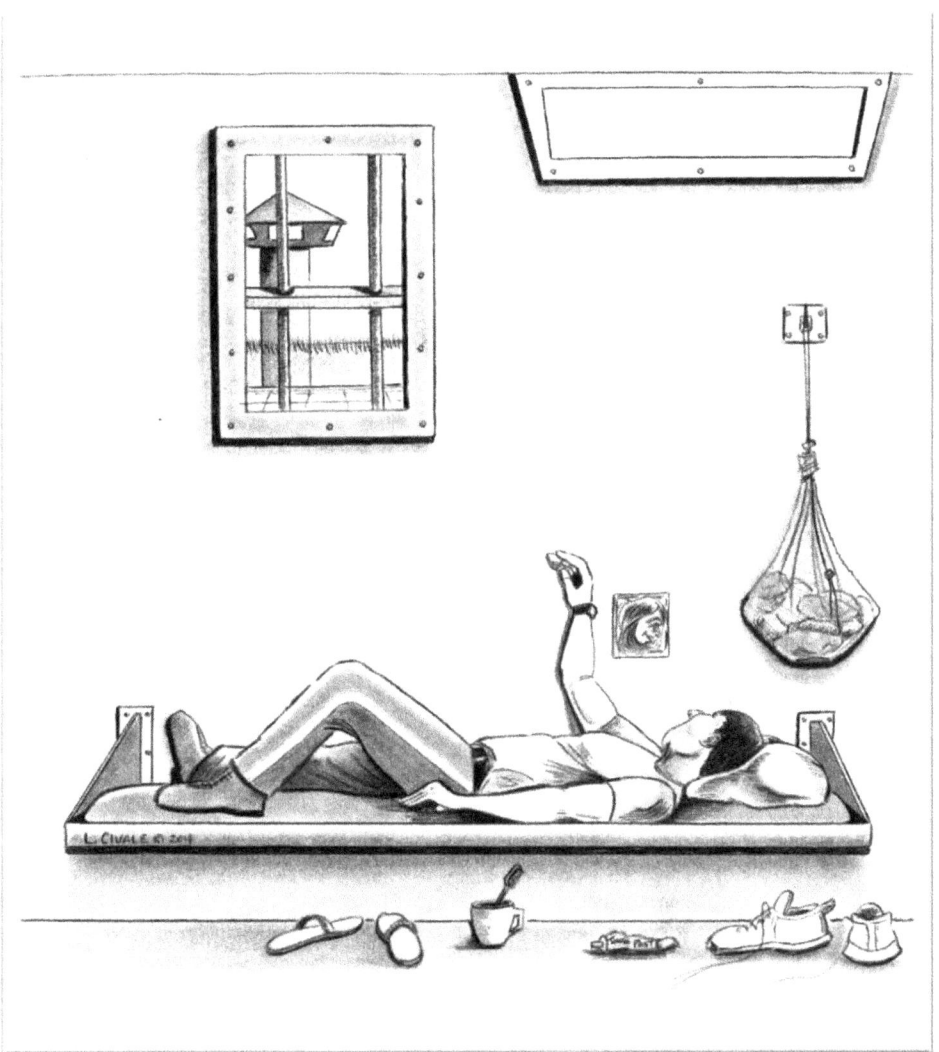

My Picture of You

Pictures worn and faded
Even burnt down the side
Guess that I got mad
More than a couple times

Tear stain in the corner
Scratched a little too
But it's my favorite picture
My picture of you

Toothpaste on the back
Keeps it hanging on the wall
I wouldn't part with it
for anything at all

Everywhere I've been
It's been right there with me
It's been my only comfort
In times of misery

Pictures worn and faded
To me, it's good as new
My most precious possession
My picture of you

That Must Be You

My telephone's not ringing
So that must be you
Who's not calling
To say hello or how do you do

The mailman never leaves
Anything at my door
That must be you
who doesn't write me anymore

Today, I was the only one
that no one came to see
That must be you
Who's not missing me

Yes, that must be you

Where Are You Now?

Your favorite song is playing
On the radio
I wonder if you're listening
Or if you even know
The memories come rushing back
And make it pretty hard
I stare into space and wonder
Where you are
What Father time would sell me
I'd buy it all
I'd sell my soul
If only you would call
You've been gone
For far too long
And I still haven't figured out
what went wrong
You'd always find an answer
To my questions somehow
But what I want to know
Is where are you now

I Think About You

I Think About You
I Think About Us
I Think About Me
I Think About You

I Think About Family
I Think About Friends
I Think About Lovers
I Think About You Again

I Think About Then
I Think About Now
I Think About When
And I Think About You, Once Again
I Often Dream, Regret, and Ponder
Then my mind begins to wander

And I Think About You
I Think About Us
I Think About Me
And I Think About You…

Learning to Appreciate

Prison was an ugly place to be in but being there has brought a lot of beauty to my life as well. Those harsh environments taught me to appreciate so many of life's little details.

You have no idea how much someone will dream or fantasize about just being able to walk barefoot on a plush carpet once again. Or barefoot on grass. While they are locked up. The luxury of being able to sit and watch just one show on tv each week that you can both, hear and enjoy, all the way through is simply unrealistic.

Being able to sit on the toilet alone. Or being able to wear something other than the color blue. There are so many things to appreciate in life and being in prison has taught me to do that.

I walk barefoot on my grass daily because for so many years, I was unable to. It is often the best part of my day. Another small detail I appreciate being able to do today, is being able to go to the refrigerator anytime that I am hungry. Free world food comes at a premium while incarcerated. Prison food is so bland and bought at such cut-rate prices the quality is not anything that would ever receive rave reviews.

One time I got my hands on a large order of McDonald's fries though and I had never been so thankful. Let me tell you about it.

One of the so-called 'perks' of living in the Jitterbug dorm was the fact that the State of Florida considers anyone under 21 to be a 'child' and in need of extra nutrition. Therefore, Breakfast and Lunch were requirements for us. At Breakfast, we all received an extra serving of fruit and we all received an extra milk at Lunch.

Desoto CI received extra funding from the Federal Government for every inmate that received the extra nutrition, and because money was involved, they made it mandatory for each and every one of us living in B Dorm get up out of bed and go to the chow hall and be counted for those two meals. They did not care if we ate or not, but they cared a whole lot about us walking in that building and them getting financial credit for us being there.

When in prison, if you do something against the rules the way they punish you by writing you a Disciplinary Report otherwise known as a D.R.

When an officer writes you a D.R. the Sargent of the shift has 24 hours in which to investigate the incident, else the D.R. is automatically dismissed. Once an investigation takes place, then the prison has seven days to give you a full hearing on the matter.

At that hearing, guilt or innocence is determined and punishment is applied. Usually, the incident will result in the loss of gain time (time earned off your sentence), possibly being locked up in confinement. Or both.

So, D.R.s are a bad thing, and you do not want them, and in my first twelve months there, I received fourteen of them.

Anyway, there was this one Saturday morning that I slept in and did not go to Breakfast. For that 'crime' I was written up and given a D.R.

Breakfast started at about 7:00 am and the midnight shift for the officers starts at midnight and ends at 8:00 a.m. Therefore, Breakfast is served at the end of the Midnight shift – *any D.R. that is written is investigated by the same shift Sargent.*

So, the next night when the Midnight shift came on, I was called up to the Sargent's office shortly after their shift began for the investigation.

As I am walking across the compound at Midnight, unescorted (they did that sort of thing back then) an officer coming on to the shift just minutes before me had brought in McDonald's and happened to drop a large order of fries on the ground. Not on the dirt, but right in the middle of the sidewalk and there they sat, right in the middle of my path.

Hot, salty, and crispy made only the way that McDonald's can make them. I thanked the Lord for this blessing and scarfed down every single one of them and had never been more thankful to eat food off of the ground. *Those fries were worth the extra 30 days that I had to do at the end of my sentence because of that particular D.R. too.* Perspective.

There was another time that a single packet of Mustard made my day. As you can probably imagine prison food is somewhat bland and prisons are somewhat short on amenities. So most anything that can be found to offer the slightest bit of comfort or pleasure, comes at a premium. Like packets of Mustard for example.

Mustard is one thing I do take delight in and would usually have a few extra packets lying around to take with me to the chow hall. No matter what bland meal may be served that day, a pack of Mustard could usually make it at least digestible.

Little tiny packets of Mustard were not served in the chow hall, nor were they provided by the State. They were a luxury that we were charged .05 cents for whenever we bought a microwavable hamburger from the commissary.

A single pack of Mustard was not something I ever took for granted. Having one could be the literal difference between having a good day or a not so good day; and it just so happened that on this particular sunshine-filled day, I was walking back to my dormitory coming from someplace else. When I happened to look down on the ground and there one was, a bright shiny single pack of yellow Mustard.

Unopened, untainted, and freshly fallen out of someone else's bag that had already walked on ahead. I reached down, scooped it up, and put it into my pocket. When I got back to my dorm, I put it in my locker, waiting to enjoy it with my next meal.

Later in the day when I called my grandmother. She asked me how I was, and I replied very casually "I'm good Grandma, I

found a pack of Mustard on the ground today, so it was a good day". She got the biggest kick out of that. Though the irony of it escaped me at the time she replied, "Wow it must be really bad in there if finding a pack of Mustard on the ground qualifies as a good day". We both chuckled together and still to this day, I smile when remembering that story; and am thankful each time I make a sandwich, that I have an entire jar of Mustard in the refrigerator, or that little packets come free in convenience stores or fast-food restaurants.

Prison taught me to be grateful for things that most other people give no consideration to. That has been a gift throughout the rest of my life. I appreciate a lot.

I can remember reading a poem once back then that I could relate to so well. I do not remember the title of the poem, how it went, or who the author was, but I do remember its message. The poem was written from the perspective of an inmate looking out into the world and seeing a guy just getting home from work and the author went on to describe a frustrating scene, by most accounts.

The grass needed to be mowed. Kid's toys were strewn all about the yard. Two babies were screaming when he walked in the door and one sibling was racing to tell on the other sibling. While the wife greeted him in the kitchen still wearing that morning's housecoat and breathing the same Dragon breath from the night before.

The guy is greeted by a stack of overdue bills on the table as his wife sets down dinner that she bought with dime-store coupons. The author then concludes by saying "Man, What I'd give to just be that guy." *One man's floor is another man's ceiling.* I could so very much relate. I wanted to be that same guy too.

I am thankful for each day, even when it is the worst of them. I have had worse. I have friends who would gladly exchange my troubles for theirs. Therefore, every day I see is a good day. No matter what it may bring. Being in prison taught me that.

Addict in The Box

It is no secret that I smoked weed during the first few years of my incarceration. I was down with doing anything that might help my mind escape being there. This led to some close calls. I was even almost caught once. This led to me having to ask the Pōlice to give my weed back, and they did. I could not believe it!

So, I have a poem to share and a couple of funny stories about smoking weed while in confinement and then I will move on - because shortly after this, I turned Twenty-one. When I did that, everything changed but these stories predate my twenty-first birthday and they're funny. So here goes…

I was in Administrative Confinement (AC). Also known as 'The Box'. This is where you are isolated and confined to a cell that is separated from the General Population. In AC you can still have your property, make a phone call once a week, order from the commissary, etc.

I would sometimes go there on purpose just to get away from the chaos of the Jitterbug dorm, catch up on sleep, and read books for a month.

So, I am locked up in confinement and the guy in the cell next to me has smuggled in an Ounce of weed. Now, let us stop right here for a minute. You are probably thinking 'How in the world did he do that?' I will explain.

What the weed smugglers usually do, is have someone from the streets bring it to them during visitation inside of their body cavity. Usually, this is a wife or a girlfriend. In preparation for this event, the wife/girlfriend will buy some weed out in the free world. Then remove the stems and seeds to make it as compact as possible. Then they chop up the Marijuana in a coffee grinder. Then pack it inside of a quarter roll, like the ones you get from a bank. Once compacted inside the quarter roll. They wrap the package in a generous amount of black electrical tape, and just before entering the prison, they insert it like a tampon.

Once inside the visiting park, the visitor goes to the bathroom and removes the package, and passes it off to the inmate with whom they are visiting. The inmate then goes to the bathroom and is saddled with the task of reinserting the package into his 'Exit only' body cavity. This method is referred to as 'Suit Casing'.

Lots of contraband has made its way into the prison system via the 'suitcase'. That, and the officers who walk it through the front gate each shift. *They bring in a lot of contraband too.*

You may think this is a bit extreme. However, once back out on the compound with an Ounce of weed. The owner of the package is King of the compound for as long as he has it. Not to mention the return on your investment. A bag of weed that goes for $100 in the Free world is worth four or five times as much on the inside.

I knew people that would support their families on the outside, from the inside, this very way. Now with Cash App, Venmo, Pay Pal, and the like. People have their people send other people money and the product gets delivered on the inside. You would be surprised at how often this occurs.

I never smuggled anything. I just bought it once it hit the compound, was unwrapped, the nastiness disposed of, and the product repackaged for distribution. These were called sacks. You had $5 sacks, $10 sacks, $20 sacks, and $50 sacks.

I was in confinement and the guy next to me had an Ounce of weed that he had smuggled in earlier. Through ingenious engineering, we had developed a way to pass back and forth and I spent the week buying weed. After all, I was alone in a confinement cell twenty-four hours a day with nothing much to do except stare at the wall. I could not see the harm.

This was back when the D.O.C. allowed you to get approved care packages from home and I had just received one. In it, I received a brand-new pair of shoes, some socks, stamps, and a few other things that I had traded for weed.

Plus, I ordered my friend things he requested from the commissary list. I then called home and had some money sent to his account, and after exhausting all my resources. I found myself with nothing left to barter with, but it was a new day, and I was bored in that confinement cell and wanted desperately to smoke another joint. So I wrote him a poem.

The guy was so impressed with my poem that he sent me back a fat dime sack complimentary. Therefore, I refer to this as the first time I ever got paid for my writing.
I call it 'Addict in The Box'.

Addict In The Box

I'm just an addict in the box
I needed a sack, so I sold my socks
I didn't care that it was small
I didn't care, no not at all
I smoked all my stamps and then my shoes
Had they been willing I'd have sold them my blues
Alone in my cell, I pace the floor
Racking my brain on how to get more
I've already sold everything that I've owned
And even a few things that I had been loaned
This is my story as pathetic as it seems
I've nothing left to sell except a few dreams
So rather than lie, and later regret it
just send me a sack over on credit

Hanging Out the Window

Another story that ended well, was another time that I was in confinement. I had been there a couple of days by myself when I got a roommate who coincidently, had a $10 sack on him when they brought him in. He told me, and we decided to save it until after they showered our wing. As we did not want the smell to alert anyone.

In confinement, they only let you out to shower three times a week. Monday, Wednesday, and Friday nights. We were towards the end of the hallway and were nearly the last to shower. After we showered and returned to our cell, my roommate handed me the sack of weed and asked me to roll it up and I obliged. The officer was making his rounds and making sure all the cells were secure.

Each cell has a 12" x 12" square hole in the door for officers to walk by and view inside. Just as he was walking by our cell, I had finished rolling a joint and was reaching up to place it on top of the towel rack. The officer seen me, stopped, and said, "What was that?" I looked and replied, "What was what?"

The officer reached for his keys to open the door and I put the joint in my mouth. I did not swallow it, due to it being the only one we had, but I was prepared to had he advanced any closer. Instead, he stared at me, and I stared at him. Finally, after our little stare off he said, "that's it! You are going to regret that" and out the door, he went.

I had to act fast because he was going to get the 'Goon squad' and they were going to tear our cell apart. Not wanting to lose the only joint we had when they came and tossed our cell, I grabbed a roll of dental floss and ripped off a segment about twelve inches long and tied one end to the joint, and tied the other end to the tiny expanded metal diamonds that covered our window and out the window the joint went, hanging down the outside of the wall.

They came in, handcuffed us, and told us to step outside in the hallway. Then they proceeded to tear all our stuff apart, flip our mattress, unroll our socks, flip through the pages of our books, check the spines of our Bibles, open our pens to check inside the ink barrels, took a mirror to check under the lip of the toilet seat. They looked everywhere they could think to look, *except outside the window!*

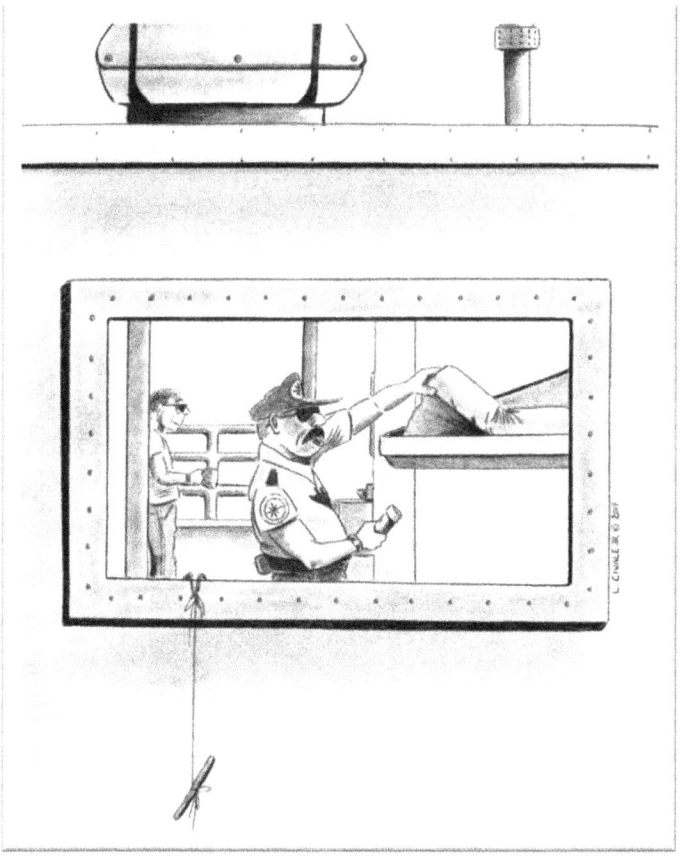

The Night the Cops Gave My Weed Back

One last short story, only because of the audaciousness of it all. This is the time I talked the cops into giving me back my weed. I was nuts!

The compound had been dry for about a month. Meaning no one had any Marijuana to smoke, or for sale, in what seemed like an eternity. Then one day, someone I knew brought some in and only had a small amount for sale. I was fortunate enough to score a dime sack.

Several of us had gathered at the North end of the dorm to play cards and smoke weed. I rolled a joint and folded the small amount of remaining weed back up in a piece of paper the size of a postage stamp and slipped it under my watch band, lit the joint, took a toke, and then passed it Left. to my Cuban buddy, Santiago.

Someone else shuffled a deck of cards. When suddenly, an officer peeked in the window. He had slipped outside and come around the side of the building to sneak a peek at what we were doing through the window. He appeared just as I was passing the joint to my left, and our eyes locked.
I yelled Five-Oh! *(prison slang for Police).*

Santiago ate the joint I had just passed him as the officer unlocked the door that was right next to the window. I slipped the remaining sack from under my watch, into my mouth and swallowed it, just as he lined us all up for a 'shakedown'. The officer knew we had been smoking weed. He seen it, he smelled it, but he could not find any evidence of it. After thirty minutes he left us to resume our card game.

Now all I had to do was throw the sack back up, dry it out and roll it up again. Sounds easy enough. Except, I could not throw it back up, no matter how many times I stuck my finger down my throat, no matter how many times I gagged, and coughed. It would not come up.

This called for desperate measures. I went to my locker, took out my PERT 2-in-1 shampoo and squeezed a little bit into a cup, added a half cup of hot water, stirred lightly, so as to mix but not lather; and with every ounce of 'wanting to get high' that I had within me, I tossed it down.

That warm shampoo water hit my stomach and came right back up in no more than an instant. Along with everything else that had been in my stomach within the last twenty-four hours.

When I was done yacking, there was my little folded up little sack. Floating right on top of all that mess in the center of the toilet bowl. I snatched it up, rinsed it off, unfolded it, and found it to be very much still intact but much too moist to smoke. I opened the sack, so it could breathe, and placed it on the windowsill to air out. My crowd of friends had lauded me as a hero for drinking the PERT shampoo and saving the weed. After which we resumed our card game, all waiting anxiously for the weed to dry out enough to smoke.

Then, that same officer decided to make another round, out the back door of the officer station and around the side of the building and then parked himself right back in front of our window. This time he saw it. There it was plain as day. A little pack of paper unfolded and sprinkled with marijuana sitting on the window sill. He came in and confiscated the last of my weed.

He could not pin it on anyone person, so no handcuffs, no D.R. but he did take it back to the officer station and throw it away in the trash can; and to any less determined person that may have been it. However, I have never in my life been described as a 'less determined person.'

There was no way I was going to just give up. I still had one more play. Right up to the officer station I went. I knocked on the door and they let me in and asked me what I wanted, So I told them.

"I have a 22-year sentence and It's only just begun, I have to live in this crazy jungle of a world and even crazier dorm and the only thing that helps to keep me sane is the occasional toke on a joint, and this compound has been dry well over thirty days and my anxiety is through the roof. I used the last little bit of money that my family sent me today to buy $10 worth of weed. When you walked in the back door a little bit ago, one guy swallowed half of it, I swallowed the rest. When you left, I put my finger down my throat to throw it up but was unsuccessful. Then I had to resort to drinking PERT shampoo to throw it up. Finally, it came up, and out into the toilet. I scooped it out and had to put it in the window to dry, and then you came along and took it, now it is sitting right there in the trash. You are not going to do anything with it, it does not make a difference to you, but giving it back would make a huge difference to me. So, I came in here to ask you to please give my package back. I have just simply gone through too much to lose it like that."

The two officers in the station were stunned, they looked back and forth at each other, shook their heads, and finally, the senior officer spoke and said "You really drank Pert Shampoo?" I replied "Yes". He looked at me a minute longer and finally said – "There's no way I'm reaching my hand into that trash can and pulling that sack of weed out and handing it back to you. However, what I am going to do is step out this back door and smoke a cigarette and when I do, I am going to invite this other officer to step outside with me. If you want to go ahead and empty our trash can while we are out smoking, then you are welcome to do so. Just bring it back clean, and with a new bag". So, I did! The rest of the evening they both left us alone. No one at the card table believed they gave it back to me, not until I lit it up and we all laughed and high fived. That could have played out so many different ways. I guess the Lord just protects those that are courageous and naïve or both.

There are many things I did at the beginning of my sentence that I would never have dreamed of doing in the middle of it, or near the end. This incident is one of them. I kind of felt like 'what's the worse they can do, lock me up?' I would come to learn later that there was a lot they could do and would do, but those lessons did not come till later.

This chapter started with a funny story, a funny poem, and then I shared a couple more audacious stories that happened to work out in my favor. However, by and large, getting high has not worked out in my favor at all. It has provided some momentary comfort but at the cost of even longer-lasting insanity. The next two poems were written as I began to realize exactly how much it had all cost. My influences are readily apparent in both.

Going Over the Rails

Lost and Found

Then turned around

Back in black

A monkey on my back

Good intentions

Bad decisions

Reap what you sow

I can't break free

Because it won't let go

Dazed and confused

Used and abused

Pretty picture

Deceptive paint

Thinking I can

When I know that I can't

Fool's gold

I was told

I'm going insane

On this crazy train

Nowhere Bound

You're running from yourself or from the truth
You figure what the hell, you've nothing to lose
You're above and beyond the legal limit
You don't care, you're living for the minute
Too many problems got to leave this town
You don't know it, but you're Nowhere Bound

Heads full of fantasies and dreams
You need a fresh start or so it seems
Inside your head, you've got it all figured out,
But you've no idea what life is really about
Chasing your tail going round and round
You don't know it, but you're Nowhere Bound

Nowhere is where you're going, and you're getting there fast
It feels good for the moment, but it doesn't last
You can run from yourself, but you won't get very far
Cause no matter where you end up, there you are
You're running out of places to lay the blame
When the root of your problems begins with your own name

You think you're climbing higher, but you're only falling farther down
You don't know it, but you're Nowhere Bound

Turning 21 In Confinement

On December 28, 1994, I woke up in a confinement cell. It was my Twenty-first birthday and I had not a single reason to celebrate. The best decisions of my life had led to me being alone in solitary confinement, inside of a prison about seventy miles from my home, my friends, and my family on this milestone of a day.

If there was anything good about it, it marked a day of enlightenment for me. It was the day that I decided enough was enough. As I lay there in my bunk taking inventory of my life, I realized that in 21 years I had not accomplished very much.

- I had received a driver's license at 17
- I had earned my G.E.D. while in the Lee County Jail.
- I had managed to receive a 22-year prison sentence.
- Oh, and I had a trophy for Most Improved Student in the 5th grade.

Other than that, I could not count a single accomplishment that I had achieved in my 21 years of living.

I had an epiphany that day. It served as a U-Turn in my life as well as a shift in my thinking. As I lay there in peaceful solace. I vowed my next 21 years would be different, and they were.

From that day forward, I never again got into any trouble within the D.O.C. Never another D.R. *not any that I did not beat on appeal anyway.* My release date began to get closer, instead of farther away. I would go on to serve another 9 years and some change after this day, but those years were served quite a bit differently than the first two were. Less than 2 months later, on Valentine's Day 1995. I transferred to Marion Correctional Institution, located in Ocala, Florida, and joined the Tier 3 program. Which was the D.O.C.'s version of an In-Patient drug treatment center.

All the participants were housed separately from the rest of the compound and though we did all interact at times. They tried to make the Tier dormitories a positive environment. A 'Therapeutic community' if you will. I was also enrolled in a vocational Drafting course during this time as well and spent 18 months learning AutoCAD (Computer-Aided Drafting).

From there I became a certified Literacy tutor and had a job in the Education Department helping others who were learning to read. I would also go on to begin correspondence legal courses and would later earn a Paralegal Certification from the Blackstone School of Law in Dallas, Texas. From that enrollment, I developed a fondness for litigating with the D.O.C.

I became what's known as a 'writ writer' meaning I learned the laws, the policies, and the procedures that governed the Department of Corrections and would constantly write up the officers, and the institution, in hopes of suing them in court. I purposed to make myself a very real pain in their rear end.

I did not realize it then, but I was honing writing skills that would go on to serve me well throughout the rest of my life. *Even today, as I write this manuscript.* I communicate best when writing.

From Marion, they sent me to Baker, and then on to Washington, and finally to Cross City before I eventually made it to Work Release. Everywhere I went, I enrolled in Education and Vocational programs.

Being there was already a 'waste of my life' or so it seemed. I could not do anything about that. But I could do something about it not being a 'waste of my time.' I purposed to use this time to learn as much as I could.

It became my personal mission and policy to seek out job assignments that benefitted me, more so than it did 'them'. I avoided hard labor like the Plague.

When Education was not an option. I worked in Food Service. At least there I could eat and sell sandwiches, so even then, I was working for me, and not them.

I earned a second G.E.D. I learned Windows, and became certified in Microsoft Office, and earned a Vocational Certification in Computer Programming as well. I attended many different Life skills classes, business classes, AA, NA, Weekend Chapel retreats. You name it. I enrolled in it. I even attended a smoking cessation class and I did not even smoke. All in preparation for the day that they would let me out.

I believe that it was these experiences that laid the foundation for the entrepreneurial journey that I have embarked upon since my release. This is not the end of the book though. I still have a lot of stories to tell, and a lot of poems to share. Like this one called 'My Reflection'. I wrote this one as an assignment while in the Tier 3 program at Marion. I remember being in the 'hot seat' as it was called.

This is when one person sits in a chair in the middle of a circle and all your peers confront you about your behaviors and attitudes. It is usually not a very comfortable position to find yourself sitting in because you are not allowed to speak. They can say whatever they want. Confront you on anything they desire to, and all you can do is listen. Some of the feedback is beneficial, some of it is not. You silently absorb it and go back to your bunk and process it.

It was during this time, that someone being slick, stood up and said "Mark with all this writing that you do, and all these poems that you write I think you should have to look into a mirror and write a poem about what you see there."

So, there it was, an assignment. The counselor thought that was a great idea and I was instructed to go back to the dorm and do just that. He further stated that I also had to read what I wrote to the group the next day.

I decided to give them what they wanted, and in this one poem I got more real than anyone else in that room ever had or expected me to. They all thought I would be funny, or sarcastic in some way. When I finished reciting the last line It was a mic drop moment. They had nothing else to say once I was done. They left me alone after that.
Here is what I wrote.

My Reflection

Walking past a mirror, I caught my reflection in the glass
And I saw the eyes of the one they call Mark Cass
His eyes were tired and lonely, a little scared and confused
They looked like they belong to someone who really wanted to use
However, closer inspection revealed that wasn't necessarily true
For through his eyes, I could see his heart, and all the good he wished to do
Then once I got past his wishes and good intentions, I could see a heart filled with pain
And late at night when the lights were out, it caused tears to fall like rain
Then looking closer at his face, I noticed it'd been days since he last shaved
Nothing more than a façade to cover all the pain he had stuffed and saved
Hoping the hair on his face would somehow prove him to be a man
And no longer a simple child to be damned
Moving on, I noticed two little holes in his ear
They were in his left, of course, so no one would think of him as queer
A symbol of my independence, his mind justifiably said
And simultaneously, the word Rebellion flashed through my head
As he stood and held that solitary pose
I remembered the overdose he inhaled through his nose
And I saw it as I had time and time again
With vomit spewing from it and dripping off his chin
This was certainly not the first time he had used to the extreme
Trying to just end it all, or at least that's how it seemed

Then I couldn't help but notice, the mouth that said never again
The same mouth that would make that promise over and over again
Swearing that each time would be the last
Only to forget that promise once the nausea had passed
I began to walk away having become uncomfortable beneath my own stare
Wishing it were possible to just walk off and leave my reflection standing there

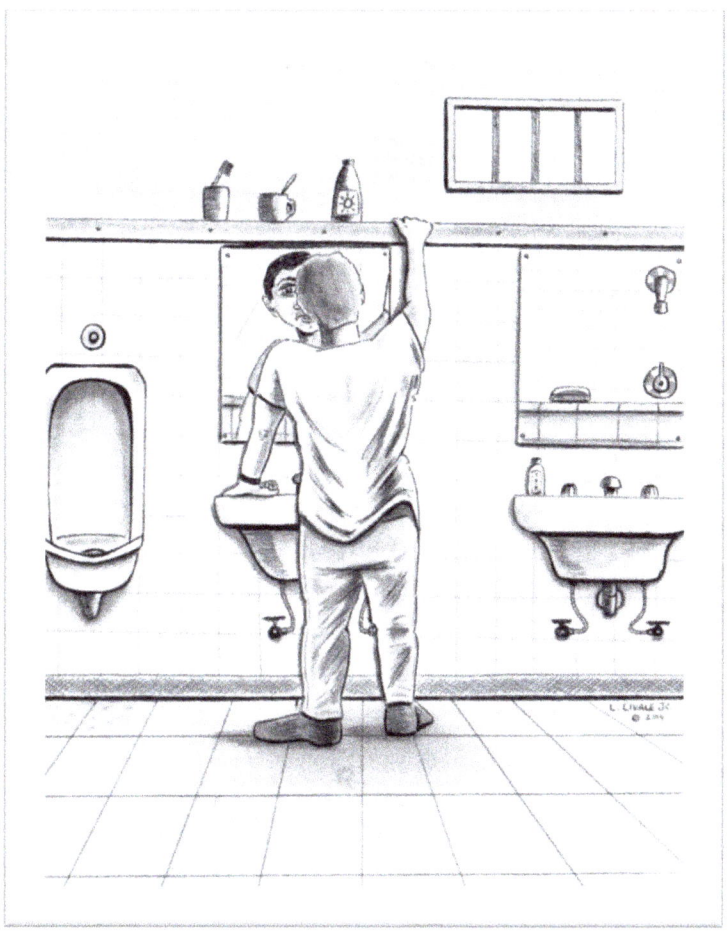

Psalm 91

He that dwelleth in the secret place of the Most High shall abide under the shadow of the Almighty.
2 I will say of the Lord, He is my refuge and my fortress: my God; in him will I trust.
3 Surely he shall deliver thee from the snare of the fowler, and from the noisome pestilence.
4 He shall cover thee with his feathers, and under his wings shalt thou trust: his truth shall be thy shield and buckler.
5 Thou shalt not be afraid for the terror by night; nor for the arrow that flieth by day;
6 Nor for the pestilence that walketh in darkness; nor for the destruction that wasteth at noonday.
7 A thousand shall fall at thy side, and ten thousand at thy right hand; but it shall not come nigh thee.
8 Only with thine eyes shalt thou behold and see the reward of the wicked.
9 Because thou hast made the Lord, which is my refuge, even the most High, thy habitation;
10 There shall no evil befall thee, neither shall any plague come nigh thy dwelling.
11 For he shall give his angels charge over thee, to keep thee in all thy ways.
12 They shall bear thee up in their hands, lest thou dash thy foot against a stone.
13 Thou shalt tread upon the lion and adder: the young lion and the dragon shalt thou trample under feet.
14 Because he hath set his love upon me, therefore will I deliver him: I will set him on high, because he hath known my name.
15 He shall call upon me, and I will answer him: I will be with him in trouble; I will deliver him, and honor him.
16 With long life will I satisfy him, and shew him my salvation.

Son of a Preacher

The 91st Psalm is the one passage of scripture that meant more to me than any other passage in the entire Bible. This was handwritten out and mailed to me on a piece of paper by someone special when I first got locked up. I kept it posted in my locker and would read it daily for encouragement, strength, and comfort. Reading it kept me going when I wanted to give up. It gave me strength when that place got dark and scary. It kept me safe underneath a hedge of protection when everyone around me turned to violence to make their point.

When I was missing home, and wondering if I would ever see daylight again, I read the 91st Psalm and found comfort. It was a long, hard, difficult journey but this passage of scripture sustained me.

As you might have surmised, lots of people 'find Christ' in prison. I did not find him there. But I did get to know him there. It is where He taught me to look towards Him and proved Himself to be trustworthy. He went down deep into the foxhole with me and brought me out on the other side, safe, sound, and a better man for the experience.

I grew up the son of a well-known and well-respected preacher. My dad is Billy Cass. An incredible singer/songwriter, guitar player, and Pentecostal preacher.

I grew up attending many church services that made me feel good emotionally while there and on throughout the week even, sometimes.

My dad would hold 'street services' on the weekends and would pull a trailer behind his truck and out into a grocery store parking lot/plaza set out chairs, set up lights, play music, and then preach the Gospel to anyone within earshot of his microphone and loudspeakers. I would play drums behind him. As he and my stepmom, Harolene would lead the singing and worship service, and my dad would preach. I grew up looking forward to our Friday night street services. It was something I was proud to be a part of.

From there my dad went on to Pastor several churches and throughout all of them, I became more and more involved in church. Sometimes, I went because I wanted to know more about Jesus. Sometimes I went to sell weed to my friends in the youth group. Sometimes I went to see the new girl, and other times I went simply because it was required, but I always went.

Growing up as a preacher's son, I had a solid foundation and understanding of who God is. I had listened to words describing him. I played music and sang about Him. I was even given the pulpit on different occasions and preached a few words about Him myself. But I had never had to depend on Him for survival. This is where He became real for me.

It took a miracle for me to come out of that place a better man. One who is appreciative of so many things, and one who is convinced beyond a shadow of a doubt that Jesus Christ is real. He died for the remittance of my sins and He walked with me through this place. He kept me safe and taught me to trust Him. This is where He revealed the depth of His love for me, and this is where we got personal. Prison is where I went from knowing about who Christ was to knowing who Christ is.

At various times throughout my incarcerated journey, I would lead Bible studies, prayer groups, or would find myself holding a service in the chapel or on the Rec field. I'm far from a proper example of what a Christian should be, but I have no doubt that it was His mercies that kept me safe, and it's His mercies that gives me breath to write about my experiences now. The Bible records God using a rooster, a donkey, a murderer, a traitor, and many other 'unthinkables' to all deliver a message to the people. Why wouldn't He use me? So of course, I wrote poems about my relationship with Christ and his Divine protection.

When He Was on The Cross…We Were on His Mind

Some odd two thousand years ago, a King left His throne
To travel to this wretched earth, condemned to die all alone
His blood was undefiled, his name knew no shame
to become a sacrificial lamb was the reason why he came
His life was low and humble, he never did anything wrong
He went about doing good, yet he knew all along
That one day soon his life would come to a tragic end
His very own friends and neighbors
would be the ones who'd crucify him

He never said a word as the soldiers plucked his beard
And when they stripped him of his clothes, he only shed a tear
The crowd began to laugh and mock, as the soldiers spit upon him
He just stood and waited patiently for this humiliation to end
One thought it might be funny,
to place a crown of thorns upon his head
He offered no resistance, He only stood there and bled
With a 'cat of nine tails', they tore his flesh apart
But the sins of this world are what really broke his heart
At last, the crowd was satisfied, the soldiers had their fun

They were now ready to kill Gods beloved son
To an old wooden cross, they nailed his hands and feet
And between two thieves he hung, in the suns blistering heat
All this pain he had to suffer to atone the sins of mankind
For when he was on the cross, we were on his mind

Right There with Me

I'm sailing across awful stormy seas
But I won't worry because I know you're with me
Water rages, as the mighty winds blow
My little ship is tossed to and fro

These winds and waves are hard to understand
But I know it's all part of your master plan
For you have me covered underneath your wing
Protected from harm. I'm safe from everything

I only see things as they are right now
Hope and pray it all works out somehow
But you see my world, as it soon will be
And you're only doing what is best for me

With my entire situation, you're in total control
For I gave you my life when I gave you my soul
I know there's no way you would allow me to drown
Or pick me up just to let me down

For you are the Father from heaven above
Your heart is filled with mercy and love
Help me to remember the next time at sea
That I'm not alone, you're right there with me

Unanswered Prayers

Despite my deepening relationship with the Lord and having had a change in attitude and behavior both since turning twenty-one. The Universe decided I needed further testing still. As I was being hardened and forged. Just like steel.

It didn't take me long after having arrived in prison to begin second-guessing myself. I had come to sorely regret my decision to accept their term of 22 years in prison for a crime that I did not commit. The more I reflected, the more I began to think, that I could have beat the charges altogether if I had gone to trial.

I figured the passage of time would work in my favor. So, I rolled the dice and filed a 3.850 Motion for Post-Conviction Relief hoping to set aside my plea and take these charges to trial. I based my claim on "Ineffective Assistance of Counsel". I prayed about it and then sent it off in the mail and a few months later, much to my surprise, I was granted a hearing before the Judge on the matter. This is how God was going to work, I was sure of it.

A short time later after having received the notice. I was transferred from Marion Correctional Institution, back to the county jail, to await my hearing. I remember feeling very fortunate on the morning of my court appearance. The officers in the Lee County Jail had brought me downstairs to the area of the jail referred to as 'booking' to hold me until after breakfast, after which time I'd be escorted through a labyrinth of hallways and into the courtroom.

Booking is where all the new people coming into the jail are held until they are assigned a permanent dorm or cell block to await trial, or until they are bonded out. Most people in this area are still in the same clothes they were wearing when they were arrested and are only held a few hours before some disposition is assigned to them. It is a holding area.

While waiting, I was in a holding cell with two other guys who had been brought in overnight for public intoxication and would soon be released. When breakfast was served, It just so happened to be biscuits and gravy. An old favorite of mine. That day, I got three plates. Mine, and both of theirs. They marveled at how enthusiastically I ate the jail food. I marveled at how wonderful this day was already starting to be.

Later on that morning, when I made it in front of the Judge. I explained that I wanted to withdraw my plea of No Contest. I demonstrated how my attorney had been biased against me and had failed to adequately represent me due to that personal bias, and then listed all the reasons why I should be allowed to withdraw my plea and given a date for trial.

My courtroom performance was spot on. I had presented my case, I had answered their 'gotcha questions' with great poise. The Judge even managed to crack a smile and chuckle once or twice at my witty responses. The courtroom was full of my family, friends, and supporters. I could not have felt better. The Judge said he would let me know his ruling by mail. There was nothing anyone could do but wait. I had done my part, there was nothing left to do now except wait for God to 'Show out.'

Upon the conclusion of my hearing, I was escorted to another holding cell. This one was on the fourth floor of the Lee County Jail and had a window with a view of the 'Outside'. As I stared out the window and took in the view of the city and the street that sat just on the other side, I wrote another poem.

Outside

I'm looking at the grass and the tall tall trees

I'm looking at the Sunshine

Wish it was shining down on me

I'm looking at the cars go by so so fast

Oh, how I wish that I could relive my past

Outside, I'm looking out at you

What I wouldn't do to be with you

Outside will you still be there for me

Will you still be there when they finally set me free

I've been looking out for oh so long

I almost forgot about you

Thought you were gone

I never thought I'd see you again

Outside, you're my long-lost friend

Outside I'm looking out at you

What I wouldn't do to be with you

Outside, will you still be there for me

Will you still be there when they finally set me free

We have all heard the saying 'Light at the end of the tunnel'. It was kind of hard for me not to feel that way. I had been in a dark place, I had been alone, feeling my way along very much as you would in a darkened and unfamiliar tunnel. When suddenly there was light.

I was excited, I was hopeful, I just knew this was how God was going to work. I was going to have a miracle story. It all made sense now. There was an end to this relentless suffering and isolation. I just knew it. Except, I was wrong!

I was later informed by Legal Mail that the Judge denied my motion, and that light that I had seen shining turned out to be a train. It ran me over, but before it did, before I knew for sure what the oncoming light was, I wrote this…

Light at The End of The Tunnel

Darkness surrounds me
As my hands guide the way
Don't know where I am going
Just that I can't stay
I must move forward
Because I can't go back
I've never been here before
Though it looks to be a well-worn track
I cannot see in front of me
Though I can see behind
I don't understand this paradox
It is too much for my mind
There is no mercy or refuge
In memories of home
They only serve to remind me
That I am now alone
Wait, is that a noise I hear
A thunder of distant jubilee
No, I've heard it before
It's just my mind playing tricks on me
When will this craziness stop?
Will this madness never cease?
I'm caught in the throes of insanity
Wondering If I will ever see release
A glimmer of hope, and a sparkle of light
Are shining just ahead
Finally, an answer
To the many tears that I have shed
I see a light
At the end of this proverbial tunnel
A birth to freedom and an end to pain
I just pray to God that it's not a train

It was a train and a pretty darn big one. It did not just run me over, it flattened me. Like a penny on a train track flat. The Judge's denial shook my Faith. It meant that I would have to serve out all the rest of my time.

I was hurt, and confused. I felt alone and abandoned. Like I was the butt of one of God's cruel jokes. I hurt in ways that I do not have words to describe. I cursed God, and with emotions all a rage. I wrote poems and letters not fit to print.

I became very acquainted with feeling like God had not only abandoned me but was now just having further fun at my expense. Like He did not care about me at all.

It wouldn't be until later, that I would learn that He had not forsaken me at all during this time, but was instead shaping my future.

"You are going to meet a lot of really great people in there"

- ***Uncle Tony***

Some of The Greatest People That I Have Ever Met.

When the news broke that I had gotten into some trouble and would be going to prison. The first words out of my Uncle Tony's mouth shocked me and had me shaking my head in confusion. After I told him my bad news, he looked at me and exclaimed, "Oh Mark, you're going to meet a lot of really great people in there." I thought it was such an odd response, but he was right! I did.

I did not understand it then, but I certainly do now. While in one sense, I was surrounded by society's worst examples of humanity. There were a few people that I met along the way that have remained lifelong friends. Many people lightened my load or lit up my path one way or the other, and they deserve honorable mentions for sure.

This book would be too expensive to print if I told you about every one of them, so I have selected just a few people of interest that I have met along the way and am proud to call my friends.

Turn the page and I will introduce you to some of the greatest people that I have ever met.

'Jeremy Spoken'

Jeremy sent me this photo shortly after he was released. It was the first time he played guitar as a free man. He learned to play while inside.

In my life's hall of fame, I would be remiss if I did not begin by introducing you to one of my best friends ever, Jeremy Anderson.

Jeremy was one of my two best friends. We met on my birthday. It was the evening of December 28th, 2001.
I slept on a bottom bunk in D Dorm at Cross City and the bunk right next to me had been open for quite some time.

It was a ritual every Friday, to come back in from our morning job assignments and check to see if anyone had moved in on top of or right next to us, as Friday was shipping and receiving day.

I had managed to go nearly three months without a 'next-door neighbor' then on the evening of my birthday there was a disturbance in another dormitory and in the middle of the night they moved a bunch of people out of that dorm into empty bunks across the compound and Jeremy landed in the one right next to me. I would always tell him that God sent him to me as a birthday present. I still believe that is true.

The song by Pearl Jam, 'Jeremy Spoken' was somewhat popular at this time so I would always sing that line to him whenever I saw him as a greeting. Thus, the moniker, 'Jeremy Spoken'.

He liked the NY Jets, and I liked The Buffalo Bills, so we would make little side bets on the football games. He played guitar and would try to show me a few chords and riffs.

He was very much Agnostic. He used to say that he did not believe in God, and if God did exist, *well then, he hated Him*. That led to many conversations about God, man, and this entire universe and why we all exist. Very civil but thought-provoking conversations that we would have. His insight and perspective on things were usually quite different than everyone else's.

In prison, almost everyone has some type of nickname. A few real-life examples that come to mind are Turtle, Squirrel, Psycho, Bag soup, Swole belly, Shoestring, Bright eyes, Thin man, Hollywood, Shepard, Rebel, Johnny Reb, Mad Max, Death Row, T- Dollar, Sexxy Red, and on and on I could go. People walk around with all kinds of names in there, and Jeremy had one for me MWSSTFOC.

Yes, it is long. It is elaborate, it is humorously vulgar, and it is so very Jeremy. He would see me across the compound and yell 'Hey what's up MWSSTFOC' and he would pronounce each letter M-W-S-S-T-F-O-C and we would both laugh.

What does it mean?
Do you really want to know?
Ok, here goes.

MWSSTFOC was a name that Jeremy gave to me one day when we were talking about all these weird names that everyone had, and since I called him 'Jeremy Spoken' all the time, which he didn't really like because he hated that song, he named me M̲ark W̲ayne S̲hot S̲lap T̲he F̲*ck O̲ut C̲ass or just M-W-S-S-T-F-O-C for short. It seemed appropriate.

Jeremy worked for P.R.I.D.E. a private industry that utilizes inmate labor to make things such as soap, uniforms, boots, they even have farms and grow vegetables, etc.…

Jeremy worked for the printing division and had a job in the sales offices. His job required him to use a phone and make calls to people outside in the free world. They paid him .25 cents an hour. Which was the top pay you could attain. Most inmates do not get paid for working. Only a select few in a select few locations. Jeremy was one of the select few.

I was released about seven years before he was, and we would call each other on his office line, and we would chat. This was against the rules and if he got caught he would have lost his job and went to confinement so we didn't do it often but when we did get a chance to speak to each other it was always refreshing and left us both feeling better after the call than before.
This one particular day, I was sitting in my car in a parking lot and had only been out about a year at this time, when my cell phone rang. It was Jeremy.

He was in his office making his routine calls when he snuck a call to me. It was his halfway anniversary mark that day and he wanted to tell me that he felt just like I told him I felt the day I hit my halfway mark date.

I woke up that milestone morning at Baker Correctional Institution. I was thrilled to have made it halfway through my sentence. In one sense it marked a real milestone, and I was excited about having half of my time done. Until I realized in the next moment, that every bit of time I had just completed, I now had to go do all over again.

He was calling to tell me he finally understood what I had meant about it being more of a dreaded day than one to celebrate.

One of my favorite memories with Jeremy is the time he bestowed upon me some of the best advice that anyone ever has. We were both laying on our bunks this one particular day. He was reading a book and I was writing a letter when he looked over at me and said:

"Mark, do not ever fall for women - no matter how enchanting their eyes may be, or how beautiful their smiles are - that have numerous notebooks filled with poetry that they have written while locked up inside of various drug rehabs and/or mental wards."

That advice has served me well up to this very day, and may very well serve you well too. Should you chose to apply it.

When Jeremy was released, I went to see him and met his brothers and his lovely mother and they all accepted me as family.

As the days, weeks, months, and years, would go by Jeremy and I would stay in touch. He would come to visit me in Fort Myers, and I would go to visit him in New Port Richey, Tampa, or Ocala, just depending on where he was. I even gave him one of my pit bulls that he had bonded with. Her name was Lady Belle. She was a great dog, and he was a great friend.

She would end up being hit by a car about a year after that, and he would end up being shot by a cop shortly after that as well, but neither of us knew that then.

After a time, Jeremy came to know Jesus Christ as his Lord and Savior and that was a pretty big deal to all of us who knew him because he had been so anti-God, and anti-Religion for so long.

Somewhere along the way though, Jeremy had a personal encounter with Christ, and Jesus did what Jesus does and suddenly Agnostic Jeremy became Jesus Freak Jeremy.
It was a beautiful thing.

Later, there would be a warrant issued for his arrest for a crime he says he did not do or never even happened, and everyone who knew Jeremy will tell you they believed him.

Anyway, one day the police kicked the door in, and Jeremy was shot and killed. It was heartbreaking to all that knew him. He is missed every day by many people.

When I think of Jeremy today though, I prefer to remember the time that I was enrolled in college classes in the Spring of 2011 and work had me falling behind on my school work and I had one weekend left to do a semesters worth of work in two different classes, or else fail very badly. I knew there was no way I could do it all by myself. I called Jeremy and he came down from Ocala to stay with me, and we worked side by side all weekend long on my course work. Me on one subject and him on another. In the end, we both passed my classes with a C.

In this next photo, we had been out bowling and I had given him my favorite Guns N Roses shirt that depicted their album cover 'Lies' *because I was too fat to wear it*; and while at the bowling alley, what appeared to be a gay Elvis impersonator walked by and Jeremy proclaimed "I have to get a picture with that dude. He is so wild, come on." So, I went with him and it is one of my favorite pictures with Jeremy that I have. Better dudes than Jeremy Anderson do not exist!

'Reverend Nick'

Nick was a very stand up dude while in the joint. We were together at Cross City. He was a Chapel clerk. Meaning he worked in the chapel as an assistant to the Chaplain.

This was right inside his wheelhouse as he was one of the most devout Christians I have ever met! It was not 'Jailhouse Religion' so to speak. Nick was real. Nick was powerful, and he always used his positive influence and persuasion over people in the absolute best way possible. Everyone looked up to him and respected him. He in turn would do anything he could to help or to serve someone else in need.

Just to emphasize my point – I will deviate from Nicks' story here one moment and tell you a funny story about another guy, just to draw a contrast and demonstrate to you what Nick **was not** like.

While at a certain Work Camp *(stories of which I have yet to share with you)* I was in the same dorm with a guy we all called 'Preacher'. This guy would loudly proclaim that he was a 'Christian' but was much more representative of those inside who just used the Bible to 'hide behind', as opposed to those allowing it to make any sort of real change in their life. This guy personified the term 'Jailhouse Religion'. He made a show of reading the Bible openly in the dorm and often prayed out loud for attention. He prided himself on being more 'spiritual' and having more 'Biblical knowledge' than everyone else.

This one day came, that Preacher had applied for a job in the warehouse. The warehouse was a coveted position and could only be filled by workcamp inmates because it was outside the gate and everything that entered the institution came in through the warehouse. *So technically, things from the free world could be sent into the warehouse and picked up by an inmate, opened, and then hidden inside something else going into the institution such as bulk laundry detergent for example. Once inside the main compound and delivered to the laundry. Another inmate could receive it and distribute it throughout the compound. Weed, weapons, and cell phones are the most common types of contraband items.* So only the most 'trustworthy' of inmates were even picked for the job.

In theory, People close to getting out were less likely to risk backing up their release date over some sort of contraband shenanigans. Therefore, they assigned 'short-timers' to fill this position.

However, Realit*y* was something quite a bit different. The Sargent who oversaw the warehouse was as crooked as they come. He had been stealing from the warehouse his self for years *or so the rumors went anyway,* and because he was crooked, he only wanted crooked people out there working for him. Inmates that would help load his truck, leave certain items off the inventory lists, miscount inventory quantities. Skills like that were the ones that were in high demand at the warehouse. Stealing was an unofficial job requirement for this position.

I understand this is backward in a civilized society, but you must understand this is not a civilized society. This was the Florida Department of Corrections and the rules are different here.

So, Preacher was called out to the warehouse for a job interview with the Sargent and after a few basic questions the Sargent looked at Preacher and asked him "Do you Steal?" and Preacher loudly, and proudly proclaimed "No sir. I am a man of God. I follow the commandments. I wouldn't steal anything." And the Sargent replied, "Well I don't need you then. I steal, and everyone who works for me steals, so you can't be out here if you're not going to steal".

Preacher dropped to his knees immediately and said "*If stealing's what you want, I will help you rob this place clean. I used to be a crack head on the streets before I came in and I stole everything in sight. No one steals better than me. You want a thief; I am your man. I am the best thief there is. I'm a professional crackhead.*" Everyone bust out laughing. After that, he never did live that down.

For the opportunity to have preferable treatment he so easily compromised his beliefs. So many people there claimed to be a Christian and it is not my place to judge any man. I have enough trouble with my own Christianity, but my point is Nick was nothing at all like Preacher. Nick was real. He had a hold of something genuine. He was different. A shining beacon of light in a very dark world.

He wore a bracelet around his wrist that was blue and orange *Florida Gator colors*. That had the letters WWJD and stood for W̲hat W̲ould J̲esus D̲o and he lived his life just like that always

living by asking himself 'What Jesus Would Do' in any given situation, and then he made that choice.

He was laughed at often and sometimes ridiculed because he would not break any rule whatsoever. No matter how trivial. If you cussed around him, he would cringe and said: "Oh Bad Word, Bad Word" in this playful but still serious way. You were not offended but understood that was not appreciated while in conversation with him.

It was kind of weird how he got the bracelet because in and of itself, it was not issued by the State, so it was not allowed. There is an exception to that though. If an item in your possession is listed on any property or inventory sheet that you have, then it is legal. You can have it.

Nick got this bracelet when he went back to outside court. Someone special gave it to him during visitation, and upon his return, he made sure that they listed it on his property sheet when he left the county jail and returned to the D.O.C. Since it was inventoried when he left there. It was inventoried when he returned automatically; thereby making it legal. Since he had it listed on an official State property sheet. He had not broken a rule.

Many of the officers tried to take it from him, but he would pull out his property sheet and show them it was inventoried, and they would have to leave him alone. He was kind of known for it. It was somewhat of a big deal. He never took it off, ever. When I left for work release later and he was there to tell me goodbye, he took it off and gave it to me. I still have it.

Lots of people called him Reverend Nick and looked up to him. So, to keep it all from going to his head, I considered it my duty to be his 'thorn in the flesh' so to speak. I felt it was my job to keep him humble.

While everyone else lauded praises on him and called him Reverend Nick, I would approach him with a smile and say, "What's up, creep ass cracker?" I was the only one who would dare, but I also knew him way better than any of them did and he knew me. We are still best friends.

I just addressed him that way to keep him humble. I did not want everyone else's admiration to go to his head. I considered my friendly insults to him to be kind of like a public service that I was doing. He was better for it, and I was better for my friendship with him as well.

We spent many days and nights discussing the Bible. He was very well versed, not just in scripture but in history too. He would spend a lot of his work time in the chapel studying other religions and learning to talk with proponents of them about Christ.

Your first week at any institution is an orientation week and you see all the different departments such as the chapel, education, rec, medical, security, classification, etc. and they orientate you with the rules, what's expected, give you evaluations, etc.. and at the end of the week, you are assigned a job assignment, and a bunk.

Nick was the one who did the Chapel orientations, so he came in contact with each and every new person within two days of them getting off of the bus.
In this position, he would minister the Gospel to everyone and would often talk to the young Muslims about Jesus Christ. He had much success converting several of them to Christianity.

After a while, the Islamic leaders on the compound grew tired of Nick converting their young Islamic members and approached Nick with prison-made shanks and threatened to kill him while he slept, if he did not stop.

Now when I say prison made shanks, I'm talking about a piece of steel off of a bed rail, ground down to v type point at one end; and the other end wrapped in various amounts of duct tape and electrical tape to serve as a handle, and then had been buried in a hole, filled with human feces so that when stabbed or slashed with the blade, your wound would become grossly infected and severely complicate your healing. A vicious weapon to be sure, and there were two of them, and they each had one.

Nick was not intimidated, nor concerned when he replied to them *"Gentlemen before you can ever get to me you will have to get through each and every one of these angels that Christ has commissioned to encamp around about me.*
So, you attempt to do anything you feel you need to, and I will continue to preach the Gospel of Jesus Christ to all that will listen." And he did, and no harm ever came to him.
He walked around underneath the divine favor and protection of the Good Lord above. There is no doubt about that.

Nick would also hold Bible studies on the rec field, and everyone would come from all over the compound to hear him. Not a doubt in my mind that the Lord brought us together. My journey with the Lord has been a bit up and down and Nick has seen me at opposite ends of the spiritual extreme and all in between. I may have wavered, but he always stood fast and stood strong.

So much so, that when I got out, I first lived near to my grandparents and Nick would call about once a week, and if I was not there, he and my grandmother would talk. She even began writing to him and sending him a few dollars on occasion. She very much appreciated him and would often chastise me for not writing to him enough after I got out.

When My grandmother fell ill and was in Hospice in 2007 and the family knew it would not be long. I called the Chaplain where Nick was at this time, *as he had been transferred from Cross City after I left to go to work release.*

I had not been in touch with Nick in about eighteen months or so. He was unaware of my grandmas' condition. I called the chaplain and told him that Nick's grandmother only had a few days left. She was in Hospice, and could he come to the phone and say goodbye.

They made a special exception and did call him to the Chapel (at this institution he wasn't a chapel clerk) he was confused when the chaplain came to visit him in his dorm and asked him to come back to the chapel with him. He knew something was up because *he did not have a grandmother. Much less one that was sick that he needed to call*; but he was keen enough not to say anything and just go along with what they were saying. Once he got to the chaplain's office and dialed the number that I had left with the Chaplain, I answered on the first ring.

He was surprised, to say the least, but I explained what was going on and was then able to put the phone next to my grandmothers' ear. They spoke to each other, told each other goodbye. She thanked him for being a good friend to me and told him she would see him in Heaven. He has always wished that he had had a chance to meet her. She passed away in 2007. Six years before Nicks' release.

Another time I remember, was when I was with Jeremy *and not at my peak spiritually*. Jeremy and I were walking across the compound at Cross City sometime in 2002 when we happened to pass Nick.

We were all on our way to our dormitories as count time was at 4:30 and it was right then 4:20 pm and for any of those reading that don't know, 4:20 is considered the international time to get high, or smoke weed to be more precise. It is a whole thing that pot smokers are into.

Anyway, we were all three standing together chatting when I looked at my watch, seen it was 4:20 and said to Jeremy. "It's 4:20" we both smiled, and I said, "Nick do you know what 4:20 is?" and he replied, "Yes, it's the international time to gather around and pray for all you crazy people getting high". We all bust out laughing. That was Nick. That was me, and that was Jeremy.

In contrast, there was another time that Nick and I prayed for a miracle and got one. Nick and I were originally in D dorm together. It was an open bay dormitory and that is how we got to know each other originally. He slept only a few bunks away from me. In the implementation of new security protocols that were being put into place at the time Nick was reclassified and moved across the compound to B dormitory, which was a dorm with four-man rooms instead of one great big giant dormitory that held ninety men. A little more privacy, a little quieter. That dorm was considered an upgrade in both living conditions and security both. As the officers could lock the dorm down easier just by sending everyone to their rooms and sliding the doors closed.

I had less time left than Nick did, so I was considered less of a security risk and I remained in D dormitory. This is important because yes, we could see each other on the compound; but in prison, about 75% or more of your time is spent inside your own dormitory. They close the rec yard, and outside activities end at dusk and during daylight savings time that can be 5 pm.

So, you lived with whoever was around you in the dorm. Like them or hate them, those are the guys that you do time with. You do life with them too. So, it was a real disappointment when they separated us. We got together and began to pray about the situation.

There was no way they were going to move him back. He had been relocated on a new security protocol and nothing trumps that. So, the only chance of us being in the same dorm again was if I moved. Plus, B dorm was much preferable living quarters than D dorm was anyway.

However, it was just as unlikely that they would move me either. I was medium custody and work camp eligible (*a lower grade of classification – less of a security risk*) therefore I fit the security protocol for D dorm. This was a whole new thing they were doing. We prayed anyway.

I had submitted a request to change dorms, just trying to be official, and do everything I knew to do to get the transfer but honestly, there was not much hope of this happening through those methods.

Before the request form could be answered yes or no, either way, one of Nick's roommates got into a fight at the Poker table and then went to confinement, leaving an empty bunk right inside Nick's room. His other roommate was cool too, and we were all friends. This was the perfect opportunity. Nick came and told me on Saturday morning, we said a quick prayer again, and went to see the Captain.
Now even if they did grant my very unlikely request, they would never do it on a Weekend. Bunk changes go through classification, and they are Administrative staff. It is an Administrative action, and those only take place during Admin

hours. Like at a bank, the nighttime security guy is not going to let you in and assist you with opening an account. You are going to have to wait till Monday and see a bank representative for that. Different departments, they do different things.

In this instance, Security can do it but would have to have a compelling reason to do so. Such as a fight, an escape attempt, something serious that threatened the security of the institution, inmates, or staff. We went and asked anyway.

The Captain happened to be out on the yard, and this was an older Captain, one who was due to retire at the end of the year and he happened to be one of the nicer ones. He did not even work that shift. He just so happened to be filling in for the regularly scheduled Captain who did not come in that day. *The same day after a bunk opened in the exact cell that I wanted to move to.*

We went up to him, and I explained that I had already submitted a request to move to B dorm and it had yet to be answered and returned. However, a bunk in Nick's cell had just opened and I did not want that bunk to get filled before my request could be returned. Would he please authorize a bunk change and move me from D-48 Lower to B-08- 4 today, so that I would not have a chance of losing it.

He said "Yes" and told me to "go pack". He changed my bunk right then and there. That was no small ask, everyone thought I had 'snitched' on someone, or offered up some sort of information on something nefarious going on because it was an unlikely bestowment of favor.

There was no snitching though. It went down just like I said it did. **Prayer arranged the circumstances, doing my part**

engaged faith, and once engaged, Faith moved the hand of God. I believe that!

Through that, I learned that God cares about even our smallest desires. You cannot tell me God did not look down from heaven and show favor on two men incarcerated in Cross City, Florida that had Faith to ask Him and then the courage enough to believe it.

God did not deliver me from that 'fiery furnace'. I suppose I needed to go through it, but he certainly walked through it with me. Providing me strength, wisdom, courage, and occasional favor all while teaching me to rely on Him.

I remain thankful for having known Nick and the influence that he has had on my life. Unfortunately, Nick passed on August 7th, 2020. *Just a couple months before this book was published.*

No doubt, he and Jeremy are awaiting my arrival to the other side. Though I miss them both. I am still hoping it will be a while longer before I see either one of them again.

Turtle

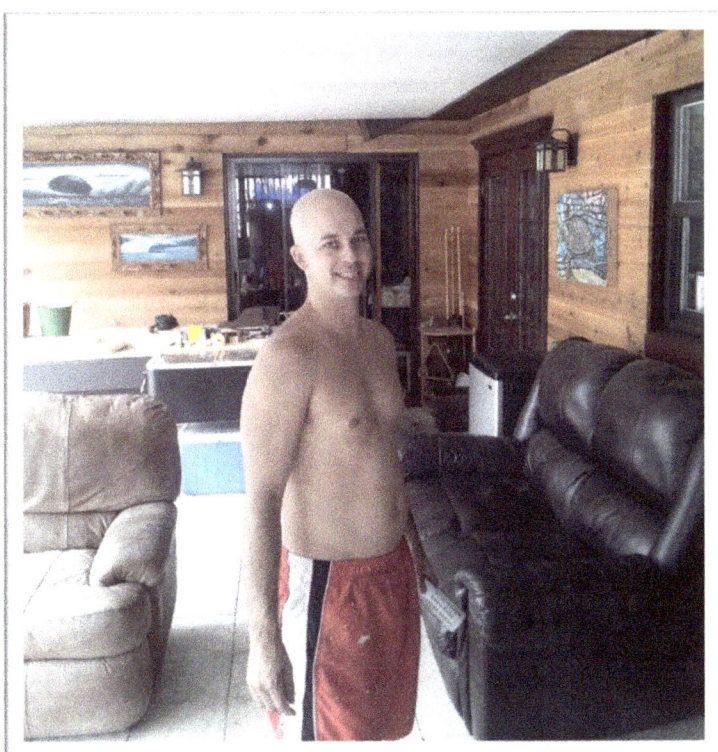

Turtle is a guy who deserves all kinds of recognition and accolades. His real name is Randy, but no one calls him that, except the law. He is one of the coolest guys that I have ever met, and we remain friends to this day.

He is by far one of the most talented people in the world. He draws, paints, tattoos, and builds with wood. Anything he touches turns into an artistic masterpiece.

He is super mellow and is also a fellow handball aficionado. Turtle was always considered one of the better handball players at Cross City.

We would have handball tournaments often while in prison and he was always one of the top three players on the compound. I played him and played him, and never once beat him. Not while we were in any way. I did eventually after we got out, but it was mostly luck. *Or so he says.*

I have been up to North Florida to visit him a few times since each of our releases and he has come down to Fort Myers several times. We play each other every chance we get. We are both extremely competitive but these days we just huff and puff as we run around the court like 'old men'.

There was this one particular day that stands out in my mind that sums my friend Turtle up perfectly. I had borrowed a few dollars from him and was due to pay him back on a certain Friday, but my money from home was mailed a few days later than anticipated and did not arrive when I originally thought that it would. So, I went over to his bunk to explain why I was not going to be able to pay him when I said I was and to tell him of the new expected payment date.

He was lying on his bunk, had his sketch pad in hand, his headphones in, and was drawing some sort of magnificent masterpiece when I approached him. He slid one earphone off of his ear, and continued to draw as I explained why I couldn't pay him that day (not that he even asked) and he cocks his one eye up at me after I conclude and reply's "Dude, you're harshing my mellow".

That was Turtle, never one to stress too much about anything. Slow-motion, steady progress, mellow vibes. He is still one of my favorite people to be around and to go visit.

After each of our releases, I would bring him down to Fort Myers and would host tattoo parties. Here, there, and yonder. Once we had one at the bar/restaurant that my mom and uncle owned called Mulletville. Turtle had come down to visit and I had him follow me in my new Camaro that had recently been involved in an accident and we proceeded to go buy me a new car.

Then we drove to Mulletville, where he proceeded to sling ink on all the hot chicks, I collected cover charge at the door, and my mom tended bar. - *she is gangster like that.* Good times were had by all that night, and each of the three of us made a lot of money. Me, My mom, and Turtle.

On another occasion, he took me surfing, up near Cocoa Beach in North East Florida and there was a rare storm approaching and the waves were nothing an experienced surfer should have been out in, much less, a first-time rookie like myself, but I went anyway.

Those waves pummeled me, and eventually, we lost sight of each other, and I fought the waves that were trying to drown me all the way to the shore. Once I made it, I walked up to the little beachside bar and grill and sat with two ladies, and had drinks. An hour later, here Turtle came. He was so happy to see me, he was worried I had drowned. We smiled and laughed, both happy that the other one was alive.

One of my favorite post-release memories with him though is when I had an extra ticket to see Slash at the Orlando House of Blues. Sometime in 2010, I think. So, I invited him to go, and before we went, he memorialized the event by giving me a

tattoo of Slash on my arm. Matter of fact he tattooed most of the tattoos that I have on my music arm.

As far as his artwork goes, it's amazing and when deciding to put this book together I asked him for a few samples from his collection that he drew while we were at Cross City together and he was kind enough to allow me use of a few for this project Please do take a moment and enjoy his Mastery.

Most of his drawings were done with colored pencils alone. He would rub certain areas with tissue paper to soften up the look a little bit, but these are all hand drawings using colored pencils, tissue paper, erasers, and things like that.

His work follows:

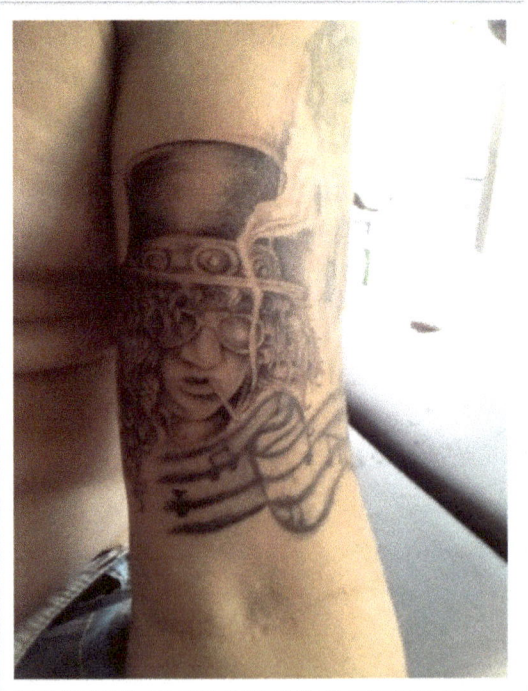

Jay

Before there was Jeremy, Nick, or Turtle, there was Jay. I met him first. He had already been at Desoto for a while when I first arrived in 1993.

We became fast friends. He taught me a lot of the ropes and gave me many pointers on how to carry myself and how to 'do time' without letting the time 'do me'.

He was a bodybuilder type and was quite the authority when it came to nutrition and exercise. We became regular work out partners. We slept in different dorms but would hang out together whenever the yard was open.

I can remember one time there was some tension on the compound. Some dude had stabbed another dude's lover and now a bunch of people was preparing to go to war and kill each other about it. It was a dangerous time to be out on the yard or in open population. But we were. Such was our fate.

Jay and I stayed posted up with our backs against the wall at the commissary the entire time the yard was open. I kept my hands in my pocket, while wearing a pair of homemade 'brass knuckles' that Jay had procured for me from a buddy of his who made them in the welding shop.

I say 'brass knuckles' to give you a better idea. But what they really were, were 'Rebar knuckles. Some guy had welded pieces of Rebar together so that they could be worn on the fist.

Jay had given them to me in case I was attacked in the middle of the night while I slept in that crazy Jitterbug dorm that I lived in. There were many nights that I went to sleep wearing them, with my hand underneath the pillow. This was all against the rules of course. It may have even meant additional time had I ever been caught with them, but being caught *without* them would have been much worse. It was 1993 and Desoto was that kind of place.

Not every day required savagery though. It just depended on the tension level at the camp. Some days were very chill. There were many days that Jay and I would go to the far side of the compound by the library, where no one could see us and smoke weed.

Then one day, they called his name on the loudspeaker and told him to report to the back gate. The Feds had come to get him. He had several 'Trafficking in Narcotics' charges pending in the Federal Court system and just like that he was gone.
He was happy about it, as doing Federal time is much more preferable than doing State time.

I was sad because I have never seen him since.

One day about nine months later he sent me these photos.
Which was cool because Desoto provided no opportunities to take pictures. I have kept them all these years. He is still in, and much older now. He is hoping that his sentence will expire in 2023 and is lucky to be getting out at all.

I say lucky because after his court procedures in Federal court. He was returned to the Florida Department of Corrections and was sent to Everglades Correctional Institution in 1998 and was there with his good friend and co-defendant from the streets.

His co-defendant was getting out soon and wanted to 'look-out' for Jay, as he was responsible for much of the trouble that he and Jay had gotten into in the first place. Together, they concocted a plan to escape that would involve his co-defendant getting out as scheduled and then stealing a semi-truck, and enlisting the help of his mom, and sister who was his friend's girlfriend.

Then one Saturday, during visitation, they did it. Jay's co-defendant stole a semi-truck and drove it right through the fences at Everglades CI and then got out of the truck shooting at officers with a shotgun, as Jay came running towards the large open hole in the fence, His co-defendant threw him a shotgun so both he and his co-defendant were laying down fire while Jay's mom drove up in a getaway car. Just like in a movie, they jumped in and were gone.

There had never been another escape attempt like that in the history of the world, much less within the State of Florida. It caught so much national attention that different television shows and movie companies have contacted him for the rights to his story.

Google it "1998 Florida Prison Escape, Everglades CI" see what you get. He made all the tv and cable crime shows. His story is much more than those shows though. As much drama as that was. As a youth, he was on track to represent the sport of boxing in the Olympics.

Unfortunately for them, the next day after the escape. They were spotted on the streets of Fort Lauderdale and a high-speed chase with law enforcement would ensue and a car accident would happen, and an innocent man would die as a result.

Jay and his co-defendant, who was driving at the time, were both indicted for murder and received Life Sentences. Jay later took that back to court, and beat the entire case, and succeeded in giving the Life sentence back. Thus, the reason why he now has a release date of 2023. That is why I say he is lucky to have that.

Upon his return, the D.O.C. placed him in their highest form of lockdown reserved for the most dangerous of all inmates called CM1. He was in a cell all by himself for 11 years.

Jay on the streets before being locked up

We are still in touch, and I plan to help him realize his business dreams and goals upon his release. *He has certainly had plenty of time to think about them.*

We are still in touch. He has written a book about his life and has plans to get it published and direct a film about his life based on the book.

He truly was an All American who got caught up in some stupid adolescent ventures and has now spent almost 40 years behind bars.

My mom knew Jay too, as we would both often have visits from family on the same weekends back then and they had met then. After all, this happened my mom came up to see me when I was at Baker in 1998 and I told her all about the escape and his mom driving the getaway car; and when I finished she replied "I am very sorry to hear that it was them; but I sure am glad that it wasn't us" – *She was gangster like that.*

Cotton

This guy is super important. We were roommates at Marion CI in 1996. He was my roommate when the guy 'attacked me in the shower, which I mentioned in an earlier chapter. He went by his last name and was somewhat of an infamous 'chain-gang lawyer'. He had a life sentence and had devoted himself to studying law, and filing legal briefs, to pass the time. He was at war with the Department of Corrections and was very often involved in one lawsuit or another against the D.O.C.

When I met him, he had already done 30 years. He too, is still in. He fell way back in 1967. He was an old-timer, a true Chain Gang Veteran. In that time, he had become famous for having won a big lawsuit, and he had helped some other guys get their life sentences overturned.

People develop reputations inside that follow them from institution to institution. Cotton was infamous, and he was my roommate. Because of this, and because I was trying to take my case back to court, I became somewhat of an understudy to

Allan J. Cotton - Prison Esq. He was my mentor in a lot of ways.

It was at this time that I began a correspondence Paralegal course through 'The Blackstone of Law' and would go on to complete a two-year paralegal program in just one year.
I was living, eating, and breathing law. Learning how to properly grieve the Department of Corrections, and then file lawsuits.

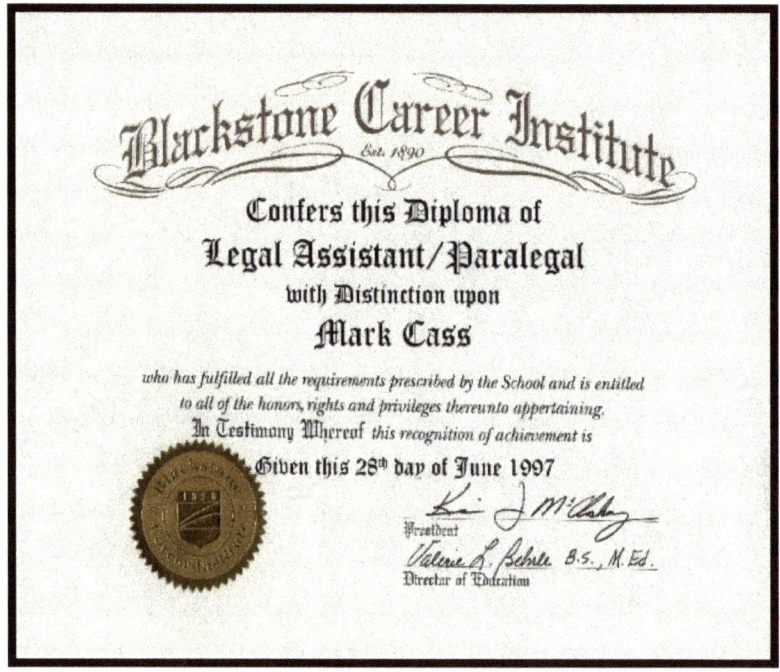

I did file paperwork in my criminal case on occasion and help a few others with simple filings regarding their case. I preferred to stay away from criminal courts though. I was still learning, and I did not want to bear the responsibility of doing something wrong and hindering someone's chances of getting out sooner. I preferred to focus on Administrative Law. Meaning most of my growing legal prowess was concentrated on fighting the D.O.C.

For my birthday, Cotton gave me my very own personal copy of the Florida Administrative Codes Chapter 33. That is the chapter of Florida's Administrative codes, *i.e. rules and regulations* that Governed the D.O.C. and I had studied it every night. It was the equivalent of Google for anything related to the Department of Corrections. There were copies of Chapter 33 kept in the law library and made available for check out upon request, but no one had their own personal copy. No one, except for me!

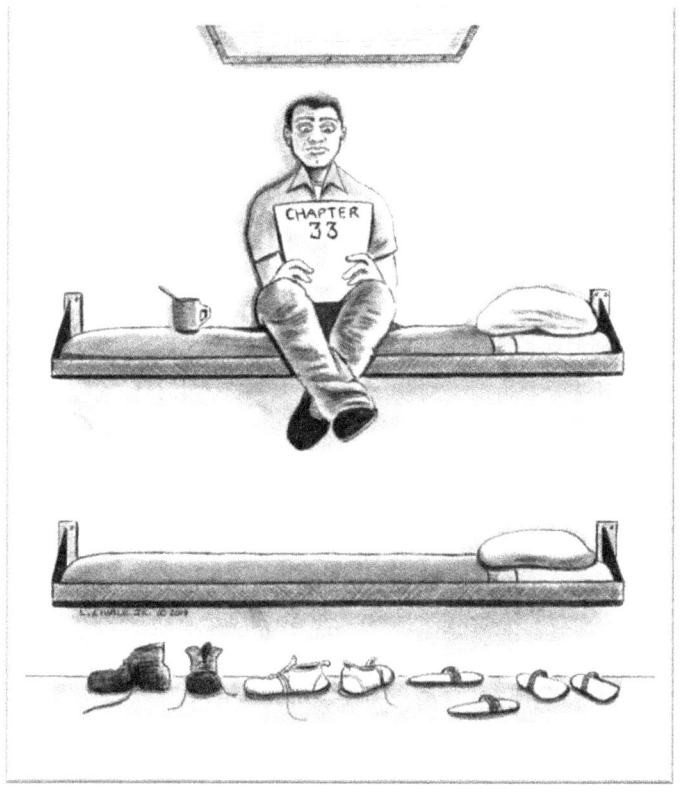

I began to read it line by line and chapter by chapter every day during count time. *They had four or five counts a day, each one lasting thirty minutes or so.* No talking or walking around is allowed during count. The whole compound becomes a ghost town. I used this time to study Chapter 33.

I stayed up to date on what the officers could and could not do. And I became the 'go-to' guy for any sort of disciplinary report appeals. *If you are convicted of a D.R. you have the right to appeal the team's decision to the Superintendent, then to Tallahassee, and from there into the courts.*

I had developed quite a reputation for 'pencil whipping' the D.O.C. I turned it into a little side hustle and began to charge for my services. People were all the time getting in trouble and coming to me to get them out of it. *I stayed knee-deep in chips and cookies.*

As part of my training, Cotton encouraged me to write a grievance on every meal the chow hall served (3 meals a day) for 30 days. In addition, I'd grieve the officers for petty uniform non-compliance issues. Such as not having a whistle (none of them ever carried one), or only having one pen instead of the required two, Boots not shined, etc... I was trying very hard to be a pain in their rear end.

It was important for me to bring the fight to them. I did not act out physically or openly defy the system, but I fought back none the less. I tied up their time and wasted their energy and their efforts. The more paperwork that I could bury them in. The more legal bills I could cost them, The happier I was.

I was full of rage about being locked up and having my life stolen from me. I was motivated by Passion. Every D.R. that I

Mark W. Cass- Prison Esq.

got overturned for someone was a victory. Every motion of 'Sentence Mitigation' that I filed, and some judge granted was a victory. Every appeal for 'Restoration of Gain Time' that I helped someone apply and argue for, was a victory. I was helping everyone get out but me.

I had become a bonafide 'Writ Writer'. I felt like, if they were going to keep me there against my will, then I was going to make it as difficult for them as possible.

What Cotton did not tell me, however, was what they do to 'writ writers'. One Friday I woke up to orders of 'Cass pack it up', I was being transferred. I had no warning, not even a clue this was coming.

This was an Admin transfer, otherwise known as a 'nuisance transfer'. It is true that the squeaky wheel gets the grease. However, my daddy always told me "if it squeaks too much, it gets replaced". That is what was happening. I was being replaced. They were tired of dealing with me and my grievances. I was headed straight to F.S.P – Florida State Prison. Up till now, every facility I have referred to has been named such and such <u>Correctional Institution</u>. This is the one facility in the State that is actually named as a Prison.
It is in North Florida, inside the 'Iron Triangle'. *An area in North Florida that has 4 major, hardcore, Correctional Institutions (prisons). All within a triangular radius and FSP sits right in the middle of them.*

Florida State Prison (FSP), Union Correctional Institution (the Rock), and New River Correctional Institution East and West. *New River is comprised of two different prisons.*

None of these prisons do you want to end up in.
They are for the worst of the worst and they are very intense environments to live in. The entire population is full of 'lifers', *people who are never going home.* No one is new.

Every one of these cats has major time under their belts and most have major time left to go. These places are not about rehabilitation or bettering one's self. These places are the designated dumping grounds for humanity. Warehouses full of hardened criminals, and F.S.P. was the worst of all of them. That is where Florida's Electric Chair is. That is where they were sending me.

I did not want to go there of all places, but that was my reward for being such a pain in their backsides. None of my pettiness hardly seemed worth it now. This is why they say, *'Hunting's no fun when the rabbit has the gun.'*

As you have probably surmised by now, I am not your average cat and I had a powerful family support system on the outside. I was blessed to have someone in my life that cared about me and would correspond with me often. Her name is Wendy, and she is certainly one of the 'Greatest people I have ever met'.

Wendy

I believe God had a hand in orchestrating our meeting. He knew that I was very soon going to be in desperate need of a friend. Someone strong. Someone determined to help me, type of friend. As one year prior to my incarceration, when I was 17. I had traveled to Virginia Beach, Virginia with my grandparents to participate in their annual Neptune Festival. Otherwise known as the 'last weekend before they close the beach'. My Grandmother had a craft booth, and I went along to help set up the tent and to lug heavy stuff around.

My grandmother would later claim that I had come into my own that weekend as without any coaching from anyone I just began helping her sell the little girls outfits that she would sew and sell called 'Dorables' *baby talk for Adorable,* to the passerby's, and that I brought in so much business that weekend. It was her all-time best sales weekend ever. She sold out of everything. I was born to be an Entrepreneur. *This prison thing just got in my way.*

The lady in the booth right next to us was Wendy and she was a Calligraphy artist and would create and sell her crafts as well. Which were incredible pieces of art that usually incorporated a saying, quote, or a scripture verse.

I found myself chatting her up in between the sales that I was creating for my grandmother. She was about 20 years my Senior and found herself just laughing at me.

She entertained my conversation probably only because I was funny, and she was bored. Once the show was over, we all packed up and went home. I never saw her again. Two years later when my grandparents returned to the Neptune Festival. They ran into Wendy again. When she asked about me, my grandparents had to regrettably inform her, that I would not be there that year as I had been incarcerated. She was sad to hear it, and passed along her address, just in case I wanted to write. I did, and she did, and she would come to be one of the most meaningful friends of my entire life.

We wrote to each other often, and whenever she was in Florida she would always try to stop by and see me at whatever institution I was at. She became a strong advocate on my behalf and was no stranger to calling up prison officials and checking on me. She lived in Indiana, but she would give these Florida people an earful. She was a dear friend whom I believe God sent to me in an hour of need to help me make it through this season of my life.

One of the coolest things she ever did for me was to attend a concert by my most favorite artist in the world at that time, Travis Tritt. She journaled about the entire experience, what the arena was like, how the opening band was, and wrote down each song that Travis Tritt sang, and in what order. As well as any commentary that he made in between songs, and wrote about the grand finale, and how much she enjoyed the show. Before seeing him live that night, she had no idea who he was. She just bought a ticket and went, because I could not go, and she knew how much I liked him. She went, just so she could write to me and tell me all about it. How cool is that?

The next super cool thing she did for me was when she heard I was being transferred from Marion was to get on the phone immediately with the head of Classification in Tallahassee and went to bat for me. She used my vocational program as the angle to try and get my transfer stopped.

For the past 12 months, I had been taking Computer-Aided Drafting and was about 6 months shy from graduating this vocational program and FSP did not offer any vocational classes.

Wendy argued that it was not right to pull me out of the class so close to graduation. Could they at least send me somewhere that offered that vocational program, so that I could have the opportunity to graduate.

Tallahassee agreed but unfortunately, the next nearest institution that offered AutoCAD drafting, was Baker Correctional Institution and that was no picnic either.

Like it or not, I had graduated to the 'Big Time'.

I haven't had many occasions to see Wendy since my release but she was my go-to person when I was in. She wrote to me, she sent me money, she visited me, she prayed for me, and she knew the rules as well as I did. So, when she got on the phone on my behalf, she had a knack for getting things resolved and this instance is just but one example.

She drew me this piece of art knowing how much the 91st Psalm meant to me.

The Rest of The Story

At this time in my history, I was nearing my halfway point. My mindset changed as did the way I was doing time. I still had five and a half years to go, but that was a whole lot less than the ten I started with or the twenty-two that they originally gave me.

The thought of maybe being able to survive this thing and maybe being able to go home one day somewhat soon changed my attitude, my outlook, and my strategies.

I was also much more familiar with the do's and the don'ts of prison life. I had become well acquainted with the system. I had grown wiser and just in time. As Baker was not like anywhere else, I had ever been. Keep reading and I will tell you why.

Baker
1997 - 1999

I dodged a bullet by not ending up at FSP yes, but Baker was just outside +that Iron Triangle and was the same caliber of prison as all of the ones previously described. This was still a problem.

In Florida, the further South you are, the looser and laxer the institutions tend to be. Certain rules are relaxed, and more liberties are allowed. The security staff have more pleasant attitudes down South.

Up North, it is not like that. The closer to Tallahassee that you get. The worse the institutions tend to be. The officers up there are of a different breed too. They would just as soon kick a hole in your head as not. Makes no difference to them. Don't believe me? *Go ahead and Google "Florida Department of Corrections abusive guards"* See what kind of headlines you get. Then click and click and click and see for how many pages those headlines go on and on for. I do not have to click. I already know, I was there.

I knew what was about to happen when 'that' Sargent took me back to their 'beatdown shed'. A place that was, *shall I say, for purposes of legal liability*, 'rumored' to be a place of seclusion, in which they would take inmates to, handcuff them, and commence to distributing their perverted brand of 'justice' to whatever inmate they felt needed it.

I was there, I was handcuffed, and I knew full well what was about to happen to me when I started praying and asking God to please not to let them kill me. I was battling within myself as to what to do when they hit me. It was not within me to just let them beat on me, but nor could I hit one of them either. That would be a trap.

That would be what they wanted me to do. Then they would call the County Sherriff and have him come arrest me, take me to the county jail, charge me with assault (if they didn't kill me first), and then I'd get even more prison time. No one ever knowing the wiser. It would be my convict word against all their most honorable words. They would make me look like a liar, and themselves heroes. Probably even go back and give each other heroes awards and accommodations, commending each other for the bravery that it took to gang up and beat down a handcuffed inmate, who dared to strike back in self-defense. Yeah, No I could not fall into that trap.

I was in an impossible situation. I did not know what I was going to do. I was scared! No one could help me. Then they messed around and asked me a question. *That is all I needed was a chance to talk.*

Normally, they thump you first and never even get around to asking you anything. But not this time. This time, they saw fit to allow me to speak about the situation at hand before they thumped me.

What was going on, was an officer who was assigned to oversee my work squad. Had written me up for a bogus D.R. when I declared a medical emergency out on a job, causing him to have to bring me back in. This led to a volley of write-ups and reprisals that I will get into when I come to it but for now, suffice it to say that they were going to bring an end to our squabbles right then and there. This would eventually lead to my transfer away from Baker but for now, I am getting way ahead of my story.

By the time, I got through explaining why I was doing what I was doing. Miraculously, they uncuffed me, apologized, and shook my hand. The Sargent even told me that he would 'have a talk' with the officer who was harassing me and make sure he would not do that again.

Wow, that was God! He was the only one that could have turned that Sergeant's heart around like that. That certainly was not me. Me talking was what had got me in this predicament to start with.

This would all happen at their work camp a few years after I arrived. I did not yet know any of that. I was just staring at the large looming gun towers, rolls, and rolls of razor wire, and everything was painted a very dismal color grey, and outlined in rust. This place was very intimidating, and it was cold and wet on the day that I arrived. I will never forget it. I felt ridiculously small and very far away from anyone that had ever cared about me.

My days of writ writing and going out of my way to be an overall pain in their behind was over. Those days ended right then and there. I had attained the formal knowledge and would continue to appeal D.R.'s and help people in the law library, as a side hustle; but the days of being a 'pencil warrior' and fighting against the system, just to fight it, because I was bored and pissed off, were over.

I learned to pick my battles. I also learned that there are consequences when you go to war. This was 'them people's place'. I left the police alone and started trying to do my time as quietly and as unnoticeable as possible.

Much of my prison experience happened while at Baker. This may even become the longest chapter in this book.
I went through many transitions, challenges, and growing pains while there. I spent longer at Baker than I did any other institution.

The first thing I had to do though upon my arrival was to deal with the issue of my co-defendant. He was also at Baker. His name is Aaron.

We should have never been sent to the same institution together. The D.O.C has protocols in place to prevent potential hostile situations between co-defendants. Our files should have been flagged to prevent this. Except they were not, and here we were. I had a temporary advantage in that I knew I was there, but he did not. Not yet. He would by morning though. I had to find him before he found me.

Neither I nor my co-defendant was found guilty by a jury or by a judge. As I stated earlier, I pled No Contest after spending a torturous year inside the County Jail and was then given a 22-

year sentence. Aaron however, pled Guilty to Second Degree Murder and received the 40 year sentence that they offered me.

Therefore, neither one of us testified against the other one, but we both had reason to feel as if it was the other one's fault that we were there. It was imperative that I find him first. I only had a few hours before he would know I was there.

Whenever you arrive at a new institution your name goes on a 'Transfers' list that is placed on a bulletin board inside of each dorm. A copy of the 'daily transfers' list was distributed to each dorm nightly Monday – Friday. My name would be on it. His dorm would get a copy. He would know I was there by tonight one way or the other.

I didn't run into him before they closed the yard that night, and he wasn't in my dorm, but a friend of his was and he told me that he lived in D dorm and went by the nickname 'Nerd' because of his thick glasses.

D dorm was on the other side of the compound. So, he was far enough away that I would not be getting jumped in my sleep but as soon as the yard opened the next morning, I was standing out in front of D dorm. Waiting on him to come out. When he did, I approached him and said:

"We might as well get this over with. We are both here. Let's do whatever it is we are going to do. Are we going to fight? Are we going to kill each other? Or are we going to be friends? Whatever it is, let's do it right now. Your call." He stuck out his hand and I shook it, and that was that. We each had our own burden. We had both been locked up about 5 years by now. I was nearing the halfway point of my sentence and did not want any trouble if I did not have to have it. Nor did he!

Later, he even wrote out a full confession. Acknowledging full responsibility for what happened and telling the Judge, the Governor, or anyone else concerned that he was responsible for the events that happened and that I had nothing to do with this act of violence whatsoever. He then met me at the law library and had it notarized and gave it to me to use any way I saw fit. Of course, I still have a copy.

Me & Aaron – 1997

<u>Affidavit of Aaron Hewitt</u>   3-15-98

To Whom it May Concern,

My name is Aaron Hewitt. An inmate of Baker Correctional Institution, and the co-defendant of Mark Wayne Cass. I'm not writeing this to speak of Marks virtues or to give testimonies of why Mark deserves clemency. I'll leave that to those who know him best.

I write this for myself mainly. No, I'm not asking for anything. Just easing my conscience by getting the truth to those in a position to use it for the better good. The following is the first statement I've made. Please keep in mind I have my full witts and have not been put under any duress. This is my idea and my choice. My truth and my words.

Mark did not kill anyone. I did it. I wish I could take it back, but can't. I pay my dues though. Mark owes no dues. He wasn't even at the scene of the crime. He left a few minutes before a crime was committed. When Mark found out about Alton being killed he went to the police as a proper citizen should. He went to the police and I went to Indiana. Eventually I was caught but kept my mouth shut. Because Mark had knowledge of the crime he was charged with me on murder. Still, I kept my mouth shut and here we are. I won't be going back to court and see no problem with telling

→

what needs being told. Should have been told years ago. Mark is not a killer. He does not have the curse of blood on his hands. Now that I've put this on paper I no longer have quite the burden of guilt. I can't return the dead, but I can help an innocent man.

Under the penalty of perjury, I swear and affirm that all statements made in this Affidavit/letter are true and complete

Dated 3-13-98

Aaron Hewitt
Aaron Hewitt A-139261

State of Florida
County of Baker.
The foregoing instrument was sworn to or affirmed and subscribed before me on March 15, 1998, by Aaron Hewitt, who provided a Florida Department of Corrections inmate I.D. card # A-139261 as identification

Carol Ann Luger
Notary Public

Aaron elected to write front and back on a single sheet of paper so that the Notary stamp, his signature, and the words would never get separated. He really did want to help me.

He was trying to make amends, and this handwritten confession was the only way he knew how. By writing it and admitting guilt he gave up any chance he may have had for an appeal or a resentencing. It was a big deal. Up until this writing, he had followed his attorney's advice and remained quiet. No one had yet heard from him. He was no stranger to the court system though. Immediately upon arrest, he invoked his right to remain silent and had yet to speak to anyone about what happened that night, until he wrote and handed me this confession on March 15, 1998.

I filed for Clemency, while at Baker Work Camp in 1998, and asked Governor Jeb Bush for relief. In that packet of information that I submitted. I included the original copy of Aaron's confession. I had a signed confession. I had a lady helping me who was personal friends with the Governor at the time. I had a specialized Clemency lawyer. I had completed several vocational programs, and correspondence college courses. I was already past my halfway point at this time.

I had family travel from South Florida to Tallahassee and speak for me. I had a fiancé and job waiting for me upon my release. No one was a better candidate for Clemency than I was at the time. None of it mattered. They still denied me, and that is where the original handwritten confession is now and that is who has it. The State of Florida!

The temperature really turned up for me at Baker. There were times I felt God to be both near and far. He may not have delivered me 'out of this prison experience' that I had to endure, but he certainly remained close to me. He protected me and walked with me through each day. He made himself known to me in little ways, tender ways. Ways that made me appreciate Him and know that it was Him telling me that He loved me and that though the storms may rage in my life, He had me nestled in the palm of His hand and that He was working everything out for my good. I will share one example of our intimacy.

That girl back home that had completely ghosted me and was the source of so much of my pain in those early days. Remember her? Well, this one morning that I woke up was her wedding day. I woke up feeling as if I were going to be crucified later in the day. It was Sunday, there was no job assignment that I had to get up and go to. I just laid there in my bunk with my headphones on. I desperately wanted to hear Clay Walker's song 'Where Do I Fit in The Picture.' A song about an ex-lover's wedding day and the pain and heartbreak that the guy feels wondering where he fits in this new picture and then realizing he doesn't fit at all. Music and writing were the only forms of therapy that I had, and most of you can relate to wanting to hear a song so bad at a certain time.

The problem was, I had no way to hear it. It had been released on the radio four years prior in 1994 and was in no way relevant, or recent. I had no way to call and request the song. There were no downloadable songs in the world at that time. I had no CDs, no tapes. Just FM radio and whatever the DJ decided to play alongside a heavy rotation of the top 40. I uttered up a simple request "Please God, let me hear this song"

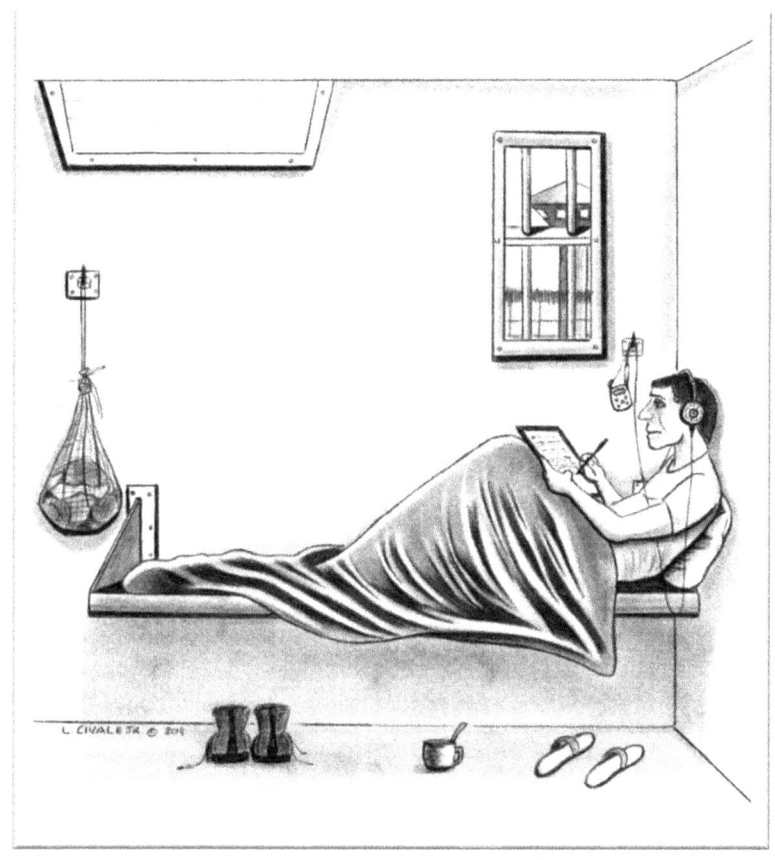

and people I promise you, with my hand before God, within the next few minutes that song came on the radio.

You take that any way you want to; but I was awed, comforted, and humbled. Because it made real, the thought of this great big giant God who ruled the Universe, and the fact that He cared enough about me, an inmate a Baker CI, going through some hard times and just needing to hear a song to feel better, to make that so. Instances like that made real to me that God loved me, and that I was not forgotten, or alone.

What a Heavenly Father that is. What an intimate experience? Something so minute as my desire to hear a song could matter enough for God to make it so. I was moved! God is real people, and he cares about the things you desire, just as much as you do.

Though I did meet lots of great people on the inside. Not everyone I met there had good intentions. Matter of fact most did not. It was only a very few that did. Most of the inmates there were Predators and looking to force their will upon you in some kind of way. Whether it be sexual, extortion, intimidation, or some combination of the three.
I had been tried a few times at other institutions. I had fought, earned respect, and then pretty much was left alone as I was in the Tier program, Education Dept, or on compounds that were laid back for the most part. And a little easier to get along at and mind your business if you were so inclined.

I did not enjoy such a luxury at Baker. There were Predators everywhere. A Predator is usually someone who has been down a long time and has romantic inclinations towards 'pretty White boys.' I was 24 or 25 at the time, slim, trim, and athletic. In the free world, these would have all been plusses. Desirable traits to have. Who does not want to be 'young and good looking'?

However, this incarcerated society is backward, and things do not work on the inside the same way that they do on the outside. The rules and culture are different.

Being young and good-looking here are no advantages at all; and the only time, I ever had someone step to me and try to 'put down' and make me their 'boy,' happened at Baker. I do not remember his name, but he was one of the biggest Black dudes on the compound. Always working out and had a real 'thug life' type of mentality. He decided that he liked me and approached me very disrespectfully.

He then began to follow me everywhere. He would wait in the chow hall after his dorm ate and until mine came in, then he would seek me out to sit at my table and just stare at me, blow kisses at me, try to bump into me and touch me whenever he could manage an 'accidental occasion' to do so. He would jump in line with me when I was headed to the chapel service, and then sit next to me.

I gave this guy no civil conversation at all, cussed him out on several occasions, and discouraged his every attempt to talk to me or be near me, but the situation was getting worse.
I was going to have to stab this dude.

Violence is the only language some people understand.
This guy was one of those. He was overly aggressive and determined to force his will on me. I was just as determined for him not to. He would win a test of strength, so fighting him was not an option. That would also mean me getting into trouble as well, which I was trying to avoid at all costs. I had not yet filed for Clemency at this juncture, but I had plans to do so very soon, and getting into a fight would blow any hope I had of getting relief from the Governor at the time.

His level of aggressive disrespect called for me to stab him though. *Prison protocol demanded that else there would be more Predators after him,* but the legal consequences would be even worse if I did that and would result in me getting additional charges and even more prison time. I was in a no-win situation, through no fault of my own. Sometimes in life trouble just finds you, and here I had a lot of it. It needed to be dealt with immediately.

I had tried avoidance, I had tried explaining "I'm not like that." This guy just kept coming. Each day brought an increase in his aggression, libido, and disrespect. I had to think.

I needed to pull a rabbit out of the hat. I had to stop him, and I needed to do so without getting myself into trouble and it causing me to back up my release date any farther than it already was. I was past my halfway point.

I believe this pressure-cooker environment, is where my problem-solving skills were honed. Figuring out how to overcome impossible situations was often a daily occurrence and something, I am quite good at today.

The situation with this dude had come to a head and I knew the next day would result in a showdown one way or the other. I had to make my move that night when the yard closed. We were in separate dormitories and I only had a few hours to act before the yard opened again and he would be at the front door of my dormitory calling for me and making a big spectacle of himself, forcing a confrontation. Then it came to me.

I devised a perfect plan, but it involved the help and cooperation of my Grandma Judy, my mom's mom. *She was gangster too.* I called her and asked her to send this guy a check for $500 in the mail. I did this for two reasons.

1) The D.O.C. does not accept checks on behalf of inmates, and they would return it to the sender. *There was never a chance of it being cashed.*

2) The second reason that I had her send a check was to prove extortion. *Which just so happened to be a felony punishable by new charges and more prison time.*

After I made her promise to go out and put it in the mailbox right then, knowing the check would arrive in three days. I went to the officer station and asked to speak with the Captain. I explained to him that this guy had a knife and had been attempting to extort me into having my family send him $500 or else he was going to stab me and even pulled out a knife to show me he was serious. Being intimidated I had my Grandmother send him the money but was now afraid that without their intervention the extortion would continue each month and my Grandma is on a fixed income and cannot afford to send him money every month….and bla bla bla on and on I went.

Acting on my information, they locked me up for my own protection, *which I hadn't anticipated*, and then went to this other guy's dorm to lock him up under investigation, and lo and behold what did they find in this guy's locker?

Yep, you guessed it. A knife.
Completely coincidental, as I had no idea if he really had one or not, though it did not surprise me at all. However, that just worked to serve as confirmation of my story. When my Grandmother's check came addressed to him in the mail that was enough evidence for them to call the County Sheriff and haul him down to the county jail and have him charged with 'Felony Extortion'. I later heard that he got another 10 years added on to his sentence as a result.

Baker decided to keep me locked up throughout the entirety of his ordeal, however. Which would lead to me spending about six months in solitary confinement. Six months alone, inside of a cell very much like this one. Only getting out to take a shower on Monday, Wednesday, and Friday nights for five minutes. This would have been enough to break a weaker man and I did go crazy for a while.

I spent a lot of time talking to myself, counting bricks in the wall, writing letters, writing poetry, praising God, cursing God, crying, sleeping, acting out movie scripts, singing, banging out beats on the wall, making playing cards out of the four squares of a milk carton and saving them up for 13 days to collect 52, make a complete deck, and play Solitaire to relieve some of the boredom. Then when I reached my breaking point and I absolutely could not take the isolation or the incarceration one-day longer, I poured out my heart in a letter to the judge begging him to please let me out. He never replied.
I just had to wear it.

My buddy Jay spent 11 years locked up in a cell-like that all by himself. I cannot even begin to imagine the horror of that. It is so easy for them to lock you up in one of these cells, throw you away, and forget about you. Being trapped like that and being able to let it make you a better person and not a bitter person is no easy task. Even there though and in those circumstances, I found a way to laugh and make others laugh too. I would sing or tell jokes while standing at my door, for all the others to hear. Some laughed, others told me to shut up but I entertained none the less.

I remember one night, I was listening to my FM radio *that I was mercifully allowed to keep, being as I was locked up for safety reasons and not for disciplinary reasons.* A guy we all knew who had just gotten out from our confinement wing the day before, had called into the classic rock station that we all listened to and dedicated Black Sabbath's song 'Fairies Wear Boot's to all of the D.O.C. officers at Baker CI. I laughed and laughed about that. It was so funny. He had told us all he was going to do it and we were all waiting and listening. Solitary confinement does not provide many reasons or occasions to laugh, perhaps that is why I remember that incident so well.

Aside from the going crazy part though, this type of solitary can also be very therapeutic as one is forced to get to know themselves intimately, and reflect on the past, as well as plan and contemplate for the future. It also allows you plenty of time for creativity as well.

I managed to get a 55-gallon garbage bag from a confinement trustee. I stood inside of it one day and used my drinking cup from breakfast and filled it full of water. One cup at a time, from the push button sink. By lunchtime, I was waist high and was able to sit and submerge myself by 3 pm. Kind of, I managed to tie one side off to the side of the bunk, but I still had to hold the bag up with my other hand.

There was no purpose for doing it, except it was summer and I was hot. All the officer stations had Air Conditioning but none of the inmate dorms or cells did.

When they finally let me out and I rejoined the compound it was like a brand-new day. Many people had left and many more had replaced them. No one even remembered anything about why I had been locked up in the first place. It was over. I had survived and come away from it all with a brand-new appreciation for Freedom, even in its most limited form.

Then they lowered my custody.

Baker Work Camp
1998 - 1999

My custody level was downgraded from Closed custody to Medium custody. Every inmate is assigned a custody level grade based on their length of sentence, time already served, and threat level assessment amongst other behavioral, legal, and psychological factors.

Closed custody meant I **could not** go outside the gate without handcuffs, leg shackles, and two armed guards accompanying me. It also meant that I resided on the Main Compound behind two rows of Razor wire fences. Under the watch of a gun tower or armed patrol.

Medium custody meant I could go outside the gate and work anywhere on State grounds, under the supervision of one unarmed guard. Medium custody meant I was Work camp eligible.

It represented a whole new way of doing time, one that I had not yet been acquainted with. Doing time with short-timers. Which was a completely different vibe altogether.
One that I had not yet experienced. All the guys you are surrounded with are leaving, most within the year. Except for me, my release date was still 8 years away *on paper*.

'On paper' meaning on paper, my release date was officially 8 years away but this 'on paper' date was not necessarily an accurate reflection of how much time I had left to do, as my date 'on paper' took into account gain time awards that I had already earned but not the ones I had not yet earned but likely would.

Being as I was new, I was given a job inside the gate. As they were not ready quite yet to let me go outside the gate. They assigned me to the kitchen instead and kept me there for six months to see how I would adjust. Turns out, I adjusted quite well.

I had just come from a population of about twelve hundred guys never going home and full of hate. To a population of about one hundred and eighty guys all going home very shortly and most had positive attitudes. During the day about a hundred and seventy of those people left the compound to go work jobs that were outside the gate.
They were contracted out to other State agencies such as road maintenance, cleanup crews, public works, state parks, etc.

That left me and about nine other people on the entire compound all morning and afternoon. Talk about peace and quiet, I loved my mornings!

I worked in the kitchen, but my job was 'swill man'. All the food that gets scraped off inmate trays when they are discarding them after a meal, goes into a large 55-gallon trash can and saved for the pigs. It is called 'swill'. A local farmer would drive in twice a week with a large swill trailer, and it was my job to pick up the swill cans and dump them into a special trailer that he had built for just such a purpose.

Then he would take it back and feed his hogs and I would wash out the cans and keep the swill room clean where the cans were stored.

So, after every meal, I would roll out the can to the swill room and bring in a fresh clean one for the next meal.
That was my job assignment. All the rest of the time I was free to do what I wanted to. Plus, I had kitchen privileges.
Again, I was working for me, not them!

Working in foodservice is a preferred job assignment because although some labor was required, you also got special privileges and authorized access to all the food inventory. Working with a small group of guys every day, the Food Service officer was cool and would often look the other way when we wanted to make ourselves special food that was not on the State menu. Or when we needed to take out some special creation that we had made and sell it for a few dollars. As long as we did our job, kept the kitchen clean, and did not get him into any trouble with his superiors. It was a mutual understanding that we all had for each other.

I ate lovely, worked out, and played handball daily. This is what they referred to as 'sweet time'. I was locked up yes, but life was as comfortable as I could make it. I had no complaints.

My typical day consisted of taking out the swill can after breakfast, working out, or playing handball all morning while it was cool, eating lunch, taking out the swill can again, and then going inside to write a letter to my pen pal love interest. It had become a nice little daily routine. I was adapting. Life as I had come to know it, was well.

I will take time here to share two short stories with you about the staff at the work camp. As I said before most inmates had positive attitudes, as most would be released within 24 months. So, there was not much trouble. Most of the time, guys left to go out on their work squads and just left their lockers completely open. There was no thievery, everyone got along, *for the most part.*

However, the staff had not changed. Most of them at the work camp were decent because the vibe was different, but you still had a few bad apples. I will give you an example of two incidents that stand out in my memory.

Most dorms have the same shift Sargent day after day and it is their dorm, they run it. However, no one works seven days a week. So, on the normal shift Sergeants day off, they have a swing shift Sargent who fills in, and that Sargent just rotates dorms depending on who they are filling in for that day. Two days a week we had this replacement Sargent come in and he prided himself on how much grief he could cause us.

On one such occasion, he came in on the Midnight shift and every shift begins and ends with a count of the inmate population. At Midnight most everyone was asleep. I have already explained a lot of people did not even take the time to close their footlockers. This Sargent decides to walk through the dorm and slam these steel locker lids closed that he sees have been left open.

If you are on the bottom bunk, then the footlocker is at your head against the wall and in between your bunk and the bunk to your right. If you are on the top bunk, then your footlocker is on the floor at the foot of the bunks.

I slept on a bottom bunk. With a locker next to my head. My buddy, who slept on the bottom bunk to my right was lying in bed awake when the Sargent came through slamming locker lids closed. He told me that he watched as the Sarge slammed each one closed. The inmate to which it was assigned, would usually jump, and wake up with a startle to the noise and the Sargent would laugh.

He had slammed ten or twelve so far and was getting closer and closer to mine. My buddy started watching intently to see how I would react. When he got to my bunk and slammed my locker lid, right beside my head, I hardly stirred at all.

I am a hard sleeper and had gotten used to sleeping in a dorm full of loud noise by this point. The Sarge was disappointed at my lack of response and my buddy said he then proceeded to pick up my locker lid and slam it down three more times, just trying to wake me up. Bam, Bam, Bam

All this occurred six inches from my head and I kept right on sleeping. My buddy told me all about it the next morning. We laughed about it because I had frustrated the Sargent without even intending to. We thought that was funny. *Score one for the convict.*

On another occasion, this same Sargent came in on a Saturday night and turned off 'Smackdown'. You know WWE, Wrestling, *The Rock, Undertaker, Triple H.* Two things rule the tv in prison. One is football, and the other is 'Smackdown'. Neither one of those things gets changed or interrupted EVER. *They are more important than religion.*

Saturday night count was informal, and the officers would often count us in place, as the day room was open until 2:00 a.m. This dorm Sargent, trying his best to be as ugly as possible came on duty and walked into the dayroom and yelled count time – everyone back to their bunks *and that meant we would miss Smackdown.*

No one moved. Every other Saturday of the year we were counted in place and now tonight, when the big match is coming on this guy wanted to send us all to our bunks - *Just to be ugly.*

We were not having it. No one moved.

So the Sargent, wearing all the bravado that his uniform afforded him, walked up and turned the tv off just as 'The Rock' was entering the ring and the biggest black dude in the dorm picked up a metal folding chair and swung and hit this Sargent upside his head, just like they do in the ring on 'Smackdown'.

There were two hits.
That dude hit the Sargent, and the Sargent hit the floor. As a result, they sent us all back to our bunks. They took the black dude to confinement, took that housing Sargent out of that dorm, and outlawed 'Smackdown.' Never again was anyone allowed to watch wrestling on tv at Baker CI, *and from my understanding, the entire D.O.C.*

It was the work camp, it was laid back, yes; but it was still a prison, and you could still get your whole head split wide open if you got someone's timing wrong. It did not matter if your uniform was brown or blue. That principle applied universally.

Working Outside the Gate

A short time later, they sent me outside the gate!
The Dept. of Corrections gets paid for the inmate labor that they provide to other State agencies and the local municipalities' public works departments.

The inmates do not get paid, but the D.O.C. does.
Inmates are given time off their sentences for job compliance. How much time depends on what set of laws were in effect at the time their crime was committed.

The more inmates that they can provide for work, the more hours they can bill for. So, the entire point of the work camp is to send inmates out to work. So the Dept. of Corrections can make money. Usually, if the work assignment can be done in an unnecessarily long and difficult way, that is the way they prescribe for it to be done.

It just was not my vibe. The first month or so was cool because it was a new experience, and one that was quite surreal, but the novelty quickly wore off.

I remember my very first day lining up with the work squads in the morning and then going outside the gate to work. Initially, it was incredible because I had spent so much time behind double fences, layered in razor wire, and now I was walking around outside the fences without handcuffs, shackles, or an armed guard. What?

"Do these people realize I am not one of the ones going home this year? I could run. I could run right now. No Stupid, you better not do that. You only have 4 years left to go. You can do this. - Ok, you are right, but I could!"

These are the conversations I found myself having inside of my head all morning long. By the afternoon though I was walking alongside the road picking up trash.

Baker CI is right next to the Olustee Civil War Battlefield. It is now a State park, tended to by inmate labor, and every February they have a Civil War reenactment weekend and that includes busloads of school children coming through for a field trip.

The work squad that I was on was assigned to walk along the side of the road and pick up any trash that may be there. They wanted a clean front entrance for everyone. That's what we were all doing when the first busload of kids came driving by and all the kids opened their windows on the bus, stood up, and sang out in unison "AH-HA YOU'RE IN PRISON - AH-HA YOU'RE IN PRISON" in the very sing-song type voice that children use when they join together to be little smart-alecky brats. I will never forget it.

The second day, they decided that I could leave the compound and go out with a D.O.T. ditch cleaning crew. This crew was assigned to clean out ditches within the City of Jacksonville. This one ditch was more like a river. It ran in between, and in the back of, two sets of apartment complexes. It was full of litter and trash and had backed up so much that it was now threatening to overflow its very steep banks. Our job was to jump in, go down to the bottom, and retrieve the debris. We were swimming in this water. We pulled out everything you can imagine. Tires, bicycles, trash, bottles, cans, condoms, syringes, car parts, broken signs, a couple of shoes, broken limbs, and the list could go on.

Despite the filthiness of the water, we had a ball swimming that day. It was a rare treat. As there is almost no set of circumstances imaginable where we would ever go swimming while incarcerated.

On another occasion, I was holding a stop sign and flagging traffic. When two girls in a convertible pulled up at my stop sign, said hello, and then lifted their shirts and showed me all the things that I had been missing. They then waved and drove off as they told me to have a nice day. So, there were perks to being outside the gate, but they were rare. The hard work and the bag lunches were a constant, everyday occurrence. I was working for them, and I did not want to do that anymore.

Even the van rides to and from the city got long and boring after one of the funnier guys on the crew named Barnhill tore open a hole in the bottom of his brown paper lunch bag, unzipped his pants real quietly, and slid his 'trouser snake' up through the bottom of the bag and hollered out to another guy named Art *who pulled pranks on everybody all the time and would ask for everyone's lunch leftovers.* "Hey Art, do you want this extra sandwich"? and holds the bag open towards Art - *but not at an angle that allowed Art to see inside.* Art replied "sure" and reached his hand back and into the sack for the sandwich and wrapped his hand around Barnhill's 'trouser surprise' instead. They both hollered and yelled, and everybody laughed. Art got mad at Barnhill, and then quit talking to him.

The daily commute got quiet and boring. The hours were long, and they worked us like Hebrew slaves every day that they could. I wanted no more of it. The problem was, I had been downgraded in custody.

I had a gate pass, and I still had four years left to do. They had me around to work and make them money for a long time. There is no way they were letting me go back to a job assignment inside the fence. Not once I had been issued a gate pass. *Once you are issued a gate pass – they very rarely rescind them.* I was between a rock and hard place, but I also knew from studying the rules for so long that one of the criteria for being able to go outside the gate was that you must wear boots. You were not allowed outside the gate in tennis shoes or anything else except the State issued Brogans.

I also knew that if Medical issued you a 'soft shoe' pass, then you were prescribed to wear tennis shoes and could not be compelled to put on a pair of work boots. Thereby, by attaining a soft shoe pass, one can ensure they do not receive a job assignment outside the gate, ever.

Guess what I did? I went and got a 'soft shoe' pass.

Now they do not just hand these out to work camp inmates for free. I was not the first inmate to utilize medical to avoid a work detail. They knew the game and would not issue a 'soft shoe' pass without a compelling reason to do so.
So, I gave them one.

One night, after a particularly hard day outside the gate.
I took out a pencil eraser and rubbed blisters on both my heels and the knuckles of my big toes. The next morning instead of going out with my work crew, I requested to go to medical and complained of blisters being caused by the work boots. They gave me a temporary 'soft shoe' pass and a seven-day lay-in. Meaning, I had been prescribed bed rest for seven days. It gave me seven days off work, to write letters, listen to music, read books, and lay in bed to let my feet heal.

After my seven-day hiatus, and my feet healed. I had to go out one more day. Upon returning to the dorm that night, I did it again. I took out the pencil eraser and I rubbed more blisters and right back to medical I went. I complained about the Brogans again and they issued me a permanent 'soft shoe' pass. My gate-pass was rescinded. I was back in the kitchen and back to playing handball every day. Life was good.

Having become skilled at navigating the system aside, I was working hard to follow the rules, and stay out of trouble. Overall, I had been doing an exceptional job at that. I had several things that I was working for. Clemency for one. Restoration of gain time that I lost in my first year, while at Desoto for two, and a transfer closer to home for three.
As inmates, we were graded each month on behavior and dorm cleanliness as well as by our job performance. Receiving an 'Above Satisfactory' rating in both areas equate to maximum credit awarded for each month's gain time disbursement.

There were 3 possible ratings. AS (Above Satisfactory) S (Satisfactory) and U (Unsatisfactory). One grade comes from our housing Sargent and the other our work squad supervisor. With how my sentencing was structured. I was eligible to earn up to a maximum of twenty days off my sentence a month. I worked hard to be graded AS each month in both categories. Further, I had been rated AS and had been earning twenty days a month off my sentence pretty consistently ever since I left Desoto.

A D.R. as I have explained is a major write up that goes into your permanent file and you have the right to a hearing and an appeal process if you do not like the outcome. Receiving a D.R. automatically meant an Unsatisfactory rating from either Security (housing Sargent) or your work supervisor *depending on who wrote you the D.R.*

A CC, however, is an informal write-up. CC stands for Corrective Consultations and these are minor write-ups that do not equate to anything except a written record that a verbal warning took place. However, receiving a CC will downgrade your monthly security rating from Above Satisfactory to just Satisfactory. Thereby, causing you to earn less than the maximum amount of gain time available.

One CC would usually cost someone seven days less than their maximum available gain time award. Officers with ill intentions would often weaponize CCs because there was typically no recourse, no appeal process.

An Unsatisfactory rating in either area would yield no days awarded *and there was no appeal process* here either.

An Unsatisfactory rating did something else too besides just result in no 'gain time' award for that month.

I was scheduled for an official progress report meeting every twelve months. This was the prescribed time to request a transfer, and I had been working hard to earn one. I wanted to go back down to South Florida where my family lived. I had been at Baker for three years. It was time for me to go. I was sick of being there.

I obeyed every rule that needed to be obeyed. I walked the line. For twelve months I sweated out what my monthly ratings would be, and I had been perfect everywhere and met every criterion. Except for my last month working outside the gate.

My work squad supervisor and I had gotten into a 'power struggle' of sorts. *This is the incident I was referring to at the beginning of this chapter when they took me out to the 'Attitude Adjustment' shed and God saved me.*

I was on a mowing squad and had been weed eating Poison Ivy vines all morning. Right after we ended our lunch break and started back to work, something had got into my eye while weed eating and I declared a 'Medical Emergency' because it was burning.

Declaring a 'Medical Emergency' while out on a work squad is a big deal. It means everyone stops what they are doing, and they put you in a van and bring you back in to see the institution's doctor immediately. It is a real disruption in their very routine days. No work gets done and the D.O.C. loses a day of billing for our labor. It is a serious thing to declare; and so are the consequences for declaring one under false pretenses. That is called 'Lying to Staff.'

'Lying to Staff' is a serious violation that can result in the loss of ALL gain time. Plus, they lock you in confinement for 30 days, and that is just for the first time. It is not something anyone does lightly. I had almost 10 years' worth of gain time at this time. I was scared to death of a 'Lying to Staff' charge.

This officer was somewhat of a hardliner. *Or at least he tried to be anyway.* He told me if I declared a 'Medical Emergency' while out with him on the job he was going to write me a D.R. for 'Disobeying a Direct Order' because he told me to wear my Safety glasses and he claims that I did not, and therefore as a result of 'Disobeying his Direct Order' I was injured.

My eye was burning, I was cutting Poison Ivy. His threat was not my primary concern. My eye was. So, I declared the 'Medical Emergency' anyway.

I went to medical and got it flushed. The Doctor verified it was a legit emergency and my work squad supervisor wrote me a D.R. anyway. As a result, they locked me up in confinement. I appealed the D.R. and eventually won and had the entire incident expunged from my record *but not until after I served 30 days in Solitary confinement.*

As sweet as winning the appeal was and getting that stain removed from the otherwise good prison record that I had been building for the last four or five years. I had still received an Unsatisfactory rating that month from my job supervisor.
I had appealed the D.R. and won, but I could not appeal the monthly rating. There was no mechanism in the rules that allowed inmates to challenge a Supervisors' monthly rating.

Only the officer who issued the grade was authorized to change it. There was no way I could get him to do that. This guy took pleasure in hard timing me.

I grieved the entire incident all over again, as it was the only Unsatisfactory rating on my record in several years and would stand as a hindrance to all three of the before stated goals that I was trying to accomplish Clemency, Restoration of Gain Time, and a transfer.

My grievance was denied. I then filed another grievance, grieving the fact that they denied my previous grievance. When I did that, is when they decided to take me out to the beat down shed that I mentioned when this chapter about Baker first began.

In essence, that one Unsatisfactory rating made my other 23 ratings of Above Satisfactory null and void. They told me to give them another twelve months there earning Above Satisfactory ratings and I could request a transfer next year.

Friends, fans, and neighbors, I do not take defeat very well. This dude's vindictiveness was enough to keep me from earning a transfer closer to home and keep me away from my family, and in this horrible place that I had grown so tired of. I was powerless to stop it. There was nothing I could do about it. This was them people's world. They run it any way they want to.

Except, I knew the rules and how to navigate the system and had just enough 'pissed-offness' to motivate me into taking matters into my own hands.

I have developed quite a knack over the years for wiggling myself out of what are otherwise impossible situations. In this instance, because of my familiarity with Chapter 33. I was familiar with the different types of transfers that the D.O.C would use and the protocols that triggered each of them.

> **A. Earned Transfer**
> Usually every twelve or twenty-four months an inmate will have a scheduled progress report with their Classification officer. The Classification officer will go over your progress since your last Progress report and then they go over your release date, any detainers, plans upon post-release, etc. This is also when we can bring up any special requests or needs. We can do such things as update our visitor lists, make changes to our telephone call list, request a transfer, a bunk change, etc. This is the proper way. This is the way I tried to do it.
>
> **B. Disciplinary Transfer**
> This is when Security decides to transfer you. Perhaps you were involved in an altercation, and it is no longer safe for you to be there. Maybe you keep getting in trouble and they want to move you on down the line. Either way, Security makes these calls – *for any reason that they want to*. This is how I left Desoto.
> Forcing this kind of transfer would have been counterproductive to my goals as it would have required me to get into trouble and lots of it. Which is exactly what I was trying not to do.
> So, this was out.
>
> **C. Admin Transfer**

This kind of transfer occurs when the Administration themselves decide that you have worn out your welcome and that having you around is not worth their aggravation anymore. They find a way to justify the request, but it is usually punitive in some form or fashion. This is how I left Marion and ended up at Baker to start with. I did not want to go someplace worse. So, the only transfer option I had left was a…

D. Psych Transfer

Each inmate has a psychiatric grade assigned to them by classification.

Psych 1 is someone considered to be 'normal' and well adjusted.

Psych 2 is someone that needs to speak with a Psychologist on occasion. It can be once a week, once a month, or once a quarter. Whatever seems appropriate for the individual. However, no medication is required. *No overall big deal.*

Psych 3 is someone that has been prescribed some type of Psychotropic medication(s). These inmates must be housed at a facility that is specifically designated as a 'Psych 3' facility. Meaning their staff is trained to deal with mentally disturbed inmates and they have a Psychiatrist on staff to write medication prescriptions.

Psych 4
Not sure what a Psych 4 is.
I have never known anyone to have that grade.

Psych 5 means you are on suicide watch. You are isolated from the population and have been stripped down to nothing but your underwear and have nothing in your cell at all. You are under constant 24-hour supervision.

Inmates would often play crazy to force the D.O.C. to transfer them. This is because there are only a few institutions within each Region equipped to deal with a mentally ill inmate population and if they reclassified you and raised your Psych grade then that is where you'd have to go. Immediately. These were known as 'Psych camps.'

Baker was not designated a Psych camp, so if I could make them question my mental stability, I could make them transfer me.

Pulling a 'Psych move' as they are referred to, is old hat inside the chain-gang. The officers are all aware of the games people play when pretending to 'go psych'. Popular methods of trying to convince the staff that you are crazy or are a threat to yourself or others are to cut your wrists, try to hang yourself, Or for those less inclined to self-inflicted bodily harm; many have been known to defecate in their hands and then rub their feces all over themselves or all over the walls. *I was not doing any of those things!*

Further, if I made my attempt at 'going crazy' less than believable then I stood the chance of being transferred to another institution punitively. There were still lots of places less desirable than even Baker was. Take Florida's panhandle for instance. Which despite my best efforts to thwart, is where they sent me anyway.

Here is the story…

I had filed for Clemency in 1998, while at Baker and had hoped to go before Governor Jeb Bush and his Cabinet to plead my case. I felt that this was my best chance yet for any sort of relief, as I felt that I had several things going for me by this time…

A. The court records reflect that I did not kill anyone, participate in any violence and that I was not even present when the crime occurred.
B. I had a notarized confession from my co-defendant absolving me from all wrong or responsibility.
C. I had already served more than six years at this time.
D. I had completed many different vocational programs, education programs, life skills programs, as well as drug rehabilitation programs.
E. I had a close family friend on the outside who happened to be personal friends with Governor Jeb Bush and had personally lobbied my case before him.
F. I had had a clean prison record for the last several years, which was quite the contrast to the first year I was in when I received fourteen DR's in just twelve months.
G. I had a pen pal girlfriend that hired an attorney from Tallahassee who specializes in Clemency appeal matters.
H. I prayed, and I believed that this was going to be the vehicle that God used to deliver my miracle.

It was not!

I was given a hearing though, and my family drove from South Florida to Tallahassee and my dad spoke on my behalf. Jeb Bush had taken an interest in my case but in the end, I was denied.

Had I been granted clemency and released, my pen pal and I were going to be married. Instead, she told me she just couldn't do any more time with me, and she was very shortly engaged to someone else.

The clemency board did not issue a decision right away. They took a few days, and my family on the street knew about the denial before I did.

I called my pen pal on the phone. Her name was Dena, and she was by far the most beautiful chick, that I had ever seen in my life. She would drive up to visit me every other weekend, we would write each other love letters every single day. 8, 9, 10, 12-page letters. Both of our lives revolved around writing to each other.

Dena was my stepmom's nail tech, and my stepmom would very often talk about me to her, and one day she happened to ask her if she would want to write to me. She said she would, and we ignited like wildfire after that.

She helped the days not be quite so hard. Every day at mail call there would be a letter from her, with photos, stamps, and several pages of her telling me how much she loved me.

She was a singer in a Rock n Roll band and had an incredible voice. Often, in the visiting park, she would sing to me. We were in love, and my Clemency appeal looked like it was likely to be granted. We were making all kinds of plans for life after they granted my Clemency. She used her personal funds and hired me a Clemency lawyer. The absolute best one in Tallahassee at that.

Through all my wheeling's and dealings, I had managed to procure a pair of ½ ct. Diamond stud earrings. Then proposed to her out in the visiting park one Saturday. She laughed, she cried, and she said Yes! That was a great day.
But on another day, she delivered me the news that the Clemency Board had denied me.

As I hear it told, Governor Bush voted in favor of granting me Clemency, but his cabinet members did not. Therefore, I was denied because, in Florida, you must have the Governors vote, plus the votes of two other members of his cabinet, *which I did not get*. She cried and said Goodbye to me, and I slumped down the wall, still holding the phone. God Tricked Me Again!

Not too many phone calls later she informed me that she could not hold on and wait any longer. She had met someone else and would not be accepting my calls any longer.

It was a very depressing weekend. However, after a few days, I was ok. Life had taught me to take those kinds of blows and just keep moving forward.
I could not blame her. She had already been way more of a friend than I deserved, and I am forever grateful for the time in her life that she did allow me to share. She was beautiful and free. This was my time to do, not hers.

With my recent Clemency denial and Dena's decision to move on I had plenty of reason to be down, depressed, and no longer wanting to live. This was not my mindset! I really was ok. I had gotten used to a life where you hope for the best but always expect the worse. But that didn't mean I couldn't see opportunity!

By Monday I had bounced back in my spirits but was still upset that this officer had messed up my chance of transferring. There was no way that I was going to stay there for another twelve months. So, I hatched a plan to go 'Psych'. I tied up a few loose ends on the compound. Said goodbye to a few friends, and by Friday I was ready to go.

I wrote a letter home. In the letter I poured on the woe is me. I talked about being denied Clemency. Dena leaving me and how I hurt so bad, my Faith in God was shaken, and I just did not want to live anymore. I did not want to do one more day behind bars, and how death would offer such a sweet release.

Then I placed the letter in an envelope, addressed it, and put a stamp on it. Then walked it up to the mailroom.

The officer in the mailroom was one of the cooler ones and we all liked him, and he would do whatever he could (within the rules) to help anyone of us out.

I told him I wanted to transfer, and that officer so and so had blocked me with an Unsatisfactory rating several months ago and that I needed a favor that would only require him to do his job. Nothing outside of his normal daily duties.

As the mailroom supervisor, his job description required him to read and/or scan all outgoing letters and report anything suspicious. That is all I needed him to do. Read the letter and bring it to the attention of Security as concerning.

He did, and I was on a bus being transferred to South Florida Reception Centers Psych unit within 15 minutes.

See they had no reason to suspect that the threat to harm myself was not legit. I had written a letter home and did not seek attention. In the natural course of doing his job, the officer discovered my threat of suicide and the attention was brought to my letter by Security, not by me. My threat seemed credible enough, and they moved on it immediately. *A little to immediately, if you ask me.*

They raised my Psych grade to level 5, and I was on a van headed to Miami in very short order. Once there, I would be stripped down and placed into an isolation bubble. All my possessions were removed. I was issued a type of suicide prevention garment. *Which is nothing more than a very heavy blanket that you wear as a dress and straps together with Velcro. The garment is too thick to be torn apart and used to hang yourself, and it is nonflammable.* I put the 'suicide dress' on and stepped into this fishbowl of a cell that would be my residence for the next four nights.

The one miscalculation in my plan was that I turned the letter into the mailroom on the Friday before Labor Day. Meaning all Admin staff was off duty that Friday evening when I arrived and on Saturday and Sunday as they normally are, and then on Monday too because of the Holiday. So, I could not see the Psychiatrist until Tuesday morning and he was the only one that could lower my Psych grade down from a 5. I have never experienced a weekend any longer or any more miserable than that weekend was.

Tuesday morning though, I was interviewed by the Psychiatrist and he determined I was not crazy and was not a threat to myself or others but should be sent to a Psych 3 camp anyway. *Just in case I had a relapse and began to entertain harmful thoughts again.*

So right back on a bus I went and started what would be a two-week journey from Miami to Washington CI. Which is deep in Florida's Panhandle in what is known as Region 1. *I wanted to get closer to home (South), instead, they sent me North West to an entirely different time zone.*

I got my transfer though, and I did not have to cut my wrists or rub dookie all over myself. So, there was that, but to this day I am still not sure I won that one.

Washington was horrible. By far the worse place that I had ever been. Thankfully, it was the place that I spent the least amount of time at as well.

Washington
1999 – 2000

Not a lot stands out about Washington CI except it was very far from home, I was surrounded by crazy people, and because they raised my Psych grade, they raised my custody too. So, I was Close custody once again. Back behind the big fences on the main compound. No more work camp. No more swill cans, no more handball. I was back to doing 'hard time'

I did not mind though, as that meant I could get into another vocational class as opposed to being sent back out to their work camp. Which I managed to avoid for the entirety of my time there, save the last two weeks.

I call that a win because that is where I learned Microsoft Office. Which has proved to be quite an advantage in the years since my release. I would go into class each day and work with PowerPoint projects, Excel spreadsheets, Word documents. Each day was a new tutorial and a new project. graduation was an MS-Office project that included elements from all the programs contained within the Office Suite. That is where the advantages of being at Washington CI ended.

All the Institutions that I had been to previously, were much older. They had been around since the '50s and '60s. They had been built out and had accumulated many things overtime when they use to provide a recreation budget for Prisons.

They had large handball courts, music programs, and musical instruments that you could check out during rec time. They had weight piles and other sorts of amenities unique to each facility. Washington was not like that. It was considered a newer prison.

In the 90s, Florida's inmate population grew to numbers that exceeded the population capabilities and they began letting non-violent offenders out without having done very much time at all. Not me of course. I had a Second-degree Murder charge. On average though, non-violent offenders were doing approximately one week for each year they had been sentenced to. Therefore, a ten-year sentence was being completed in about ten weeks. The rest of their time was being given back to them as a type of probation called 'Conditional Release'. To curb this, the State of Florida started building more prisons.

They built a whole slew of them in Florida's panhandle at this time and they all looked the same, huge open barren plots of land, closed in with double razor wire fences, several buildings to use as dorms, one or two other buildings for staff and admin, a chow hall, a tiny chapel, and a plot of grass that was referred to as a rec field. That was it. Then they were on to the next one. These newer institutions offered very little in the way of education and vocation classes. I was lucky to have gotten a seat in the computer class when I did. It was the only class offered on the whole compound besides GED classes. Which I already had two of.

I made a couple of friends here that stand out to me. One was named Eusebio. He was Cuban and we would often play Scrabble and attend chapel together. He was teaching me Spanish and required I use it when speaking to him. He would later be transferred to Everglades CI and there he would preach on the rec field and hold Bible studies. He drew this picture for me and mailed it to me in 2009 to show me how he was doing. In it, he is depicted as preaching and it hangs framed in my office today. The headline is written in Spanish but says "Nothing shall separate us from the love of God" and is especially meaningful being as Everglades CI had a fence running down the middle of the compound to separate half the population from the other half. He then wrote at the bottom. "This is how we gather in here. Can you tell which one I am?" I am proud to have it and proud to count Eusebio as my friend.

While Eusebio and I shared a dorm, he did not sleep near me. The guy who did sleep next to me was a little old man of Asian descent. Every morning, while making my bed, I would say "Good morning" and then ask him "how are you?" and he would always smile, squint his eyes, bow towards me slightly, and say "Ahh, not too good, not too bad, just ok." In a very heavy Asian accent, and every time I would burst out laughing. He made my time easier as we each ensured that each other's day always started with a friendly greeting and a laugh. His response never varied.

That taught me a lot. As this guy was one of the kindest people I have ever met. Sweet and humble. Always had a smile. No one disliked him. Weird thing is, I later learned, he had 5 murder charges and 5 life sentences. The rumor was he shot and killed his wife, mother-in-law, and children. I do not know any of the details as to how, when, or why? I never asked him about it. He never discussed his crimes with anyone, and you never ask someone about them. It is unethical. People may volunteer and tell you on their own accord what they are in there for, but you never ask. You could get your whole head bashed in by asking that question.

What living next to a guy with such a sweet disposition but who had such a terrible past taught me was that 'Happiness was an inside job'. It is a choice, and it is not necessarily based on your outward circumstances at all.

He taught me that no matter what happened yesterday, each day is a new opportunity to wake up, look forward, and find a reason to smile. *If a guy with 5 life sentences can find a reason to wake up each morning and smile, then I certainly could too.*

Then there was my buddy Terry. Unfortunately, he has a life sentence too, and we may never see each other on the free world side of the fence, but our friendship has survived the years.

We were roommates at Washington, towards the end of my time there. We both shared the same two-man cell. He worked in Laundry and the advantage to life in prison when your roommate works in the laundry is your bag gets washed with his bag only and not the rest of the compounds all at once, and they get delivered to your cell, pressed with creases. Anything that can make you feel good about yourself while inside, was usually worth the premium. Prison life does not afford many opportunities for that to happen. So, I appreciated him doing that for me. He would always say "Keep It Live". That was his way of saying 'drive it any way you want to, but keep it between the ditches'.

That is what I got out of it anyway. We lived together for about six months and he never did explain to me what it meant.

Another thing that stands out about Washington is it was very cold during the winter up there. They made us go out and walk laps around the rec field every morning Monday – Friday for three hours while the housemen cleaned the dorms.

I would just sit out on that barren rec field and feel the wind knife right through me. My teeth would chatter, and my body would shiver for warmth. There were no buildings or handball courts to hide behind and break the wind. Nothing on the rec field at all except cold, fierce, wind, and nothing to do but walk laps. It was miserable and I hated It. Luckily, I spent the least amount of time here.

Eventually, Winter gave way to Summer and I came up for my annual Progress Report. I had twelve months' worth of dual Above Satisfactory ratings. I could now request a transfer. They lowered my custody once again and then let me pick three places that I wanted to go, and I picked two institutions very close to my home in Southwest Florida and another one with a reputation for being an excellent place to do time but *was still a 4-hour drive for my family.* This is the one they granted, my third choice. Cross City. This is where I would meet Jeremy, Nick, and Turtle.

Cross City was one of the better places to do time. It was an older institution and had a lot to offer in the way of recreation and education. They had a well-established Chapel program with volunteers coming in all the time, to show care and concern to the inmates. Every Friday night brother Clyde would come in and preach the house down. Preaching just like I grew up hearing. He was my favorite.

Cross City
2001 – 2003

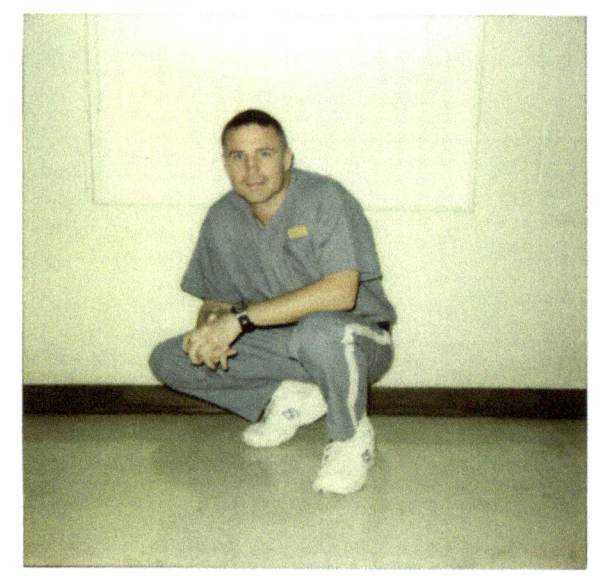

12/28/2002
My last birthday inside

Cross City was the only place that I had ever been that when I stepped off the bus and was saying hello to people, I was meeting for the first time and would ask
"How is this place?" that they would all respond and say "Sweet". I was relieved because when you ask that question at most places you hear responses like "this place is horrible", "its whack", or "better get a knife right away".

I was still new and had yet to meet any of my friends whom I introduced you to earlier. However, I did have a buddy there from Washington. He was Hispanic and we were down. He was a friendly face and a welcome sight in my dorm because if any trouble kicked off, or if anybody jumped me, by being friends with him, I had the backing of all the other Hispanics on the compound as well. My liking for the place was increasing more and more.

Cross City offered a lot in the way of Education, Vocation, and Recreation all three. It was the sweetest place I have ever been, as far as prisons go. I had to get into a Vocational program as soon as possible though. Washington had lowered my custody to Minimum *which meant I could now work outside the gate with no supervision* and my soft shoe pass would not be valid here. I would be at the work camp by the end of the week if I did not act fast.

Monday morning, I already had a request into Classification to join the Computer Programming vocational course and it was approved. I was good. I was not going anywhere, not until I finished that class anyway, and it was a twelve-month course.

But before that happened, on my first morning at Cross City my Spanish buddy asked me if I wanted to go see the movie with him. Those were words I had not heard since 1993 at Desoto.

See way back when I first started doing time, institutions had a budget and funding for Recreation, and the Coach would always rent a couple of movies from Blockbuster or some other such place and would show the movie in the rec hall at routinely scheduled times throughout the weekend. That practice had long been eliminated though. There had been no movies any longer at Desoto, Marion, Baker, or Washington; but Cross City was one of the oldest institutions in the State and they had a large rec hall with an entire collection of movies that they had bought back when there was a budget or that people had donated over the years. So, they still showed movies every Saturday.

What was showing that Saturday morning on the rec halls 10-foot screen? Titanic! Yes, the epic movie with Leonardo DiCaprio and Kate Winslett. It was an amazing moment to be sitting at Cross City amongst friends both old and new watching this incredible movie in such a grand fashion, after having just been at Washington, a hell hole of a place, just a week earlier.

I don't expect any of you can truly appreciate just how surreal that experience was but the movie Titanic is one of my favorite memories from when I was doing time and never do I watch it, without teleporting back to when I saw it for the very first time.

Cross City also had tennis courts, handball courts, as well as a music program and I, spent many days strumming the guitar out on the tennis courts playing R.E.M. 'Losing my Religion', practicing going from D to F and making that chord change on the guitar. Or trying to learn 'Knocking on Heavens Door'. I checked out a guitar every chance I could. Jeremy and I would sit and pick with each other every chance we got.

I was at Cross City when 9-11 happened and I remember that morning having a toothache and falling asleep during morning count and failing to get up and go to my job assignment (which was my vocational class). Normally missing my job assignment could have led me to getting into trouble and having a DR written, but 9-11 changed everything. Usually, the TVs are not even on in the dormitories until after 4 pm. I was asleep on my bunk and I heard a bunch of commotion going on in the dayroom, news announcers, plane crashes, fires, building collapsing, what?

So, I got up and walked into the dayroom and stood there watching the news just like everyone else. We were caught up watching the towers fall in there, just like the rest of America was out here. We watched the towers fall, the Pentagon burn, we heard Todd Beamer say, "Let's roll", and we heard President Bush address the nation. 9-11 will certainly stand as a 'where were you moment?' in history and that is where I was. In D dorm at Cross City Correctional Institution. Laying down with a toothache when the first plane hit.

I went on to graduate from my vocational course and then took enrolled in another one. Once I completed that course there was no way they were keeping on the main compound any longer. I had been there two years with Minimum custody. I had earned two vocational diplomas while there, one in Business Software Applications and the other in Computer Programming and was down to about twelve months left to do. I had thus far avoided the work camp and having to work outside the gate. They were having no more of it. One week after graduating from my second vocational course. I was transferred to the work camp. Being there, however, opened a whole new entrepreneurial opportunity for me.

Prison is a very lonely place, and people have the weirdest pets to keep them company. Some people have pet spiders and they feed them, take care of them, and then fight them with other people's spiders, while they bet on which one will win. Other people have pet insects of all types, but most of the saner people had pet lizards. I was one of those.

I had a pet 'Oak lizard' named Pretty Girl. She looked just like a miniature alligator. They were cool pets and would often sell for $5 apiece. They could only come from outside the gate. As no trees ever grew inside the compound. Meaning, only work camp inmates could procure them and bring them back inside the gate.

On Wednesday nights work camp inmates could come over to the main unit and visit the Law Library. Nick and Jeremy would often come to the Law Library then as well. So we would visit and hang out. But before I would come, I would stick four or five lizards inside my shirt, and they would hang on my t-shirt that I would wear underneath my uniform pull over. That way the guards would never see them.

Though we are supposed to go through a physical pat-down before entering or exiting either of the two facilities, the security officers were very complacent and rarely performed this correctly, allowing me the opportunity to traffic lizards. I would bring them over, give them to Jeremy because Nick would not break any of the rules.

Yes, I trafficked in Reptilian flesh. I would also tie dental floss to dragonfly tails and sell them as 'kites' too. I was just a White boy, trying to get by and survive. I never meant any harm. I was an Entrepreneur even then though. I've always had a knack for seeing opportunities where others did not.

Then came the day I had been waiting for, working for, striving for, the day that I thought would never come. The day they transferred me to work release. One week after my 29th birthday.

Pompano Work Release
January 2003 – April 2003

Work Release is when you are housed in a State facility, but it functions more like a halfway house. There are no fences, inmates can wear civilian clothes, and hold regular free world jobs. Of course, the State finds a way to confiscate most of your earnings, but it does not even matter. Work release is almost like being out. Except you are very much still in.

The facilities are run by D.O.C. guards and most are looking for a reason to write you a DR and send you back behind the fences. Which did not play into my favor much at all as my situation was a bit different than most of the other guys who were there. The crime I got charged with happened way back in 1992 when inmates got one third off their sentence. This Gain time award was granted to them in the form of 'Provisional Gain Time Credit' right from the start.

My 22-year sentence and subsequent Gain time awards broke down as such:

22 years given by the Judge.
Minus 1 year time served in the County jail.
Equals 21 years.
Minus the 'third' (7 years) provisional gain time credit that I was awarded the day I got to prison.
Plus Earned Gain Time (the 20 days a month awarded monthly with Above Satisfactory ratings)
Plus, the actual day for day time that I had done.
All those numbers get calculated and the sum result equaled my Release Date. By the time I got to work release, I had well over 10 years' worth of gain time that I could lose. I was forevermore worried that they would find a reason to take it back and return me to prison to serve out another 10 years.

Others who were there had fell (or been sentenced) after October 1st, 1995 when the 85% law went into place. *In the prison boom of the '90s. In order to keep all those new prisons full. The Florida Legislature passed a law requiring inmates to serve at least 85% of the time given to them by the courts.* Meaning there was very little Gain time that new people coming into the system could earn or lose. As the most that could be taken off, or taken back was 15%.

While I had a boatload of Gain time that they could take from me at a moment's notice. I was surrounded by others that only had a small amount of Gain time that they could lose. *We were not the same.* Our attitudes about the police and the rules were vastly different.

I walked around work release on tippy toes. Careful to obey every rule. I had come so far. I had been through so much. I did not want to give them any reason to send me back. I had too much to lose. Just because I was not looking for trouble though, does not mean that trouble was not looking for me…

I remember the morning I packed up at Cross City Work Camp and was shuttled over to the main unit to await the transport bus. While waiting, Nick and Jeremy, both came to tell me goodbye. I had spent eleven years telling other people goodbye, and now it was finally my turn to move on and leave my friends behind. When the bus came, we all said goodbye. Then I went, and they stayed.

I arrived on a Friday and the air was electric. I was finally here. I had made it to work release. People were eating McDonald's, Pizza Hut, Chili's. There were vending machines, people had cash money, and were walking around in blue jeans and tank tops, wearing shorts and sandals. Calling girls on the telephones.

It was Miami, on a Friday night. Freedom was shining its face on me. It was real. I was here. I had made it. No tricks, no let downs. My family was coming down to see me the next day, Saturday. I could hardly sleep at all.

They had already bought me blue jeans and everything.

My Grandmother had gone to Walmart and bought me several pairs of Rustlers. Now, most of you know that is a generic brand. I had not a care in the world. I loved those Rustlers. They fit great, they looked good, and I slept in them. The next morning after my visit, I woke up still wearing my brand new Rustlers.

Several people in the facility worked at a Chili's Restaurant right down the street. One guy that I talked to thought that he could get me on being as he was cool with the Manager. When Monday came, I got a pass to leave the facility and checked out. I was on my way to fill out job applications.

I walked a couple of miles down the road and I have never felt so grateful for the sound of city traffic or the warm sunshine. I was in the middle of downtown Pompano on a major thoroughfare, in street clothes, walking down to Chili's restaurant to apply for a job. How could life get any better than that? *Still to this day, very few moments of my life have lived up to the significance of that one.*

I was grateful for every step of that mile or so that I walked. I wished it were five miles or even ten.
It was the first time that I could just go walk down the street and I wanted every step that I could get.

When I arrived, the manager was expecting me and interviewed me verbally, but he never asked me what my charge was. Then he asked me to fill out an application. He was used to hiring people from the work release center and just assumed we all had petty crimes. Then I wrote Yes and Second-Degree Murder on the application when it asked if I had ever been convicted of a felony and for what.

The expression on his face taught me not to do that ever again. To say he freaked out would be putting it mildly. Where I had just come from no one blinked an eye when I told them my charge. I was back in the free world though and here it hangs around my neck like a Millstone.

I began writing 'will discuss at interview' after that. That charge Second Degree Murder looks bad when written in ink. It makes people nervous and makes them want to tell me No right from the start without ever even giving me a chance. When I explain that I did not do it, they just look at me even more suspiciously.

He interviewed me again and then brought in his assistant manager to interview me a third time after reading my application. In the end, he hired me and gave me a chance. I will always be appreciative of him for that. He hired me as a busboy and man did, I ever love that.

I met new people in the restaurant every night and would charge all the servers ten dollars apiece to do their side work at night. They were all happy to make that deal. I was making an extra fifty to sixty dollars a night that I did not have to report to the D.O.C. *as the manager kept an envelope in the safe for me that I could put my side cash in.*

I would come in early before we opened and scrub the dumpster pads, and I would stay late after we closed rolling silverware. I stayed gone from the facility the maximum number of hours allowed each day. I was stacking cash both on the books and off. I was getting out in June and it was now February. Then it was March. April, and finally May. In May I was transferred, but before I go there, I need to go over a few more things that took place while working at the Chili's in Pompano.

While at work release and gone on a job assignment. You are not allowed to go anywhere else except directly to your job and directly back. Easy enough rules to understand. Remember if I am caught deviating, I stand to lose more than 10 years' worth of gain time. So that being the case, one day just before 11 a.m. when we opened. The Manager handed me two Twenty-dollar bills and asked me to go next door to the bank and get him Forty dollars worth of dimes.

I was floored, humbled, honored, scared, excited, flabbergasted, and anxious all at the same time. No doubt I put more thought and seen more meaning into that request than was ever intended. He just needed change. To him, I was there, nothing more than an errand boy, but to me, he had just anointed me.

Here I was an inmate that he was handing money to. Asking me to go to the bank for him. The trust he was putting into me blew my mind. To you reading this book, it was Forty bucks with very little risk. To me, he had just entrusted the entire financial operation of the restaurant to me.

I did not want to say no to such a big ask or such an exciting adventure either. Imagine me, a convict, with a murder charge, inside a bank. I could not wait. I was so excited, but I could not get caught either. This errand could cost me ten more years of doing time, but I had permission. Technically I was still on the job site, even though I was not. In the end, I quit overthinking and just ran next door to the bank.

I presented the two twenties and they gave me two zipper bank bags full of dimes. The teller never even suspected I was an inmate with a murder charge. She did not act scared or suspicious. She never called the law or acted alarmed in any way. Wow! I was sure it had been tattooed on my forehead.

Upon exiting the bank with two large and bulky money bags, I realized I was a prime target to be robbed, and right then in the next forty feet from the bank entrance to the Chili's entrance I made up my mind I was willing to die defending these forty dollars in dimes. This man trusted me, and I was not going to let him down.

Turns out all my bravado was for naught. I left and returned all in about eight minutes. Without any sort of incident whatsoever. All that big head trip I went through was as unnecessary as it is fun for me to look back on and laugh.

Another time, I finished my work about an hour early and was waiting until we closed before calling the work release center to come pick me up. One of my buddies' from inside the restaurant drove this cool car. He gave me his cell phone and his car keys. He told me I could go sit in his car, listen to music, and use his phone while I waited on the center to come pick me up *because after dark they did not allow us to travel alone.*

So here I am sitting behind the wheel of this way cool car, talking to a friend on the phone when suddenly, I noticed the Anti-Theft light blinking in the car.

All it meant was the doors were locked and the alarm was activated. However, I did not know that. I thought some alarm had been tripped and the police were on their way, and when the center got there to pick me up there would be cop cars all around me with flashing lights and I would have to explain why I was not actually trying to escape. I would lose all my gain time. I freaked out and ran back inside real quick and told the dude all out of breath and secretive like. That his anti-theft light was blinking and what does that mean?

He laughed and reassured me that everything was ok and that it was just an informative beacon letting me know that the alarm was on. I felt stupid but he understood I had never seen anything like that.

When I fell in 1992 the internet was not even really a thing and cell phones came with side bags and shoulder straps. Now, it is 2003 and everyone has a cellphone and there is this thing called the internet. I had a lot of catching up to do.
You may ask, was I ever tempted to just leave, run, or escape? The answer is 'every day, but not really, except twice.'

In general, we all fantasized about leaving or escaping every day. So yes, I thought about it constantly, but in terms of fantasy not in terms of making any plans or putting any sort of plan into motion. That never really happened, except twice.

The first time was in my first few months inside the County jail which is a completely different animal altogether. I broke a steel table off a wall, and we were all swinging it, taking turns, trying to knock a hole in the concrete wall, big enough to climb out of and escape. Then tried to cover it up with a poster when the officers came in to check on all the noise we were making.

I told them I was new and had nothing to do with what other guys were doing in my cell. They were all bigger than me, I could not keep them out. Miraculously that was that and nothing ever came of that incident and I never acted on any such stupid plan again. The temptation grew less each day.

The closer I got to getting out the less I thought of leaving in any way that was not authorized. Except for this one particular night. Now my feet stayed planted right where they were supposed to, but only because I was fighting against every impulse and emotion that I had inside of me. Which were all screaming in unison for me to leave, LEAVE.

Let me tell you what happened. There was this one bartender chick there at Chili's who had a roommate that was an exotic dancer down there in the Fort Lauderdale area and they were both Bisexual.

This one Friday evening when we were closing, the bartender's roommate happened to stop by to pick up her friend the bartender. The bartender needed a few more minutes as she was finishing up her side work and I was sitting on a barstool waiting on the van from the center to come pick me up and the roommate strikes up a conversation with me.

One thing leads to another and she invites me out to party with them both that night. My heart jolted with excitement and the bartender replied to her friend and said, "He can't go anywhere with us, he's a criminal" and her friend said, "What do you mean a criminal?" The bartender explained that I was at work release, the roommate then got up and came over and started teasing my hair and said, "ooh I like criminals, they're hot". Then they both walked out of the door but before they did, she turned and looked at me and said "too bad you have to stay. I'd love for you to come."

People, that moment right there caused this guy who had been locked up for almost eleven years to nearly lose all common sense and run out that door and tell the police "Catch me if you can". Except I did not!

I stood still. Frozen, elated, shocked, and wowed, with every nerve ending on fire until the van showed up and took me back to the center. I almost threw it all away. All the hard work, all the effort, all the tears. Almost gone with one impulse. But almost does not count. Thankfully.

In all those years spent behind the fences. I had come to understand that one impulsive reaction could ruin your entire life. I failed that test in 1992. This time, in 2003, I passed.

I never saw either one of those girls again. They transferred me once again very soon after that night. Turns out sometime within the past few years my dad had some fishing poles stolen out of his garage and technically that is 'burglary'. I did not know anything about it. My parents had never mentioned it in phone calls or visits but the guy who did it was at my same work release center. So as a security precaution, they transferred both of us when they became aware of it.

I only had six weeks left. When the van from the center pulled up to my job assignment at Chili's and told me to get in, I was being transferred. They took me immediately to another work release center called Miami North Work Release Center. I only had a few weeks left and I was glad. It was dirty and grimy and felt a lot like living in a dirty bus station.

Before that happened though, my dad and Grandpa came to visit me. Instead of going to the center, my Manager scheduled me to work *but really gave me the day off.* So instead of a visit in the visiting park as we had so many times before. I got to sit and have a real meal in a restaurant with my dad and my Grandpa for the first time in eleven years.

We talked. We laughed, ate, and carried on with each other for several hours. It was a great time. Two days later I was transferred.

Miami North Work Release Center
May – June 5th, 2003

This place was horrible!
It was Work Release, yes, but they ran it very much like a prison. Addressing individuals as 'inmate' *which they only do when they are trying to be belittling.* Whereas Pompano was laid back and the officers did not go out of their way to harass you. They enforced the rules, yes but if you respected them, they respected you.

Miami North was a lot more like Baker or Washington. They had North Florida type attitudes. They did not keep it North Florida clean though. This place was filthy. and there was this one Sargent that worked in the property room. He liked to take everyone's stuff. It was a personal game of his to try and confiscate as many items of an inmate's property as he could. It was rumored that he would steal people's jewelry all the time. Use the power of his uniform to confiscate it, and then it would just get 'lost'.

Pompano would allow us to have any sort of clothing we wanted as long as it did not depict anything rude, crude, or vulgar. Miami North would not allow any clothes that had labels, logos, or writing on them period.

Everything had to be solid plain colors. I only had about four weeks left at this time. So none of it mattered to me, except when he took my hat. I had a cool cap that was black and had a checkerboard streak that went around the side and the front said, DC Crane. Evidently, it was a hat for a crane company located in DC, but none the less it was cool, and my roommate had given it to me when he left at Pompano and we had become friends so that hat meant something to me. Because my hat was not plain and had writing on it, he confiscated it.

By rule, whenever something is confiscated it must be held for 30 days to give the inmate a chance to appeal the decision to confiscate and I got out in less than 30 days.

He wanted a reaction out of me, I did not give him one. I think he was disappointed. A lot of them were like that. They would provoke you and then write you up when you reacted. I was not going to give him the pleasure.

I was able to transfer to another Chili's in the North Miami area called Doral. I was also able to get on the schedule and go to work right away. Except now my bike ride was a much longer trek. As this Chili's was across town and took me about 45 minutes to pedal there. I crossed major intersections, rode underneath overpasses, through the ghetto, past The Pink Pony Strip Club, and then on through an industrial section of town, and past a bunch of car lots. Finally, I would ride up and into the back end of a huge shopping plaza that Chili's sat in the front of. Next to a Hooters, and a Wal Mart. It was quite the commute, but I put my headphones on and just pedaled.

Every day I passed the Pink Pony, and I could not help but wonder what went on in that place and what a Paradise it must be. I kept telling myself the day I get released I am going to go in and see.

Remember I was barely Eighteen when they locked me up. I was now knocking on the door of Thirty and had never been inside a fully nude club. Or experienced anything of the sort. Riding a bicycle past the club every single day put a spell on me. My curiosity grew.

I had to go in, I had to see, but I was not going to deviate. No sir. I would have been the biggest fool in captivity had I got sent back to prison for another ten more years because I stopped and went inside of a strip club.

Yeah, no they were not going to get me like that. I just kept pedaling every day. I pedaled and pedaled and did not stop until I got to Chili's in Doral.

…but there was this one time that I did deviate, just a little bit. I had gotten to work early and as I said there was a Wal-Mart right next to where I worked. I walked over and inside the Wal Mart. The feeling again was surreal. Here I was inside the Wal Mart shopping just like everyone else, and no one knew. So many of my other brothers were behind the fences doing their time, and I was doing my time while shopping at Wal Mart. How cool was that?

These are the head trips I endured while walking through the store. I went to the music section and bought a Guns N' Roses 'Appetite for Destruction' cassette tape *because they still had those then.* Along with a Walkman cassette deck so that I could listen to it when I rode my bike back and forth.

I paid for my items, and when I went out the security alarm went off because the cashier did not demagnetize my cassette tape. I did not stop to think about the fact that I had a receipt, and everything was ok.

I just saw ten years of gain time going away. The cops coming. The center being called. Me going back to prison for a very long time, and I ran.

I ran and I ran, and I ran. It took me 15 minutes to catch my breath once I stopped. I then realized how stupid running was but when I finally did catch my breath again. I had a Walkman, and a new Guns N' Roses tape to listen to while I rode. All is well that ends well, I suppose.

While working at Chili's in Doral, I met a dude named Spanky.

He and I hit it off. He was a portly fellow with a bald head and long beard. He was very Rock N Roll. Just like I was and he happened to be upgrading his music collection from tapes to CDs and one day he came into work and gave me all his tapes.

There was everything in there. He had a hair metal library. Guns N Roses, Ozzy, Motley Crue, Def Leppard, Bon Jovi, Warrant, Skid Row, all the tapes I had lost when I got locked up. My entire music collection had just been replaced in one fell swoop and then some more added in to boot. I was ecstatic. *One man's trash is another man's treasure*. It was one of the best gifts I have ever received.

Then it was June, and I only had four days and a wake up left. I was still working as much as possible, picking up side work at the restaurant whenever possible. When I got out I had about Three Grand saved.

The week of my release date I was at Chili's and was checking out the area's weekly newspaper called 'New Times' and ran across my horoscope for the week of June 1st – June 7th. Normally, I do not pay these types of things much attention, but this one was different, it caught my attention because of its uniqueness and I felt like I could relate. This one was personal.

> **CAPRICORN** (Dec. 22-Jan. 19): In 752 AD, the Japanese Empress Koken wrote a lyrical poem in praise of the eupatorium plant, whose leaves turn a vivid shade of yellow in summer. Recently, scientists punctured the illusion she was under, demonstrating that the lovely foliage of the eupatorium is caused by a disease virus. In my view, though, this shouldn't diminish our appreciation of either the poem or the plant. I've noticed that a lot of the world's beauty forms in response to a wound. In fact, I expect you're in the midst of that very process right now.

I got out 4 days later!

June 5, 2003
My release photo

The Day I Got Out

Waking up the morning of June 5th, 2003 felt much like any other morning. It started like all the other ones did that came before it. I got up, brushed my teeth, got dressed, and went to breakfast, came back to my cell, and then sat on my bunk for count. Except for this morning when they cleared count my good buddy, Robert was there to pick me up.

Many people offered to come get me, but Robert and I had a special relationship. He was my friend from childhood and we had remained in sporadic contact throughout my incarceration. He lived in Miami, and we had been talking about this day for months. He arrived at 8:00 am, and they made him wait till 9:00.

I made him wait another hour and a half before I would leave. Why? Remember my hat? The one the guy took when I first arrived? I wanted it back.

When the property officer was processing my belongings as part of the exit procedures. I brought up the subject of my hat. He acted like he did not remember, so I produced the property receipt that he gave me when he confiscated it.

It was dated less than 30 days ago, meaning he was still responsible to have it. I had him stop everything he was doing and go find it. He looked for more than 45 minutes before he finally came back with it. Robert and I just stood there and waited. Neither one of us willing to move an inch until he came back with my hat. I was not leaving without it. Robert was there for me and backed me up. Never one time did he say let's just go, or just forget about it, I will buy you a new one. He just stood in solidarity with me.

Once my hat was returned, we left. I said goodbye to the Dept of Corrections and hello to my new life, but before the new life started, I had a couple of things to tend to first.

Our first stop was Chili's. I had to get my money out of the safe, and then Robert and I enjoyed a steak and Chili's signature drink - The Presidente' Margarita. My manager picked up the tab as a way to wish me well and to congratulate me. It was an appreciated gesture.

Next, I wanted to get a cell phone, and in the same plaza as the Chili's was a Cingular wireless store. Not knowing the difference or anything about cell phones, that store was as good as any other. So, in we went. I was talking to the representative about a new cell phone and a plan *this was before unlimited when they still sold cell plans by the minute and in packages.* He was asking me how much I intended to talk a month and how many minutes did I think I would need? I had no idea how to answer that question. I was stuck.

He then asked me how many minutes I talk a month now. Again, I had no answer. I had just come from a world where cell phones did not exist, not for us anyway. I had never seen one, owned one, nor paid a bill. For the last eleven years, every phone call I made was collect and cut off after fifteen minutes. I had no idea how long I would talk to people if there was no timer waiting to cut me off. I had so much to say, so much to tell everyone.

How much are 500 minutes? I do not know if that is enough If I go over - it is how much? Well, I need a lot then. He was asking me lots of questions, and I had just as many for him. He would answer mine by asking ones of his own and I had no idea how to answer. My head began to spin.

He just kept talking, and then started staring at me funny. The room was spinning. I was overwhelmed. Too much information was coming at me too fast. It was too much to process.

I was out!
Oh my God, this is what real-world problems look like.
I am out, I am out, oh man, I cannot believe it, I am out.
Emotions just began to crash over me like waves during a hurricane. Years' worth of pent up loneliness, heart aching, anxiety, and frustration just crashed over me all at the same time, and they just kept coming. I lost all composure and just burst out in tears. Right in the middle of this dude asking me how many minutes a month did I think I was going to need.

I know he thought I was weird. I did not care.
Robert just put his hand on my shoulder, turned me around, and told the guy "We'll take a brochure" grabbed one, and walked me out the door. He said I could use his phone and said we would tackle getting a cell phone another day.

Why did I break down in the middle of a cell phone store and cry? I do not know. I am guessing, him overwhelming me with information, me feeling inadequate and embarrassed for not being able to answer basic questions. The emotional dam that had been held back for so long let loose at the same time, but Robert knew. He understood, and he graciously guided me right outside of that store back to the safety of his car.

He took me to a LaQuinta hotel and paid my tab for the next two days. He told me to take some time for myself, get my thoughts in order, take a night or two to enjoy myself, and then he would take me home, back to Fort Myers on Saturday. This was Thursday. It was a great plan.

Except my room had no coffee pot and I did not discover that until after Robert left. My room had a coffee maker, but the pot was missing. I looked and looked but could not find one. I checked the bathroom, under the bed, in the closet, it was not there.

Let something come up missing in the chain-gang and see what a big deal that is. They shut the compound down. Send everyone back to their bunk assignments, and they search, they search, and they search. They bring in dogs if they are looking for drugs. If it is a missing knife from the kitchen or a screwdriver from maintenance, they will turn the whole prison upside down. They will interrogate everyone, *and then they will get nasty about it*. Things do not return to normal until it is found. A missing coffee pot inside the chain-gang would be a great big deal. Not only is there no coffee, but the pot can be used as a weapon.

I was beginning to panic. I just knew they were going to call the cops. I have only been out a few hours and already I am going back to prison for another crime I did not commit. Panic was setting in. So, I called Robert. He answered, and I told him the coffee pot was missing. He did not react with near the panic that I felt the situation warranted. Instead, he held his voice very calm and steady; and advised me to call the front desk and tell them it is not there and ask them to please send you another one up.

I tried to explain to him that If I did that, they would think I stole it, they would call the police, and they would see that I had just got out of prison and they would send me right back to where I just came from.

He then explained that they would not do that. I asked him how he knew, and he explained "because you are no longer inmate Cass. You are out now. You have done the time that they sentenced you to. You're now Mr. Cass, and people don't think Mr. Cass would steal a coffee pot." I was stunned. I had never been 'Mr. Cass' before.

He then told me to call the front desk and see for myself. I had remembered no one looked at me weird at Chili's, or Wal Mart, or at the bank, maybe he was right. So, I paced the floor and built up some courage. Made sure I had a fast escape route just in case this conversation did not go well, and after about ten minutes, I called the front desk.

They apologized for my room not having one and sent someone right up to deliver me a coffee pot. Just like Robert said. No interrogations, no questions, no searches of the hotel room by room. Wow! Being 'Mr. Cass' was cool.

Later, Robert stopped back by the hotel and picked me up, and asked me what I wanted to go do, my first night out. Of course, it was mandatory that I go inside the Pink Pony. The same one that I had been pedaling my bike past for weeks.

I had Three Grand, and a compulsive desire to go spend some of it inside that beautiful pink palace. Except the inside was very dingy, and kind of gross. Girls were walking by nude, asking if I wanted to tip them, as they held out a garter. I believe I gave away $300 just in walk-by tips. I did not care, because there was this one Latin beauty with the coolest accent that I have ever heard, and she was telling me she liked my accent too. She asked me where I was from? so I told her. *I was fresh out of prison.*

She took me in the back room for a lap dance and was honored to be the first girl to give me one upon my release. She gave me the first one free, and then I bought three more. I spent five hundred dollars with her inside of fifteen minutes. Just in lap dances and tips.

After the third song, I proposed. I asked her to marry me right then and there. She had more good sense than I did because she declined my offer. She advised me to go home and see my family and if I still wanted to marry her, to come back and see her and we could talk about it.

Robert suggested we leave not long after that and I asked him if I could pull up the car. He handed me the keys and in his stick shift Honda that was parked fifty yards away. It took me a little over eleven minutes to drive back up to him.

I kept sputtering and stopping and having to restart the car. It was embarrassing but we laughed it off. My first day out was full of gaffes. They were funny. Re-acclimation was a process. I do not mind sharing it with you.

Later that evening after Robert had gone home, and I was alone in my hotel room. I was only going to have a first night out once and I knew how I wanted it to end. I wanted the company of a woman. I wanted to touch, to feel, and to smell a woman. I wanted to look in one's eyes. I wanted to have a conversation, I wanted to flirt, I wanted to let desire grow, I wanted to kiss, and I wanted sex. I did not know anyone. Or even have a phone but after the Pink Pony, I still had better than two grand left and I was in Miami. I was sure I could make something happen.

I went down to the lobby of the hotel and picked up one of the recent 'New Times' newspapers. They had the call girl/massage/escort ads in the back.
I called a girl named Holly.

I told her I had just got out of prison; this was my first night out in eleven years and I wanted to spend some time with her. I did not want her to just stop by and leave. I wanted her to hang out and spend some time with me. She replied, "What were you in prison for?" I told her drugs, and that I got arrested for hauling a bunch of pot in high school, I just got out today."
There was no need to go into the whole murder thing with her.

She took my word for it and told me she would stop by for a drink, we would talk, and she would check me out. If I was not a weirdo then maybe, but she wanted to meet me first. I agreed.

I began to hide my money. I was not sure who was coming over, what they were going to look like. Or If they were going to try and rob me. Or what circumstances I might find myself in. So, I broke my money up into stacks and began to hide the stacks all around the room. Between the mattresses, under the corners of the carpet, inside the lamps. If the worse occurred and I got robbed, and they searched the room. The chances of them getting any more than a little bit would be greatly decreased.

An hour or so later, she knocked. I answered, and surprise surprise there stood this incredible-looking black girl, and I was a good-looking white boy and neither one of us had expected that.

We quickly got over our mutual surprise though and she came in and sat down. I sat down opposite her so as not to crowd her or make her feel uncomfortable. Turns out she was from the Caribbean. Her father was white, and her mother was from Jamaica and she spoke with this very cool Calypso accent. We chatted for a bit, mostly about me and the fact that I had just gotten out of prison, and then she asked if I had anything to drink. I did not. So, we went downstairs and across the street to a convenience store. She bought a bottle of wine and a pack of cigarettes. I bought a Dr. Pepper and some M&Ms.

We went back to the room and I talked some more while she drank, and about halfway through her bottle of wine, we kissed and then ignited like a passionate ball of fire.

Our experience that night was pretty special. I will keep the details between her and me, as a gentleman should do. I will say though, that we connected. Just like real people in desperate need of passion, and in the end, she whispered "Welcome home" in my ear. That made the experience personal. Her words capped off what was probably the single best night of my life. Up to that point anyway. She stayed the whole night; we fell asleep wrapped up in each other's arms. Looking just like coffee and cream.

The next morning, we woke up together and went to breakfast. Her real name is Yvette, and she was working on getting her Real Estate license during the day.

We became friends and stayed in touch with each other for several years. I ended up crashing at her place a few times whenever I would go and hang out on South Beach over the course of the next few years, but there was never another time that we engaged in romantic activities. We had become friends and that was fine with each of us.

What I did was dangerous and I'm sure that I wouldn't make that same choice again to call a 'call girl' like that but on that day, under those circumstances, I did, and I marvel out of all the ads, out of all the girls I could've called, I called one who would stay the whole night, and would later become a good friend.

Life was working out pretty well so far, but that would prove to be temporary as well. I would soon face obstacles and challenges of a different kind.

Those I will save, however, for the next book. This one concludes as did my first night out. With me being satisfied and going to sleep.

What happens next?
You will have to read Book Two: Serial Entrepreneur to find out. It starts on page 238 of this book (keep reading), and in the same place that this one ends. Then it goes on to detail what life was like once I came home, looked for a job, how I started not one business, but several.

In the next book, you will also find out how I made the Department of Corrections pay me back money for all the days of my life that they took from me, the status of my new Clemency appeal. How I have grown, what decisions I made next, what I did then, and what I am doing now.

So, until then,
Thanks for reading.

Marion CI 1995
With my sisters Kimberly & Melody

Honorable Mentions

Upon conclusion, I would like to mention a few more things worthy of recognition. I did not make my journey alone. I had a family that loved me. No matter how far they sent me away from home, my dad always made the trip to come and visit me. Even when I was a 9-hour drive away up at Washington CI. He would still come up to see me. Not every weekend, or every month but often, and as often as he could.

2001
Me & my dad – Cross City

I must also mention the name of my stepmother, Harolene. She came into my life when I was seven and she did as much to raise me as anyone else did and proved to be an invaluable ally during my journey. Her prayers no doubt was what kept me safe on many occasions. She and my dad ended their marriage after 20 years when I was at Washington CI but she and I never quit being close.

Both of my grandmothers would write to me, and occasionally my uncle Kenny. He even took a picture of both a sunset and sunrise onetime and then wrote me a letter explaining how they were both relevant to me, my life, and my circumstances.

I had pen pals all over the world. I sought out people to write from internet searches that people would do for me. From pen pal writing clubs, magazine ads, referrals of friends. I have corresponded with professors at universities, a gay judge that lived in Tennessee, a dominatrix in London, a Pastor in North Florida. NA sponsors, AA Sponsors, as well as a dude living in Holland. I corresponded with people from my church, with people from other churches. I wrote to anyone who would write me back and got to know many people from many different places and lived vicariously through them all.

I wrote, I listened to music, and I played handball. That is how I survived, and I did not let it ruin me as a person.
I never kept it all bottled up inside. I always found a way to let it all out of my soul.

That, and I had a bunch of people praying for me. Several of these special people come to the top of my mind, the first of which is **Sister Ginny.** Ginny was kind of like another mom to me. I was at her house when I was arrested. She wrote to me very often while I was inside and would later go on to start a prison ministry and would write lots and lots of inmates and encourage them in the Lord. She grew up with my dad and often attends his church. She and I are still close and whenever I am in town, I stay with her often. Thank you, Ginny.

Sister Thelma
Sister Thelma was an old-time Saint of the Lord. She attended the church that I grew up in and would not only pray for me daily but would stand up every December and ask the church to remember me. She would then have them take up a special

offering just for me, every Christmas. One year to thank her, I wrote her the poem 'A Tool in The Master's Hand'. When I got out and came home, she had invited me to attend a church service with her. *The same church I attended and my dad pastored when I first got locked up.* I accepted her invitation, and we slipped in and sat near the rear of the sanctuary just before church started. Once it did, I looked around and wondered if anyone would recognize me. No one did.

Then the new pastor of the church, Brother Carl looked at Sister Thelma, and then at me and said, "Sister Thelma, how about you tell us who that young man is sitting right next to you." She stood up and with such a joyful glee and announced. "That's Mark Cass and I sure am glad he's here."

The place erupted. A great big gasp, a sigh, a Praise the Lord, and then clapping. They were all glad I was home. All of them except my ex-girlfriend. Yes, the girl that I wrote most all those lovesick, heartbroken poems about. She was there, and so was her mom. They were sitting near the front, on the far side. I only saw them for a second. Then the Pastor dismissed, and she slipped right out the side door without ever even saying Hi. I looked around for her, but she was gone. *Just like all the days before.*

Praise God though for Sister Thelma. What a Saint she was. I could not bear to write a book about those troublesome times in my life and not mention her. She is a hero.

Second to last, but certainly not least, is my good friend **Leah Hill.**

**Me and Leah
Cross City 2002**

Leah wrote to me on the first day that I was locked up and she continued to write too until the day I got out. I would always hear from her several times a year. She would come to visit me about twice a year. Hearing from her was always so refreshing. She was always positive and encouraging. She believed in me, no matter what the newspapers said, and she deserves special recognition at the end of my book, because she was there for me at the end, at the beginning, and in the middle too. Thank you, Leah. Your friendship will always be treasured.

The very last honorable mention of this book goes to my friend **Louis Civale**. He is not mentioned by name anywhere in this book as I have only just recently met him via email. However, he has personally hand-drawn, every illustration that you have seen in this book unless otherwise credited by me in the text.

I felt that I needed an illustrator to bring this book to life. To provide the reader with the best possible experience, I needed someone who knew what it looked like on the inside. I knew what I wanted in the scenes and I knew that I wanted the scenes to be hand-drawn but kept realistic.

So, I put the word out to a few of my friends who are still trapped behind the fence, that I was looking for an illustrator, and was referred to Lou and was told that he was the best artist on the compound. I emailed him and told him about my project, and he was happy to contribute his talent and art. So, credit where it is due. Thank you, Lou.

I am honored to feature his artwork alongside my poems and stories and adventures. He is a most excellent artist and I appreciate his contributions to this book. His expected release date is 2023.

Six For The Road

Before we say our final goodbye and move past this chapter of my life, I have a few more poems to share. Ones that I wrote and wanted to include but somehow got left out of the storylines.

The first one 'One Friend' was written for Leah.
I wrote it inside of a homemade birthday card that I had a guy make for her. She loved it and it was entirely worth the three packs of cigarettes it cost me to have made.

The second one is one of my personal favorites. It is called 'No News Is Good News'. I wrote it while at Marion CI in their Tier 3 program. I was practicing trying to write about things outside of me. Not emotional drainage. I had written enough of that. So, this poem is about what I had seen on the Eleven o'clock news.

The third one was written for Sister Thelma and the members of my church. It is called 'A Tool in The Master's Hand' and was written to thank her (them) for always praying for me and remembering me every Christmas.

The fourth one 'Desperate Need of a Coat of Paint' was written in August of 1996 while at Marion CI as well, during count time one evening. I was staring at the walls of my cell and its old, ugly, green, peeling, paint. It is written more as a metaphor about my life and what I was going through at the time. It remains one of my personal favorites as well.

The fifth, 'Hello Me' is a song I co-wrote in county jail.

I had a good friend named Dennis, he was a songwriter, and we wrote it together. We used to talk about how we were going to get out and start a band. We were both going to write songs. I was going to play drums and he was going to sing. Another dude in the cell block was down to play guitar with us too. We just needed them to let us go.

Instead, we all went to prison and the masses have been denied this incredible song that surely would have been a #1 hit and made us all three, a Million dollars in royalties. If we could just get the right person to sing it.

Someone like Greg Allman, it could have been a comeback song for him. Or Elton John, a piano tune with a lead guitar break and a soulful voice. Or even an uptown groove, with a Billy Joel type vibe.

This other dude in the cell block was a guitar player and supposed to be as good as Eddie Van Halen and had volunteered to put down a real mean lead guitar break, for just a case of beer.

We had it all worked out, we talked about our band all day long. None of us had ever heard the other one play anything, but that was ok. We were going to have a big jam session when we got out. We just needed to get out!

So, heard here for the first time by anybody who was not with us inside of Cell Block 4F in 1993 is 'Hello Me'.
Feel free to sing it any way you want to.

The last one, 'What's A Visitor to Think'. May very well be the most significant one of them all. I did not write it while incarcerated though. I wrote in high school. It is the first poem that I ever wrote.

It is a very conservative poem, reflective of my environment growing up during the 80s while processing thoughts about current events. I happened to ask myself 'What's a visitor to think?' and that was that. I wrote it I about ten minutes on a sheet of notebook paper. This is the one that made me believe

that writing may be something I just might be able to do. Everyone liked it. I liked it, and that feeling made me want to write more.
Please enjoy!
Keep It Live!
Don't Read and Drive!
Keep It Between the Ditches!

One Friend

*If I awoke in the morning
with a decision to make
I could only have one friend
which one would I take
That wouldn't be hard,
I know exactly who I'd choose
If I could only have one friend,
I'd want it to be you
Only one friend to walk with me
down life's long and winding road
Only one friend
To help me bear my heavy load
If I could accomplish some great feat
And only had one friend to tell it too
It could be anyone that I wanted
I'd still want it to be you
Someone to understand me
Someone to know me inside out
I'd want it to be you
beyond the shadow of a doubt
Someone to love and trust
And really get to know
someone who'd believe in me
and never ever go
Your friendship would be sufficient
To help me make it through
If I could only have one friend
I'd want it to be you.*

No News Is Good News

*I stayed up late one night
to watch the eleven o'clock news
and heard the story of a wino
who'd been shot and killed for a bottle of booze
Immediately following this
Was the story of a teenaged hooker
Found dead in an alley, naked,
Beside a needle and a homemade cooker
I couldn't help but ask myself
What's this world coming to?
Has society lost its conscience?
Do we no longer care what our children do?
The next story was about a politician
Who'd been arrested in an undercover sting
Seems he received probation for his part in a child
pornography ring
Ironically, the next story
Was a kid given twenty-five years
For going to an all-night convenience store
And stealing a six-pack of beer
I thought of the paper that the laws were written on
And how it had become nothing more than litter
Because of the way 'justice' was being auctioned off
And sold to the highest bidder
At this point, the newscaster smiled
And said they'd be back after the break
And I just turned the television off
For I'd heard about all that I could take*

A Tool in The Master Hand
For Sister Thelma

A Masterpiece is what God is creating inside of me
Because of you, I am becoming who he wants me to be
He is forming me in the image of his Son
I will be just like Jesus when the Master is done
He is the potter, and I am the clay
He molds and shapes me in his own special way
For he is the master with all the plans and rules
Christian brother and sisters are His beloved tools
He uses them with the utmost of skill
To fashion me after His perfect will
I thank you for your obedience and for letting God use you
It proves that your commitment to him is so true
Because you have taken the time to care
I've been delivered from the chains of despair
His word and his promises,
I'm beginning to now understand
Because you were willing to become
A tool in the Master's Hand

Desperate Need of a Coat of Paint

I sit in this concrete box
        And cannot help but ask
                Have I become all that
                      I'm destined to be

What's happened to my childhood dreams
        And my teenage fantasies
                I often find myself wondering aloud
                      Whatever has ever become of those

My life was once filled with uncertainty
        Adventure
                And blessed
                      Unpredictability

Now my every day is the same as the one before
        I wake up alone
                In a pale green room
                      In desperate need of a coat of paint

And every night is the same
        as the thousands that have preceded it
                I fall asleep wondering
                      If this is all I will ever be

        In a room that is still
                In desperate need of a coat of paint

Hello Me

V1. Hello me, how are you, just thought that I'd drop you a line
I hope you're holding on, cause me, I'm not doing so fine
You see my hearts always aching
I'm lonely as I can be, seems no cares how it's breaking
Or what it's doing to me

V2. To have to live without you has been the hardest of all
I wait but I get no letters, and you're never there when I call
And I've been feeling lonely cause I'm so all alone
Oh, how I wish I could only, still have my family to hold

V3. So, Hello Me, how are you, just thought I'd drop you a line
Cause if I didn't write to me, I would surely lose my mind
Because I truly need someone to keep from falling apart
You see I've been coming undone from all this pain in my heart

V4. And I hope that this letter helps to make me feel better
I hope it helps make me see that someone hopes that I'm alright
And that I make it through
and someone hopes you have sweet dreams tonight,
Remember I love you

Lead Guitar Break

Repeat V3. and V4. *Fade out with guitar and 'I love yooou'.*

What's a Visitor to Think?

What's a visitor to think of our mighty USA?
And the way we slay unborn children every day
Where our Veterans fought and in return
We made our flag legal to burn

What's a visitor to think?
Of the land of the free and the home of the brave
Where the Indian was deceived, and the black man was a slave
Where most kids aren't interested in school
All they care about is hanging out and being cool
What's a visitor to think of our great land?
With all the polluted beaches and the littered sand
Where it's never safe to leave your doors unlocked
Or people will rob you blind for a twenty-dollar rock
What's a visitor to think of the land in which we reside
When every year there is an increase in teenage suicide
Where children drive their parents insane
And people of all ages engage in destroying their brain

What's a visitor to think of the land in which we live
Where people take more than they give
And we have homeless people on our street
Begging and stealing for food to eat
What's a visitor to think of a place?
'where politicians lie right to your face
Where adults can't read or write
And men sleep with men and say it's alright
What's a visitor to think of a country?
Where the planet is being destroyed and nobody cares
Where a ten-dollar bill can even buy sex
It sure seems like America is under some type of hex
Tell me, what a visitor to think?

You have survived 'The Jungle'
End Book One

**Begin Book Two:
Serial Entrepreneur**

Serial Entrepreneur

Dedications

Book Two of my Memoir series, titled 'Serial Entrepreneur' is next and is dedicated to Entrepreneurs and to those that are downtrodden anywhere and everywhere.

This book is further dedicated to Mya and Marley. This is the story of your daddy, and how I overcame an unfortunate set of circumstances. I made some mistakes along the way. You will too, and that is ok. I know each of you will go on to surpass me in many ways. Your Daddy loves you!

Further, this book is dedicated to the best friend I ever had in my life, Mr. Smith. Thank you for lying right by my feet as I wrote most of this and for teaching me the meaning of loyalty, and how to love unconditionally. I hope that you are the first one I meet when I cross over to the other side.

Special mentions and thanks as well, to Tim Jacobs, Brian Solt, and Chas Wilson. You guys have all changed my life for the better. Thank you for believing in me.

Finally, this book is dedicated to Shannon and Anisity. The two women who have helped me get this far.

Waking Up Free

Having just gotten out of prison the day before. June 6th, 2003 became the first morning I woke up as a free man since the morning of July 31, 1992. Yvette and I slept in that morning until nearly Eleven. As my eyes opened. I just laid there basking in the rays of freedom and sunshine coming in through the window and smiled.

I had no plans, and neither did she, so we went and had brunch, and when we were done, I suggested we go see a movie. There were a lot of new ones that I wanted to see. She consented, as we were walking in, after we bought our tickets, her phone rang, and it was business.

She explained, as much as she wanted to hang out with me, she had money on the line. She had to go get it. We happened to be near her apartment though and she did not want to leave me stranded. So, she took me back to her place and told me she would be back in an hour.

She lived way up on the 21st floor in one of the high rises along Collins Ave. that accentuate Miami's South Beach.

When we reached her front door and opened it, I stepped inside, to the most amazing view I have ever seen. Her entire back wall was made of glass and gave the most exhilarating view of Miami Beach from that height and that large wall of glass. The sun just sparkled off the clear blue water and you could see the military vessels way off in the distance with sailboats much closer in with their colorful sails, pretty people swimming and seagulls flying by. It was an incredible nature scene alive, right inside of her living room. It took my breath away.

She was nervous about leaving me there inside of her house and asked me to please not steal anything. I was shocked that she said that as we were having such a nice time. Why would she think so little of me, then she explained?

"You just got out of prison yesterday. I do not know you, and now you are in my house. I have a right to be concerned. So please don't steal anything." I agreed she had a point once she put it that way. I assured her I would not, and I kept my word.

She showed me her computer and how to log on to the internet, as I had never done that before. This was my first time. The first thing I did when she left, was go to the Buffalo Bills website and read about the Buffalo Bills and all that was happening. As they were gearing up for training camp that started in July.

She came back about an hour and a half later and I was still sitting in the same spot at her kitchen table, taking in that magnificent view of the ocean and marveling at how much information I had been able to access about the Buffalo Bills. I have always been a super fan, even though they have not provided much reason to be during those years. I am very loyal by nature. If I am down with you, then I am down with you. Period. I was no different in my painful allegiance to the Buffalo Bills.

Adventures in Miami did not last much longer as I was anxious to return home and to see my family, plus my Grandmother was already a little perturbed that I was not home already.

The next morning came. It was Saturday, June 7th, 2003 and I was riding with one of my lifelong best friends, listening to 80s hair metal, and had 100 miles across Alligator Alley to go. Phones do not work out there. So we listened to music and

talked about all that we thought the future would hold.

By the time we turned down Cass Drive and slowed for all the potholes in the road, I could hardly contain my excitement. I wanted to jump out of the car and run the rest of the way there.

When we pulled into the driveway, and my Dad came outside to greet us, that is when I knew it was real.
I was home. No probation. No parole, over and done.
No more count time, plastic sporks, or state-issued boxer shorts. No more showering with a bunch of men all at the same time. No more phone lists, visitation request denials.
No more. I had made it. I was home. That journey was over.

Except it was not at all!
What I did not know then about being incarcerated is that it is never over. It stands out as a gigantic red flag any time you apply for a job, apply for housing, when dating, and then you come under even more scrutiny when you involve potential in-laws, and neighbors.

Having been incarcerated is a factor looked at and considered anytime someone else is deciding whether to approve you as a field trip volunteer at your child's school, athletic event, or church function.

A felony record is considered years later when applying for health insurance, and at every single traffic stop, you will ever have.

It is impossible to predict, understand, know, or catalog all the negative effects that having a felony conviction on your record is going to cause you throughout your lifetime.

For example, when I first came home, I was given a small pull behind camper trailer to live in, and my grandparents allowed me to place it on their property. Which was more like a family farm or compound. It was modest and it was small, but it had more amenities than where I had just come from, so I was happy.

Coincidently, a new convenience store had opened right down the street, and they were hiring. I had a family member who knew the owners very well. A word was given, instructions were passed back down for me to apply, I attempted, but they were out of paper applications and they opted to verbally interview me instead, then I was hired.

During my third-day training, I was asked to finally fill out an application, I did and checked yes to the 'Have you ever been convicted of a felony' question. I was let go within 30 seconds of turning in the application! That same set of circumstances would rear its ugly head over and over in my life, time and time again.

To this very day, it continues to create hindrances that stand in between me and my goals. It will never go away. It is a brand. Ex-con, or Felon.

One night of stupid decisions, not thinking things through. One night, one hour, one moment, one bad decision is all that is needed to ruin the rest of your life. **There is an incredible difference between 'enjoying your childhood' and 'ruining the rest of your forever'.** Unfortunately, Youth is often wasted on the young.

I never lied when asked the felony question on an application. Ever. I figured they would respect me more if I just told them the truth upfront. I have always been very honest. The transparency of this book confirms that.

Every job interview, I checked yes. They asked I answered, and then explained that I have not been in any trouble since, and it was a long long time ago, etc.

Never once have I lied and answered 'no' to the felony question on a job application. Except for this one time…

It would be one day, ten years off in the future before I would once again find myself in desperate need of a job.
I was homeless and sleeping on the floor of an office building that someone allowed me to share with them.

I remember very clearly it was September 2013 and life was about as tough as it could get for me at that time, and I met the General Manager of a popular chain restaurant near Fort Myers Beach. He and I shared a table at a Sports bar on the first NFL Sunday of 2013. We watched the game together. He told me he was hiring servers for the season. We talked, and he interviewed me on the spot and then told me to stop by and formally apply and he would hire me.

I went there feeling confident, thankful for a blessing. I knew I had this job, I could finally see a way out of the desperate situation that I was in. Then there it was *the felony question.*

Staring me right in the face. It was question number 7 on the application. "Have you ever been convicted of a felony?"

A lot of applications nowadays ask that question but reference it with a time period such as in the last seven years? The last ten years? Etc. I love those applications because I can always check No. The crime I was charged with happened in 1992 so even if they go back as far as 25 years. I am good!

But this one said 'ever'. No time references.
I shook my head, I sighed deeply, and for the first time, I considered checking No.

This job was life or death for me at the time. I had been out of work and desperately looking for a few months, my new business was becoming quite difficult to maintain all by myself. I could not have my kids overnight because I slept on the floor in someone's office at night. I had been submitting applications everywhere and just needed to catch a break. This was it. I could not take a chance of not getting a callback. I needed this job. I was not going to leave there without it. I had to check No, my gas tank was on E. I needed to start work immediately.

So, I did it. I checked No.
I already had the job, and I could not risk jinxing it.
I was hired. I started training the next Monday.
I was there thirty minutes early all week long.
I went above and beyond what was required. My prior restaurant experience shone through. I caught on quickly. I passed all the written tests. I passed the menu test. The wine test, all of them.

It was Friday night, and my training was done.
This was going to be my first night on the floor by myself.

I was finally going to make some tips and come home with money. Man, I needed it. I had borrowed $20 for gas from my cousin till Friday, but now I owed the $20 and my tank was on E again.

There were no groceries, my dog needed dog food, and as I was ironing my shirt, getting ready for work, my phone rang.

It was that same General Manager. He said they got a call about me and ran my background. Turns out I had been in jail for Second-degree murder and I checked the felony question No on the application, and they were terminating my employment effective immediately.

"Do not come in tonight".
"Pick up your check for hours already worked next Tuesday at 2 pm." I hung up, as I slid down the wall to a sitting position on the floor. Completely deflated. The thoughts and emotions that exploded within me at that moment are not family-friendly or fit for print.

Suffice it to say though, that example is but one of many that lie waiting for me and I would have to soon endure, and only one of at least a hundred lessons that I was yet to learn.

But for now, I did not know any of that. That was all yet to come. What I did know, however, was that I was home.

I just stepped out of Rob's car. My dad walked around the corner of the house with a cup of coffee in his hand and gave me a great big bear hug.

My Grandpa was there, and so was my Grandma, and then later came other family members and friends and we had a great big family dinner in which my dad blessed it, as we all held hands. This is how it was supposed to be. I had come to miss these moments so very deeply over the years. I was home. God was good! This chapter ends here. With a smile. 😊

The Next Few Days, Months, and Year or Two or So…

I can remember the very next Monday my Grandmother took me down to the DMV and allowed me to use her minivan to take my driving test. I passed.

From there she drove me to her bank and helped me open a checking and savings account, and then on to Radio Shack where I bought a Nextel walkie-talkie phone. It was quite an adventurous day.

Once I had a Drivers' license my aunt and uncle gave me an older model Isuzu Trooper. This was a genuinely nice gesture. They had only the best of intentions and I will appreciate them always for that.

However, this turned out to be a horrible disservice to me, as there were troubles around the corner that were unforeseen as a result, and they were coming in towards me with blazing speed.

My first month or so out was a wonderful time. Everyone was glad to see me. I was going around seeing lots of family members, hanging out with my sisters. Seeing old friends. I had money saved up from work release. Everywhere I went people were offering to help me, give to me, provide for one need or another, but that only lasts so long, and then the money runs out; and when it did, I still had no job. I discovered that prospective employers were not nearly as impressed by the statement 'I just got out of prison' as that one-night stand in Miami was.

Before any of the hardships that were yet to come. When everything was still fresh and new. The day I got my driver's license, a new cell phone, and my vehicle insured.

I went to see my mom. I put on a tie, spruced myself up, and anxiously drove off from my little camper and headed out.

My grandmother owned a very popular restaurant/bar called

Mulletville. In this little fishing community known as Pine Island. I had never been there or seen it, but they told me it was where the old Moose Lodge used to be, and I knew where that was.

So, there I was fresh out. Driving down the road in my Isuzu Trooper. Cassette tapes playing and headed out to see all my family on my mom's side.

All of whom I am very close to, and most of which are Outlaws. The Outlaw den was a rickety-looking fisherman bar that is world-famous for their annual 'Mullet toss'. An event where all the locals and tourists alike come and see who can toss a mullet the farthest. Yes, the fish. People come from all over the world to throw dead fish. It is like a crazy phenomenon, but that was not what was going on right now.

Right now, I was walking into this rough, rowdy bar full of hard-drinking, and hard living fisherman, and I walked in wearing what amounted to a suit and tie and did a horrible job of blending in.

I will never forget the way my cousin Katie greeted me when she saw me. She was behind the bar, serving drinks when I walked in and took an empty seat in between two burly fishermen who had just come in off the boat. She looked right at me and I just smiled.

She thought 'Who's this joker walking in here with a tie just smiling at me?' and then the lights turned on inside her head, she looked up again, recognized me, and let out this great big scream "Aaahhhh Mark – You're home, you're home, you're home" and she came running around the bar screaming with joy and jumped in my arms and gave me this enormous hug. It was nice.

No other feeling quite compares to someone seeing you from across the room and running towards you with outstretched hands, screaming your name, and then jumping into your arms. Happy to see you.

I was twenty-nine. Six months shy of thirty. I had no debt, no boss, no mortgage, no wife, no kids, I was truly free.

I took disposable cameras with me everywhere and took pictures of everyone and everything. I had so much taken from me while in there, everything except memories. I knew how important they were, and they would come to be, so I tried to capture everything.

My mom hosted an extravagant weekend for me that included an expensive shopping trip, and several nights at the Lani Kai hotel on Fort Myers Beach. My first month out was an incredible time of reuniting with everyone.

After the first month or two though my money began to run low, and the two or three financial responsibilities that I had accumulated, were now all due and I still did not have a job.

I wish someone, <u>anyone</u>, would have advised me to focus on generating an income, before signing up for financial obligations i.e. *cell phone, car insurance, credit cards.* **Instead, doing the right things in the wrong order was celebrated. Everyone kept telling me how good I was doing.**

I had been used to hearing that and thought for sure that I was on the right track. While I was in, I had accumulated many accomplishments and had them on record. I had remained disciplinary report free for the past seven, eight, nine, ten years. I had completed several vocational courses and Life Skills classes. I had a couple of Prison Fellowship certificates and more AA and NA attendance certificates than could fit in my file.

Outside, in the free world though, nobody told me how little people were going to care about that. Especially next to a statement such as "I did eleven years", Second-Degree Murder", "I have been out 30 days, 60 days, 90 days," whatever the count happened to be. **No one even cared that I did not do it.**

I was an ex-con, fresh out of prison, and that shut a lot more doors of opportunity than it opened. No one had prepared me for that.

Eventually, the money that I had saved at work release ran out and I began to feel a lot of pressure. I so very much wanted to do everything right and live by the book. I was not looking to run afoul of the law in any kind of way.

I became familiar with pawnshops, and payday loans, and that got me by for a little while, but then came a day when I had three bills to pay by Monday, and it was Friday. I only had enough money for two of them and quite by accident, not intending to in any way whatsoever, I tripped and fell right into the middle of a great big pile of cocaine, *and I almost did not survive that.*

I seem to have established a pattern in my life of tripping and falling right outside of the starting gate. Having to then struggle and catch my footing while running behind. Eventually, after having put in much more work than was ever necessary, I find a way to right the ship, trim the sails, and come out the other side having lapped everybody and with an epic win. I am happy to take the win in such fanciful fashion, but I do wish I would have begun making better decisions, much sooner than I began to.

I made a wrong turn here at this point in my story. I went down a very dark path and should have had my soul required of me more times than is pleasant to think about.

This dark period began, with me trying to do the right thing the wrong way. In the end, some five years later in 2008. This path that I was about to embark upon would eventually lead to me becoming a full-fledged addict. At my very worst point near the end, time would find me raving mad in a hotel room shooting Five hundred dollars worth of Cocaine a day, in my arms.

Just barely, and only by God's grace, would I remain a half a step ahead, of not just the law, but the Coroner too.

I wholeheartedly believe that my God had his hand upon me always, but especially during this time. On more than one occasion He found Himself running after me just like a mother would run to the rescue of her infant baby that had just fallen into a backyard pool.

Take just a moment to imagine that scene. It is important. I want you to see it with your mind's eye. All the family is gathered at the home of a family member with a newborn.

It is a pool home, and the infant is out on the pool patio with a family member who becomes distracted in conversation.

Momma is in the kitchen handling something hot. While Aunt Evelyn is telling her about one venture or another. When the dog suddenly gives chase to the cat and runs by and bumps the baby carrier, tips it over, and the newborn accidentally plunges headfirst into the swimming pool.

Everyone gasps, many are frozen still, but that baby's momma is on the move. She is in a full blast sprint. She drops everything from her hands, lets out a yell, and runs with all the speed she is capable of out of the kitchen, through the living room. She jumps and clears the couch and screams for Uncle Mike to move as she shoves past him and dives into the pool to grab her child and save it…
Can you picture that scene?

That is how God chased me folks, and that is how he is chasing you too. He must get to you. Just like He had to get to me. I would have drowned in my folly had God not pursued me with such passion.

I did things during this period that some people still have not forgiven me for. I wasted time. I wasted life. I wasted money and wasted opportunity.

I did things I never would have done otherwise. I was not anyone that I was proud to be, but none of it started that way. The nightmare I would come to survive started with me simply trying to pay a bill.

I was doing the best I could to pay everything on time, build credit, not fall behind on my insurance, find a job, see everyone, catch up for so much lost time.

I had a plan for when I got out. I had completed a 'life plan' project in which I described a business venture idea in detail. I was going to apply for a small business loan that was backed by the Federal Government and was available to Ex-convicts as a form of reentry assistance.

The starting amount available was $10,000. Plenty enough for me to start a pressure washing business and put ten percent of all profits aside to buy either a vending machine route or video arcade games, some sort of vending opportunity. Something that would make money by itself. While I slept.

I honed my resume writing skills. I interviewed well, I had ten years' worth of prison accomplishments to point to.

I was confident. Then reality punched me right in my mouth, hard. It left my whole life looking like a broken ketchup bottle.

There was no business loan available to ex-convicts. There was no job available for a guy who just got out of prison on a Second-degree murder charge. **I had a plan, but I did not have a plan for when that plan did not work out.**

Not having any better advice and feeling like my back was against the wall. Intending to do right. I did wrong and accepted the opportunity to buy a hundred and fifty dollars worth of Cocaine for only a hundred from my cousin. He said he was trying to help me 'come up'.

I knew I could go to my Mom's bar, Mulletville, and sell this amount to those fishermen for two hundred and make a hundred dollars, just like that. I made two or three trips back and forth to my cousins that weekend and by Monday I had enough money to pay my third bill. I was happy. Mission accomplished. One and done.

Except, I had spent all the money I had paying those three bills and was now broke again and needed gas.

Right then my phone rang, and it was another fisherman wanting to know if I had any more of that 'White Girl' which is a slang name for powder Cocaine.

Do not feel bad for not knowing that, I did not either. Not till this guy called me and I had to ask him what that was. He said, "Cocaine man, can you get me any more of that stuff you had Saturday?" And just like that, my lack of income problem had been solved. I started selling Cocaine.

I had long been honing my Entrepreneurial skills.
I began my first business in the summer between Eleventh and Twelfth grade. It was called 'Mark's Lawn Service'. I became so successful by the end of summer that my Dad allowed me to forgo my senior year of High School in exchange for a promise to continue my Senior year via Home School. This arrangement allowed me to continue growing my business.

I had furthered those skills inside the chain gang, by running lotto boards and pairing my poetry with other people's artwork. I kind of became a dealer of homemade greeting cards so to speak. My buddy would draw them, I would write a poem inside, and we would both go sell them and split the proceeds 50/50. We were business partners.

So, I was experienced with cultivating a customer base and providing timely customer service. I even had some experience in 'Trafficking'. *If you consider the lizards that I would bring back and forth across two compounds at Cross City.* So yeah, I could do this. This was just another extension of the Hustle and Grind.

I was still inexperienced and had not yet learned to cut my Cocaine or mix it with any other non-Cocaine additives as everybody else did. So, mine was always better than everybody else's. Those commercial fishermen could not get enough of it. My reputation grew. My phone started to ring, a lot. I was able to pay my bills on time, and even told myself I was being 'responsible'.

Then I started using Cocaine.
They say, 'Don't get high on your own supply'.
Except, I did and when I started doing that, my life began a slow spiral down the drain. It was slow and I did not even recognize it at first. I was able to use Cocaine and still be reasonably functional and responsible, for a while anyway.

Matter of fact I became so good at using Cocaine and not allowing it to control my life, I began to do more of it. Just to prove the dang point when others began to express concern. Eventually, though the wear and tear of being up for days and irregular sleeping patterns, and going days without eating, began to wear down my body. Then want turned to need. As it usually does when you mess around with that 'White Girl' for any length of time.

Ironically, all the friends that I thought I was making, and all the fun I thought I was having - when I search back through the annals of my mind, they are all gone. There is not even three of them that I can remember.

There are not a lot of stories that I can look back and repeat like I have been doing. This was just a dark time and I would come to battle back and forth with this addiction until I quit, cold turkey in 2008.

Not all that time would be spent in hardcore addiction though as I did spend a lot of time as a casual weekend user, and then a lot of time trying to get clean and abstaining as well. Stringing two or three months of sobriety together at a time before spending one weekend binging in a hotel room, and then having to start all over again.

I spent a lot of time searching for meaningfulness during this time. I did not want this lifestyle, I hated it, but I was trapped.

There were a lot of fun times in the beginning, but they were superficial and would only serve to lure me deeper into this lifestyle that I wanted nothing to do with.

One night I was in Miami, and the next night I was in Tampa. I made my rounds to all the strip clubs and would serve all the girls, and then move on to the next club, house party, family get together, or wherever it was people were that wanted Cocaine. I lived out of my Ford Explorer and showered at whatever chicks' house I ended up waking up at that morning.

God had delivered me from the cauldron of prison, and here I was enslaved once again. Those who know, know Cocaine is just a Succubus in disguise vying every day to steal your soul.

I was never looking to make selling drugs a career, but these were the circumstances that I found myself in when I could not get a job and had no better advice to listen to.

It was during this time that I met this cool chick from Tampa. I am not going to mention her name. I have no desire to bring her any unwanted attention, but she was my friend, and then she became more.

Whether we were ever 'boyfriend and girlfriend' or not would depend on which one of us you asked. I like to think we were, but I was in a much lower social class than she was. We had chemistry, and we spent a lot of time together but there was no way she was ever going to introduce her Cocaine dealing/ex-con boyfriend to her 'high society' friends. We became very close though and had been together for almost a year when I presented her with a ring and asked her to marry me. She recoiled, became offended, then cussed me out. Not the response I had expected. I envisioned a hundred possible responses to me asking her if she would marry me, but not the one I got.

Before that though, we celebrated Valentine's Day together. I had pretty much stopped writing poetry at this point. Except, I thought it might impress this chick.

So, I wrote a poem that specifically described her, her body, and the tattoo she had of a flowering vine that wrapped elegantly around one of her ankles.

I copied it by hand on a piece of paper, set the edges on fire to give it a burned look, and rolled it up, tied it with a string like a scroll, and gave it to her.

That poem, a dozen Roses, and a little bit of 'toot' made for a terrific lover's weekend. One that I cannot even remember. However, I did keep a copy of the poem.

It was titled with the use of her first name written in bold Calligraphy font. This reprinting on these pages does not do my efforts justice. She probably still has it hanging in her house. Though I do not know, because very shortly after that I proposed, she said No, and we broke up. To this day, I have not seen her since. No doubt though, she would be surprised with the man I have turned out to be. He is nothing at all like the fresh out of prison guy she dated.

Your skin is Fire to the touch, Lavender to the senses

Like whipped cream, rich and thick to the taste

A wonderland of delight, an amusement park of pleasure

Just like Candy Land, or Disney World, whichever

Your body is a landscape of perfection

Hills topped with rosebuds

Lightly dusted with the color pink

Rays of golden glow

Perfectly trimmed and manicured

Shining down on the valley below

There's a garden growing around your ankle

Of flowers, flesh, and ink

With colors so bright and beautiful

They run together without a flaw

Staring in amazement

I'm overcome with Awe

Inside this exquisitely wrapped package

Of sinfully delicious pleasure, that is you

Lies a woman full of elegance, grace, and class

That none can surpass

Dating, Relapse, & Marriage

Early in 2004, I was hired to run heavy equipment as part of a road-building crew. *A skill my dad had taught me growing up.* Then one day, I had taken a lunch break and did not know that a guy had pulled up right behind the machine that I was on and picked that spot to park his tiny blue truck.

Since he pulled so close to my rear, I could not see his truck in my mirror when I restarted the machine and then put it in Reverse. I ran right over the hood of his truck. Once I heard the crunch, I got down off the machine, looked, and then panicked.

I climbed back on my machine and drove back to my truck; parked their machine and left - *they were going to fire me anyway.* I just could not catch a break.

The company bought the guy another truck. So, all is well that ends well, but I just could not find my place in this world. I was spinning around and around, no job, no idea what to do with my future, I was so far behind everyone else. Nothing I learned inside prepared me for this. I was still a teenager. Now living in a 30-year-old body. I was in a world full of grownups that expected me to act just like them. But I was not them. I was Me. We were not the same.

I did try though.

When the opportunity came, it was December 2004 and the new year was bringing on a new opportunity as my Dad was hired as a foreman for a land development company in Naples, Fl. They allowed him to hire his crew and he hired me to run the front-end loader. I was making $15 an hour and being paid overtime in exchange for 48-hour weeks. Life was starting to get better for me. For the next two years, I rode to work every day with my Dad.

We were working on a new four-lane section of Livingston Road in Naples, Fl. The piece of Livingston Road that connects Vanderbilt Beach Road and Immokalee Road, right where the North Collier Water Park sits now. My Dad and I built that. I think of him and those times anytime that I drive that section of road. Hopefully, now you will too.

I cleaned up my lifestyle during this time and became an active participant in a church that I attended with my Dad. I was playing drums and even preaching on occasion. The Pastor of our church gave me the Honor of the pulpit on Easter Sunday 2006.

I came to the church in a suit, but in the intermission, I slipped into the back and put on a pair of my holiest and raggediest jeans with a Rock N Roll concert T-Shirt that I had cut up and made into a tank top. All my arm sleeve tattoos showed, as did portions of my underwear through the holes in my jeans as I came walking out the back with the microphone.

No one was quite sure what to make of me when I approached the stage and announced that the title of my message was 'Motley Crew'.

I brought out how Jesus ran with 'roughians'. The disciples were coarse men. Men that drank, men that cussed and caroused around. Just like many local fishermen that you might know today. Then I brought out how God does not care what rough shape that you may be in. He can meet you there, right where you are, and begin to improve your quality of life if you allow Him to.

I used myself as the next example and was met with great applause. It was another nice moment, that I will remember always. I still have a CD recording of the message – Somewhere, I am sure.

Life was going so well, I thought it would be a good idea to start dating again. I wanted a wife, kids, family, stability, an SUV, a mortgage, all of it. I even once dated three girls named Shannon all at the same time. The last of which, the prettiest one, I later married. I was quite fond of her smile and country girl ways. *It is still one of the prettiest smiles that I have ever seen.*

I stopped seeing all the other girls and just concentrated my affection towards this one. Not long after that decision to see just each other. I got off early one Friday at work and found myself alone, nowhere to be, no one expecting me, and a pocketful of money.

"Certainly, one little bag of Cocaine wouldn't hurt" came the thoughts. "No one will know "came another one.
"You've got several hours before you have to be home." Suddenly, I was fighting urges strong enough to have overwhelmed a weaker man, and at that time, on that day, I was a weaker man.

I rented a cheap hotel room, called my old friend up for a rapid delivery, and off to catch a train I went. **Choo Choo!**

I was not done in an hour or so. It was after midnight, and there was no going home without suspicion. My phone was blowing up, people were worried sick about me. I was unaware of course, as I had turned my phone off so that I could poke holes in my arm and get off without interruption.

Then it went on for day two, and finally on day three when I came to my senses. I was broke, hungover, and disgusted with myself. I felt such a heavy weight of shame. I hated myself.

I had done this again. It had been so long, I had been doing so good, and I just went and blew it all up. I justified my behavior with the rationale that it was the weekend, it was my money, I didn't miss any work, I didn't commit any crime, I just spent what I earned on what I wanted to.

I do realize now, however, that it is was highly irresponsible of me, it was selfish, as no one knew where I was or had heard from me, and I had been clean so long, it was the most stupid and self-destructive move I could make. Yet I did it anyway, and with great gusto.

This realization scared me, and I did not want to do it again. If I could somehow salvage this weekend, my relationship, and get through just one week with no money, then I could fix this. More enlightening would have taken place than actual damage done. I might even come out of this on the plus side and with that thought, I called Shannon. Who had been feverishly looking for me, calling me, and worried sick, and when she answered her phone, I proposed! It was the only thing I knew to do.

I thought getting married would help me gain some sort of normalcy about myself. I had no peers. No one I knew had a life was like mine. A good wife, a good job, and a family would surely be all the help I would need to stay clean and build a life worth having.

Shannon said Yes, and then I bought her a truck instead of a ring, as we needed that more.

Why she married me, under those circumstances, would be a question you would have to ask her. But I think that we were both in love with the idea of being in love, but we were not necessarily in love with each other.

Over time we came to cherish each other deeply, but at the time she represented salvation and stability to me. I am sure I represented some sort of rescue to her too, as her circumstances were not necessarily shining bright with optimism at the time either.

On the day of our wedding, our two families become one. My family was taking pictures and congratulating everyone, and her family was making side bets on how long our marriage would last. The longest-tenured wager was for 12 months. We exceeded that expectation by 7 years.

There is not much that I am going to elaborate on regarding our marriage. Except to say, we both tried hard and it was a marriage much like many of yours. There were great times, and there were not so great times. We usually found a way to work through any issues that came up. After 6 years of being together though we decided that we cared for each other deeply, and each appreciated the time we had shared, but we both wanted out. We had grown enough to realize our dreams were different. So, we separated until our divorce was finalized 2 years later.

I can not just completely gloss over that entire period from 2006 to 2012 though. A few major events took place and many lessons learned that I still have to share with you.

I will tell you about the first day of our marriage. Our first big challenge. The night I left. As well as a few other noteworthy accomplishments. This was a period of growth for both of us. After accepting my proposal, as humble as it was. We then planned for a July 4th wedding. We were also attending church together at this time and secretly got married after church one night in a home that was hosting a bible study/home church service.

Our Pastor was there and officiated. My Dad and his wife witnessed it. So, the wedding ceremony itself was July 4th but we really got married privately on June 30th because we were so excited to do so.

To celebrate we went to Wal-Mart and bought groceries on the way home and 'what kind of cereal do we buy' was our first major decision to be made together. In the end, we could not agree and just got two boxes.

That should have been a sign right there. Then for added irony when we checked out, we were all giggly and carrying on with each other when the clerk looked at us disgusted and I said, "We just got married" to which she replied, "I'm sorry to hear that." We thought that was rude and walked off to live happily ever after.

The cereal did not last, nor would the marriage. But something else happened that night that would last.
My first child was born. *Smith Nathaniel Rodriguez*

Mr. Smith

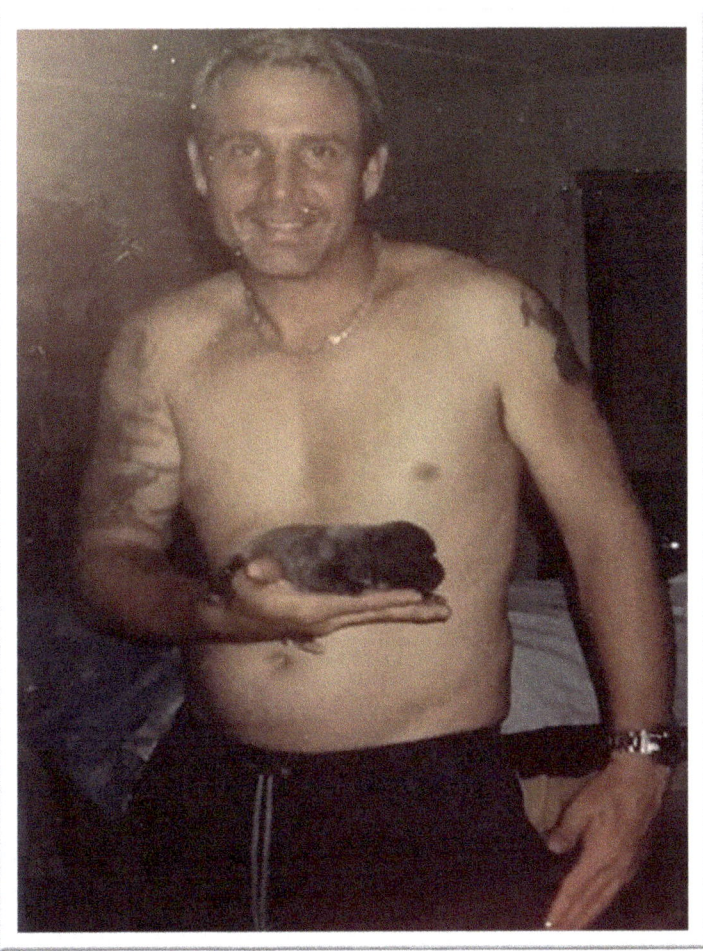

Shannon had a dog named Dixie and she was pregnant. When we came home from Walmart and the church service, we had 14 new little pit-bull puppies. 5 died at birth, and 9 survived. Out of them all, I ended up with my best friend, my guardian angel, and the coolest Pitbull to ever be the color blue.

His name is Mr. Smith. He is a pure-bred Blue Pitbull. Razors Edge bloodline. He is 13 years old and at my feet now as I write this chapter. He is much older now than he was then,

and he does not get around so well. He goes everywhere I go though. Or he certainly did for a long time. Inside grocery stores, Rent A Center, tire shops, scrap yards, job sites, in to pay my insurance, everywhere I went, they all knew who Mr. Smith was. Some even preferred seeing him over me.

'Smith Nathaniel Rodriguez' was my first child. He is the only dog that I have ever really had. There was usually a family dog around when I was growing up, but not like Smith. Smith was mine. We were down like 4 flat tires on a Cadillac. Hmm? What's that you say? Why is his last name Rodriguez? Oh, because Smith Cass just sounds stupid and I liked the way Smithy Rodriguez just rolled off my tongue.

Shannon left me on January 1st, 2008 and we separated for 6 months. When she did, she took everything but him. I walked in through the door on New Year's Day 2008 to an empty house, a deflated heart, and a dog overjoyed to see me. My world was falling apart, I was a mess, my life was a wreck. But this dog loved me and was always happy to see me. When I walked into the house that day, it was empty of possessions but full of this dog's love for me.

He had my back during my darkest period. When I'd walk in and out of places that were ill-advised for a White boy to be. He walked with me. He'd guard me and protect me when I'd get out of my mind and climb the walls inside of rented hotel rooms.

He kept the police from wanting to search my car during any number of traffic stops, he kept me warm on many cold nights when I slept alone. He helped protect me from the demons fighting for control of my mind. He slept right beside me in the bed on nights when I was alone as well as on nights when I wasn't. Made no difference to him. He got one side of the bed and I got the other, anyone else had to 'get in where they fit in'.

He was always stealing my pillows at night as he lay right beside me when I slept. Always in my passenger seat when I drove. God knew I needed a protector. Something that wouldn't judge me and would just keep me safe. Something that would love me despite my not being worthy of it. Mr. Smith excelled at both. Humans aren't capable of that type of unconditional Love. That's why God gives us dogs, and I believe that's why He gave me Smith. I needed Him. He made sure I woke up each morning.

Married to The System

There was another big surprise waiting for Shannon and me almost as soon as we said, 'I Do'. Shannon was buying a mobile home when we first met, and she would have soon owned it. Except, the overnight security officer in her community ran the plates on my vehicle when he began to notice it parked in Shannon's driveway every night, and it wasn't long before they knew who I was and called Shannon down to the community centers office and told her she'd have to sell her mobile home and move. As they did not allow ex-felons to live in that community.

I once again had to gather letters of recommendation and provided a list of character references for them to contact. I went in and interviewed with the property manager, showed her my certificate of ordination as I had recently been ordained as a Minister of the Gospel. I explained my whole life was about helping others. The property management did not budge. No Ex-Felons. Period.

Before we even took off for our honeymoon, we had to move. We sold the puppies for $250 each, and her trailer for $1,000, and we moved into a one-bedroom apartment in Cape Coral. Up until this point I had not tried to rent any place and was unaware of the hassles a felony conviction brings to the process.

We were lucky her dad worked for a property management company and they rented to us on the strength of his word. Every place I have ever been, I have left better than when I arrived, but getting in is always a difficult task. We were unaware of that when we married each other. We overcame, we survived, and in the end, we lived well but it was always a more difficult task for me or anyone with me than it need be. The incarceration never ends. It just changes forms.

For the first four years of our six-year marriage, there was only us, Mr. Smith, and any other assortment of dogs, cats, turtles, fish, and rabbits. We did not have a successful pregnancy until 2010. Up until that time we were animal parents and would usually have ten or more animals at any given point in time.

Once, I remember we had four dogs seventeen cats and two rabbits all living together at the same time and would all wait their turn to eat out of the same bowl. No one that ever came over to our house could believe it. The cat would wait on the rabbits, and the dogs would wait on the cats, and then on each other before eating. Smith kind of set the order and did not allow much ruckus. He was special.

In 2010 we graduated from being animal parents to being human parents. Our daughter Mya was born on October 1st, 2010. Then a year and a half later in July of 2012 came our second blessing. Little Miss Marley.

We both loved her, but each other, not so much by this time. Nothing was wrong, there was just nothing right anymore either. But that is the end, let me start with how it all began…

Self-Employed

Perhaps one of the best things that ever happened to me was being laid off from my job in May of 2007. I had been married almost a year when the company that my dad and I had both worked for started laying people off every week and the first Friday of May, it was my turn.

This was during the recession when the housing market imploded, and everyone lost their jobs. Mine was included. The very same day that I was let go, on my way home, I stopped and applied for a salesman job at a big used truck lot in town.

I went in and told the guy I just got laid off my job of eighteen months, and if he will hire me, I can pass a drug test, I have a valid license, and I will be here first thing Monday morning ready to challenge his number one sales guy. He hired me on the spot and told me to report Monday morning.

I arrived at 7 am the next Monday. An hour before they opened. Once the manager arrived and unlocked the doors, he asked me to formally fill out an application. I did, and it asked if I had ever been convicted of a felony and why. I checked yes and stated, I would explain in person.

When I submitted my application to the manager, he looked at it, and asked me to explain, I did. Then he explained how I was a liability.

That he could not let me go alone and test drive a car with a customer. Not after knowing I had been to prison on a murder charge. I was too much of a liability if something were to ever happen. He rescinded his employment offer, immediately.

I called Shannon for a ride and went to work filling out applications. I would end up looking for work for three weeks.

When I say looked for work, I mean diligently looked for work. I was up at 5:00 a.m. Dressed for the day compete with a tie. I would walk to the corner store, buy a cup of coffee and a newspaper.

I would walk back to our little one-bedroom apartment and scour the classifieds. I would make calls, keep notes as to who I talked to, and who I needed to follow up with, along with notes about the conversation.

I would try to set up as many afternoon interviews or meetings as I could. After the first in-person contact was made, I would send a handwritten note on a purchased thank you card. Thanking them for their time, expressing optimism about the new opportunity, and causing my name to cross their desk once more during their hiring process.

I must have mailed thirty or more during these three weeks. Nothing was biting. Times were getting desperate.

My rent was coming due, groceries were running low, I had exhausted my borrowing power, and I did not have much gas. I was starting to feel very much like a cornered dog.

I just needed an opportunity. It had been so hard for me to finally land a decent job, and now it was gone. I was feeling some pressure. I had to do something.

But if you think that I began to ask myself should I sell Cocaine again? Should I pick up a pistol and rob someone? Should I come up with a scheme to defraud someone? Then you would be wrong. I did not! Not even once! None of those ideas ever crossed my mind.

What did cross my mind though was scrap metal.
I did not know anything about it yet. Other than the fact that everyone with a truck seemed to be collecting it. Prices being paid for it were higher than they had ever been before, and I went looking for some.

I had an extended cab 4-wheel drive Chevy S-10 and began to drive it up and down the block looking for any type of scrap metal that I could find. It had recently been trash pickup day and my area was picked clean by more seasoned scrappers. So it was not easy coming up with my first load. Which did not come until I drove behind a supermarket and jumped inside of their dumpster and pulled out a bar-b-que grill that someone had discarded.

The grill was bulky and ate up a good deal of room inside the bed of my little truck. I drove straight to the local scrap yard and across their scales. They directed me where to unload at and I complied. I drove back across the scales and weighed out excited to see what my load netted; as my gas tank was nearing E.

When I presented my I.D. I was given a receipt slip and $5.42 in cash. I thought right then "This is going to be a hard way to make a living".

That day I stayed very close to the scrap yards to conserve gasoline, but did continue to drive around and check the dumpster areas of many of the apartment complexes and communities that were in the area looking for discarded scrap metal items, and by the end of the day. I had made $50.

I bought $20 worth of fuel and went home with $30 and bought dinner, and that was reason enough to get up the next day and do it all over again. So, I did. Again, and again, day after day.

I began to go into industrial parks looking for discarded scrap metal behind plumbing shops, mechanic shops, steel, and aluminum fabrication shops. I would develop relationships with the owners. I began to make notes about different neighborhoods, regarding their trash days and volume of move-outs and new move-ins around the first of the month. Plus, the contact information of landfill supervisors, maintenance supervisors, independent truck drivers, general managers of various contracting businesses.

I was building a database as well as a network.
Still, every day was a new hunt and a new challenge to find more metal. Adding to the struggle, was the fact that everyone with a truck was doing the same thing I was, and because so many people were asking businesses for their scrap, they began to become annoyed whenever anyone of us would stop by.

Other people began to steal people's air conditioners, catalytic converters, aluminum, etc., and not only did I have more competition than the law should have allowed, but I also had to deal with the stigma of being a 'scrapper'. A term often used synonymously with other derogatory terms such as crack head, homeless, druggie, etc. I knew to survive; I would need to be different.

I could not help but notice that the junk removal industry was sorely lacking any sense of 'Professionalism.' So that is where I aimed to stand out and make my business different.

I offered business owners professionalism and the opportunity to sell their scrap to a uniformed professional.

I had shirts printed up that said, 'Metal Recycling and Salvage' and would show up in 'uniforms'. I would weigh their scrap metal on-site and pay them a fair amount for their metal, in cash. As opposed to having a horde of unsavory characters stopping by their business throughout the day and night.

I invested money into having some nice glossy business cards made. Whereas most everyone else was printing their contact information on a business card size piece of paper from their home computers.

I contracted with a business called 'Mark's Dumpsters' and began to put his containers at my client's places of business. Everyone thought they were my dumpsters because they had my name on them. Of course, I did not own them. They belonged to another dude named Mark. I just saw the opportunity and begin to use them to boost my credibility.

In 2008, my side hustle went legit by way of me being arrested. Yes! You read that correctly. I was arrested and they were talking about sending me back to prison.

The Sheriff's Dept. had beef with this muffler shop that was right across the street from their field office in my hometown. They had set up surveillance, believing the owner of the shop to be a dealer of stolen property.

He was accused of buying and selling stolen catalytic converters *an anti-pollution device, that acts as a filter on a vehicle's exhaust system.*

Catalytic converters are often filled with Platinum, Palladium, and Rhodium and are considered a high-priced commodity in the world of scrap metal recycling.

I had called the muffler shops parts dept. the day before to order a needed part for my truck and they were holding it for me. When I stopped by the next day to pick up my part, that was the exact time and day that the Sheriff's Dept. had decided to raid this muffler shop. Everyone present went to jail.

They charged every one of us with dealing in stolen property. Then they plastered my photo all over the news and acted like they took down some high-profile gangsters. In the end, they dismissed all my charges, and most of everyone else's too.

As it turns out, all the purchases at that shop had been legal, legitimate, and well documented. There had been no crime committed and certainly not one that I had anything to do with.

However, the arrest remains on my record. To this day, I continue to wait on all the news stations to inform everyone that my charges were dropped and that I should have never even been arrested and for them to do so as vociferously as they announced my arrest.

Before this was fully resolved though, I ended up being banned at two of the local scrap metal recycling centers. I had customers call and cancel their scheduled pickups with me. This almost put me out of business before I had even gotten a chance to get started.

The other reason that this arrest is worth mentioning and pointing out in this book is because it was this arrest that catapulted me into the world of business.

When they arrested me. They held me in a holding cell for several hours and then brought me into a little room for interrogation.

In the discussions that ensued next, I explained to the detectives that I was just a customer buying a part for my truck. I was not an employee of that muffler shop and had nothing to do with the daily operations of the business. To prove this, I provided them with one of my business cards. This led to them asking me if I had a business license.

To which I replied "I pick up scrap metal from businesses and people's homes when they call and request a pickup and recycle it at the local recycling center. I'm picking up trash off the streets. You need a license to do that?" They replied, "Yes you do!".

Turns out they were correct! Who knew? I certainly did not. It's called a 'Secondary Metal Recyclers' license and a 'Secondhand Goods Dealer' license is also needed in that profession as well. I did not know a single person with such credentials. Having a Recycling license issued by the State would validate the 'professionalism' of the brand I was trying to create and would only help my marketing.

I went and got my licenses. Each one required a background check that went back ten years, so I was good there. I submitted my fingerprints and paid $6.00 for each license for a total of $12.00, and Presto. I had a new marketing angle. I was now licensed. I already had commercial vehicle insurance for my pickup truck and trailer, so I claimed to be insured too.

I then was informed that I still needed to go further and acquire a county business license as well as a Tax ID number. I did as I was instructed. It took about 45 days in total but in the end, I was legit. Man, it felt good!

After acquiring all my necessary licenses, the State Attorney dropped their charge of 'Operating a business without a license' too. So, I was free and clear.

That felt even better.

For the first time since being released, I began to view myself differently. I was a business owner.

Something else happened right about this same time too.
I got clean! Once and for all. But I need to take you back a few steps to better explain to you how powerful that was, and what happened to make me quit cold turkey and not ever look back.

My Darkest of Days

Shannon and I had been separated since New Year's Day 2008. *I mentioned this earlier when telling you about Mr. Smith.* I had been out for three days celebrating my birthday with my cousin and had not been home.

My grandmother had gotten upset when I told first her that I was getting married. She said there was "no way I was mature enough for that." Turns out, she was right.

Shannon had grown tired of my bs. As I was still relapsing and going on weekend binges about every 30, 60, or 90 days. I would take my paycheck and go check into a hotel room and shoot it all up my arms. I could not get ahead, because I was too busy getting high. I had not yet figured out how to get out of my own way.

I could put together about a month or two. Staying straight, sane, sober, and moving forward in the right direction. Building, making progress but then I would take one weekend and tear it all down, shoot all my money into my veins, and destroy everyone's confidence and trust.

This was a cycle that I had gotten caught up in since I became dependent on Cocaine. I had days turn into weeks without laying down for sleep, as well as had weeks turn into months in which I had stayed clean. I was very inconsistent. It was no way to live. I hated it, Shannon hated it, but I did it anyway.

It was my birthday, December 28th, 2007. My cousin came and got me for a night out, that night turned into a 3-day extravaganza holed up inside of a hotel room with my phone turned off. Later, when I came home the house was empty and nothing was there when I arrived. Nothing, except Mr. Smith. That was New Year's Day 2008. That is when it got dark.

With Shannon gone, the governor was off. I got the highest that I ever would get and the lowest that I would ever go as well. Doing time back inside the Chain-gang was better than the life I was living at this time.

With no one to come home to when I got there at night. I felt lonely and cold, empty, and bored. So, I just sat in a corner and shot dope.

I recessed into the worst state that I have ever been in and eventually lost the apartment. I moved in with the guy who worked as my helper picking up scrap metal. He was a junkie too. So, we made a perfect pair.

He would lock himself in his room and shoot Heroin and I would lock myself in my room and shoot Cocaine. You can imagine that neither one of us accomplished much. We were both going nowhere, fast!

Eventually, Shannon and I started communicating again and she would try and come over on the weekends and stay with me. We were talking about working things out. She was in my corner cheering me on. Placing her bets that I would beat this thing that had a hold of me. But then she'd lift the mattress in my room and see all the used syringes from the dope I had been shooting all week. She would then be so disappointed. The fights would start almost as soon as she arrived.

This went on for several months. She was staying with her mom during this time, and my in-laws were never big fans of mine to start with. I would make them all laugh when we were together because I was funny, but they wanted better for Shannon than what I was. I do not blame them for how they felt. I was not much good for anybody at that point.

In July of 2008, Shannon's grandmother presented her with an opportunity to move to North Florida with her and she further offered to help her get her G.E.D. and then her Realtors license. There was a catch though. She had to divorce me, and they had even offered to pay for it.

She should have taken their offer and left me to my folly, but she did not. She declined their offer. When she did her mom kicked her out and she had nowhere to go except for back to me and the 'shooting gallery' that I lived in.

I was so moved that she would choose me over help from her family and a chance to start over that I promised her that I would not make her look like a fool, or ever regret her decision. I was not going to let her be wrong about placing such a big bet on me. I quit using Cocaine that day, July 15th, 2008.

She was 'all in' on me and there was no way I was going let her down. She believed in me when no one else did, and that made all the difference. Well, that and the fact that my cousin inherited a piece of property with a dilapidated trailer on it and said that we could move into it for $100 a month.

I dove into the life of Entrepreneurship with vigor and set about turning what had been my side hustle into a legitimate business. I felt reborn once again. Like I was getting a second chance at life *for a second time.*

Building A Business

I had been living a life that required me to drive the streets and look for metal. I had bigger aspirations than that. Much bigger. Shannon worked side by side with me in many of the early days. I used to tell her that she paid the rent with her eyes. She would see junk cars in driveways and backyards from a mile or two away.

Back in those days, I did not know how to back up a truck with a trailer. When my uncle bought me my first trailer, I had no trouble filling it, but I did have plenty of trouble backing it up. Whenever I would have to back into the scrap pile at one of the scrap yards to unload. Shannon and I would have to switch seats, and everyone would laugh at me, while I had a woman back me up. It was embarrassing and it did not take me long before I learned to do it on my own. *Now I can run figure 8's in reverse.*

I did not want to have to continue to hunt for metal every day. I needed people to call me to come pick it up. So, I started marketing and began to develop inbound leads utilizing Craigslist to search for free metal and to advertise. I would also post ads offering free property cleanups and cleanouts.

From there I moved on to creating a website, then social media, and Google My Business. I wanted to know more about how this online world worked. I knew it was the future. I wanted to be taken seriously in this industry. I wanted to be a major player.

I was several hundred depths away from being able to compete with the behemoths that ran the scrap industry in my area in terms of money, assets, clout, experience, or resources, but that did not mean I could not still do it.

I understood the internet. I understood that clients came from efficient use of it. The big yards had yet to catch up to that idea. They were still spending their money on print advertising and traditional marketing. I knew before they did, that was dead.

There were many lessons that I learned about business during this time. I had days where I made $10 and days where I made $15,000. I learned from both.

I learned to hunt work and how to go get it, but I also learned how to market my business on the internet. I began to consume as much information about digital marketing as I could. The aroma of success was all around me. To illustrate my point, I will share a few stories with you.

One of the big things I use to look for, solicit, and buy were junk cars. I have towed them with a rope down the interstate for 200 miles or more. I have towed limos and even a bus or two behind my pickup truck. I have dragged cars with locked wheels. Had the rubber skid off, and the asphalt grind the wheels down to half-circles, while sparks flew as I drove down the road. Only to have the cops follow the drag marks in the road right up to the scrap yard scales while I was selling the car I just drug there.

Go ahead and shake your head, the extremes that I would go to get a load of metal to the scrapyard were bodacious. There was never a piece of metal that I ever went for and then left it. If I went for it, I took it with me. I never let it beat me, except once!

I went to Plant City *about 200 miles away from my house* to get a truck out of someone's backyard and it whipped me.
I had to leave it. However, what separates me from most, is how I responded to the failure. I turned it into a bigger win than I even imagined. Check it out. There are several lessons to be learned here. Plus, I like telling it. It involves my Grandpa.

My Grandpa has always been a jokester. He would always joke with the telemarketers. For example, someone called one time from M.A.D.D. (Mothers Against Drunk Drivers) and was seeking a donation and he replied "Well mam, who is out there advocating for the ole' drunk guy? Don't you think we should be collecting funds for him and his family, after all, he's a drunk?" The telemarketers would always get frustrated and not call anymore.

Then there was me, who was always seeking to buy junk cars. It was on the back of my card, on the back glass of my truck, it was on my T-shirts – We Pay Cash For Junk Cars. I was known for it.

So, one day while visiting with my grandpa, the phone rang, and it was a telemarketer seeking a donation. I hollered out to my Grandpa, "Ask them if they have any junk cars?"

He just handed the phone to me I asked the guy on the other end if he knew anyone that had a junk car and he said that his aunt did, but she lived in Plant City and would I go there? I said yes. He gave me her phone number, I called, and she confirmed she had an F-250 in the back yard and all was well. She claimed, it would roll right down the highway.

The next day, I grabbed a friend to help steer and took off, and drove 200 miles North East. When we arrived, I discovered that this lady had not given me an accurate description of this vehicle.

This truck did not move. Not at all. The brakes were locked up, as was the axle. This truck was not going anywhere, not without a lot of persuasion. *But it took me all day long to discover that.*

Upon arrival, we set out to try and make it roll. I tried every trick in the book. We went up to Walmart and bought tools, came back, and tried. Then went back and bought more tools and tried something else. At the end of the day, It still sat in the same spot. Mocking me.

I went through my phone and called a friend of mine who had a slide bed type tow truck. I knew he could get it. He had a tow hook in the back that would take tow a second vehicle too.

I began to scour the neighborhood for any other such opportunities. A few houses away, I spotted an old Mercedes that had grass growing up around it and leaves on the top. A sure sign that it had not moved in a while.

I approached the house, knocked, and explained that I would like to buy the car in the yard and come pick it up tomorrow. They agreed and I drove back to Fort Myers that night empty-handed but full of opportunity for the next day.

The next day came, and back to Plant City, I went. My buddy and I got the truck, the Mercedes, and made plans to come back and do an entire property cleanup for another neighbor down the road. That would yield, on another day, two cars and two large air conditioning units that were full of copper and aluminum.

When all was said and done, I made about $5,000 off that Telemarketer called my Grandpa asking for a donation.

A buddy of mine once told me - "That's what I like about you, you will talk to anybody, anywhere, at any time."

I suppose that is true, I have had a mind for marketing, and relationship building that goes back for as far back as I can remember. It has helped me greatly along the way. That would be my advice to any entrepreneur that may be reading these words now.

- **Be Bold**.
- **Do Not Be Afraid to Ask for The Business**.
- **Never Take the Word No To Be the Final Answer**.
  Today's No could very well be tomorrow's Yes.

Be Bold
Always say yes

I was brand new in the recycling game and had not yet done any demolitions. When my first opportunity came.

A busy mechanic shop in town was my client and at one time he used to have fuel pump canopies over the pumps - as is not unusual.

However, the pumps were long gone and the two canopies in the middle of his parking lot were an inconvenience and limited his parking capabilities. One day while there, he asked me if I could take those canopies down. I was excited and intimidated all at the same time but said "sure". As if I did that kind of thing all the time.

Sunday was the only day we could do the work. As he was open Monday through Saturday. We planned out the job for two Sundays in a row. He would supply the gas and torch set; I would supply the labor and keep all the metal.

I called my buddy Larry who had experience with a cutting torch as I did not, and off we went.

We decided the best route to take was to cut the four vertical support posts at the bottom, on all 3 sides – all the way through and then on the 4th side (the side furthest from traffic) we would only cut ¼ of the way through on each side and then yank it down in the direction we wanted it to go with my truck and a chain.

It worked. The canopy dropped to the ground just as pretty as you please. All that was left to do after that was cut it up in pieces and load them onto my trailer.

Except the money after being split three ways was not much. I ended up making about $400 for two Sundays' worth of work. Not horrible, but I had certainly hoped to make much more.

What I did not make in money however, I made up for inexperience, and new confidence gained. I had learned that by just offering to haul the metal off for free was leaving money on the table. Demolition services should cost extra.

I also learned that I could do all the things my network could do. I was not handy with an Acetylene torch, but I knew a guy that was, and that was just as good. That job taught me that Boldness gets rewarded.

Do Not Be Afraid to Ask for the Business
Always Be Mindful of Opportunity

In December of 2009, Shannon and I went to visit my buddy Nick at Polk Correctional Institution where he was incarcerated at the time. While there, we were talking about my business and junk removal services. When he told me about a field right beside his workstation there at the prison. There were several acres full of scrap metal that the prison had accumulated over the years and that was all the information that I needed.

The next Monday I contacted the Asst. Warden of Operations.

We scheduled a meeting to discuss it. I drove up again at the end of the week to meet him and to look over the field. We negotiated a deal in which I'd pick up, haul off, and remove all the prisons scrap metal from this field. For that, I would keep two-thirds of the net proceeds. While returning one-third of the net proceeds to the prison. We shook hands and agreed that I would start the next Monday. Martin Luther King Jr Day 2010.

I arrived with my crew that Monday morning which consisted of myself, my brother-in-law Charlie, Shannon, and Mr. Smith of course.

I immediately set about separating the metal and placing all the different types of metal into separate piles. Trying to build each pile large enough to fill a 100-yard semi-trailer full.

I filled 5 of them *plus I took several trucks and trailer loads full of aluminum, copper, and batteries in myself.*

It was a treasure trove of metal. Lots and lots of Stainless Steel. Big Stainless-Steel kettles retired from kitchen use long ago, Stainless Steel kitchen tables, piles, and piles of them. Lots of Copper and Aluminum.

An entire warehouse full of old A/C units, broken down tractors, steel frame beds, and footlockers galore. Industrial washers & dryers, truckloads of copper wiring, and batteries as far as the eye could see.

There was even an old aluminum semi-trailer or two for us to cut up, dismantle, haul off, and remove too. I was in Heaven. I had never seen so much beautiful junk.

After a few days, sorting, cleaning, and preparing the metal for recycling. I called to have semi-trucks visit the job from the recycling center that I dealt with.

In total, I grossed about $40,000 on that job in just three weeks. I was fired up! I had found a new source of metal. Prisons.

I always said 'they' stole my life from me. I was happy to finally be getting some 'change' back on what they took.

I immediately set out to catch this wave and was on to the next prison. It turned out to be the women's prison in Hernando County. This one only had about $10,000 worth of scrap metal. Still, I was happy to go get it. Then I was on to my third.

However, a couple of things happened in between these three jobs. I had been calling around to all of the prisons in the State known to have 'boneyards' offering my services. In the course of this, I had spoken with many people in charge of various institutions.

I was told that Martin CI had more than 100 acres full of old scrap metal. So, I went to Martin County Florida which is also known as Indiantown. It is way out in the middle of nowhere.

I met the Major *the Commanding officer in charge of the work camp and all outside grounds crews and projects.*

As we walked around, he pointed out a lot of the metal that they had, we talked about previous projects I had already done. He said I was developing a good reputation. He stated that he had heard that I was quick, safe, and paid the prisons their share of the money in record time. All these things pleased him. I left Martin C.I feeling good about the prospect of starting that job soon.

Further, I got a call one day very shortly after that, from the Department of Corrections Central Office in Tallahassee, Fl.

Turns out, I had been sending all of these checks to the Departments' Accounts Receivable in Tallahassee and they were surprised at not only how quick I was sending in their money, but how much I was paying them as well.
We were all making money. It was a win/win and they wanted to talk to me about entering a contract for the entire State.

I would personally make a tour of the facilities from Miami to Pensacola and arrange clean ups and leave with dumpsters in place for future scrap metal collection. This would mean that I would make a boatload of money up front and the money would just keep coming every time one of the facilities filled one of my dumpsters.

I felt like I had succeeded and was on the cusp of taking my business to an entirely different level. I even started looking at making heavy equipment purchases. I was gearing up to make a giant leap in my business.

See how God turned all these things around for my good and my favor? Hard work pays off, a good reputation precedes you, Karma, you reap what you sow, and all of that**… Except Sometimes Not Too.** Sometimes that light you see at the end of the tunnel is a great big train. Here is the plot twist.

At every prison so far, all the cleanup has taken place on the outside of the prison. There had been no need to do a background check on me. When we arrived at this third prison. They wanted us to go inside the fence and dismantle an old Chiller plant and then bring the pieces out.

Except to go inside the gate, into the actual prison, you had to undergo a background check. *They do not just be allowing anyone that wants to walk in and out of their gates.* You can probably already guess, I was radioactive!

My brother in law had never been in any trouble and he passed. So, they let him drive our machine in and out of the gate picking up the pieces that the female inmates had dismantled. I was required to remain outside the gate. So, I staged all the pieces, cleaned, and separated the metal.

It was day two of a three day clean up job and the Major called me from Martin CI. I had been expecting his call, hoping to confirm a start date for his prison clean up. So, on the second ring, I answered "Hello Sir, how are you?" He replied, "I'm doing just fine, and you don't need to ask me any further questions. I am going to speak to you and tell you something and after I do, you can erase my number out of your phone as you are not welcome to dial it ever again." I stammered "I don't understand sir, what's going on?"

He replied, "I've done some checking into you and I know who you are. I know you're an inmate who has recently gotten out, and now you're trying to call around to all these prisons and make money off our metal."

"I'm calling to tell you that you will never get one piece of metal that is here at Martin CI, from Central Office or anywhere else as far as I can help it." I was devastated!

Right when it looked like I was on the verge of some good fortune. It was snatched away from me, again. Another opportunity worked for, earned, and then lost because of my criminal record. It is serious folks. **An arrest, and even more so a conviction, carries the heaviest of consequences. It is self-inflicted harm, that never stops inflicting harm**. Felonies should be avoided at all costs.

I would eventually turn that No into a Yes, but it wouldn't be for several years later and I promise, I will circle back to that when it becomes relevant again but for now, I still had to finish this job.

I hung up the phone and went back to work. For the rest of the day, I concentrated on doing a good job and letting my work speak for itself. Upon completion though, I used the money to upgrade my equipment. I bought a new truck with a winch. As well as a used Gooseneck trailer to tow behind it. Significantly increasing my hauling capabilities.

I was bound and determined to invest their money into bettering myself and growing my business before it all disappeared. I could sense the temperature was about to change and I was right. The next week when I began my follow-up calls. People that had previously seemed warm and receptive to talking with me. Now seemed cold and distant. Then the

Warden of one of the prisons talked to me personally and told me he had received an internal memo informing everyone that Mark Cass from Metal Recycling and Salvage had been calling around to all the prisons trying to clean up scrap metal. The memo further informed everyone that I was an ex-inmate and for them not to do business with me.

He further explained; he did not have a dog in this fight. He had no personal problem with me, but I was blacklisted, and he could not go against that either. Until I could fix that, no one else was going to deal with me.

I thought very hard about that last sentence and concocted a new plan. *You did not think I was going to let that Major just beat me like that did you?*

Here is the plan I came up with.

I dropped my last name, used my middle name and had a new set of business cards made up that read Allied Recycling and put an Allied Recycling tag on the front of my truck and went back in and cleaned up three more prisons after that as Mark Wayne of Allied Recycling and then left dumpsters at each one of the prisons. So that I was sure to earn residual income long into the future as well. This brings me to my third point in this advice to Entrepreneurs series.

Never Take the Word No to Be the Final Answer.
Not if you want it

The last of those three next prisons that I scrapped out and cleaned up was Desoto CI. *Right back to where it all began.*

I was feeling quite accomplished and like I had outsmarted the Major from Martin as I was now watching several convicts, load down both my new truck and trailer, with batteries that the institution had collected over the years. To them it was trash. To me, it was $5,000. I could not resist snapping a picture of the moment.

I had once walked past that very same loading dock every morning as part of my job assignment. I was the convict under the supervision of that Sargent. Now on this day, almost twenty years later. I am driving a new 2500 Dura Max Chevrolet and pulling a trailer. Watching as it is being loaded down with money so heavy that it would later bend the tongue of my trailer before I could even get it back to the scrapyard to unload it. *It is funny how often Life comes full circle, and brings you right back to a place you use to be.*

I would move on from the prison clean-ups and get into airplane demolitions after this, but I never forgot that pile of metal still sitting in the fields of Martin CI. Nor would I ever forget the Major that said I would never get that metal…

Mya

For many years while incarcerated I was unsure if I would ever have the opportunity to even have kids. I was not guaranteed to have survived prison in the first place. After I did. I had an opportunity to be with several women over a period of time and no one ever claimed they were pregnant. I began to wonder if there was something wrong with me.

During our marriage, we endured the emotional trauma of five miscarriages. Having a baby became our hearts' cry. We both prayed for a baby.

We very often timed romantic dinners for the best time of the month for her to conceive and did all the things you are supposed to do. Finally, one terrific night in Orlando it happened! We were staying at a resort not far from Polk CI. And had decided to take a couple of days off and just enjoy a nice long weekend.

It was a great time we had that day, and a great time we had with each other that night. The next morning, we went indoor skydiving. We did not know it then, but that night had been magical. Shannon had conceived. Had we known; we probably would not have chosen a Skydiving simulator as the next day's activities, but we did not know. So, we did.

In pregnancies of the past, we had never gotten as far as being able to hear the baby's heartbeat. We had always lost the baby before that. Or had to endure being told on the first or second checkup that there was no heartbeat.
Except for this time, there was!

I heard it, she heard it, and then I cried. I was so happy.
We went home with strict instructions for her to be on bed rest and I waited on her every need. Sometimes joyfully, and sometimes begrudgingly because I thought she was milking it a little bit, but wait on her I did. She was carrying my baby.

We got through the first trimester, the second, and now had gotten into the third. This was real. This was happening. She was going to deliver, and I was really going to be a daddy.

I had suggested the name 'Justice' and that served as a popular choice until I later thought of the name 'Arizona Rain'. I loved it, and she hated it, so I asked my mom what she thought of it. My mom being the most diplomatic person I know, replied

"I think you should give her a name she isn't going to have trouble spelling in Kindergarten". *My mom is gangster like that.*

So, we went with 'Mya Marie'. I am so proud of that little girl. I had thought I wanted a boy until Princess Mya arrived. Her arrival taught me that nothing could ever be greater than her.

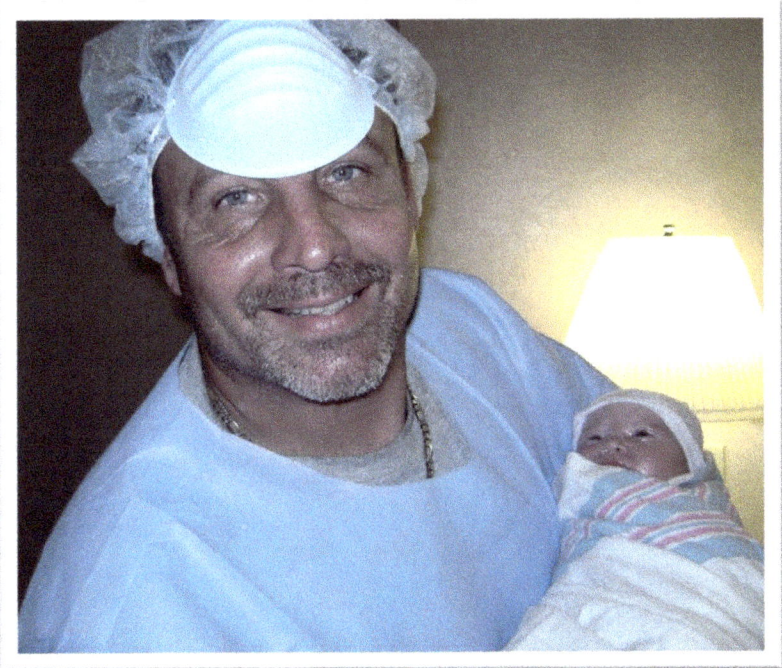

I took my baby girl with me everywhere. She slept on my chest when she was born, and later, beside me in our bed.

I remember the first time she did not sleep with us. We all three had been in the living room watching tv. Mya fell asleep in her playpen and Shannon and I had gone to our bedroom to do what couples do when the baby finally goes to sleep. Afterward, we fell asleep.

It was with quite a startle that we awoke the next morning and realized the baby was not in the room with us. We both panicked. Then jumped up out of bed and raced to open the bedroom door, which opened into the living room, where Mya lay sleeping peacefully.

There was no problem at all. We just slept in separate rooms. This serves as a great example though of how we felt about her and how close her mother and I both stayed to her.

When she was first born, I remember her mother rolling the crib into the bathroom with her when she showered so as to not leave her alone, even for a second. We were new at this and did not want to let her out of our sight. We had been through

so much to have her. She was my pride and joy then, and she remains so today.

Marley would come about 18 months later, and we make sure that they are never separated, but that first 18 months of Mya's life, was a special time between her and I.

She was my entire world, and nothing mattered more to me than spending time with Mya. She looked and acted just like me. No doubt she would grow up and rule the world. She had it in her. She was her daddy's child. I am so proud of her.

In 2017 I got to take Mya to see Guns N Roses on their "Not in This Lifetime Tour" in Miami.

Mya & I, in 2019 at a business networking meeting

Top of The Page

I had reached the top of Google as well as had the top spot in the Yellow Pages and was starting to taste quite a bit of success because of my growing marketing prowess.

I began to get phone calls for jobs that were way outside of the scope and range of jobs that I should have been taking. I took them on anyway.

That is when I learned to always say yes when asked if I could do something. *Even if I could not.*

Like this one time, in the middle of a large storm, a construction barge hauling large boulders broke away from the tugboat that was pushing it and eventually ran aground on the

pristine beaches of Boca Grande, Fl. A very lush and very hidden, Millionaire's island located in Southwest Florida.

A place known to be frequently visited by Former President George Bush and his family during the Christmas holidays, now had this eyesore of a construction barge loaded down with boulders the size of small cars, sitting on their pristine Paradise beaches. Rusting and rotting away as the waves beat upon its hull relentlessly.

Every Government agency that you could think of was involved in this removal. Or had something to say about it anyway. It came ashore and beached itself right in the middle of a patch of sea-oats. Which also happened to be endangered plant life and are Federally protected. Meaning they could not be uprooted or disturbed in any way without incurring the wrath of the Environmental Protection Agency (EPA).

All the alphabet agencies including the Island police, the County Sheriff, D.O.T., EPA, FDLE, OSHA, U.S. Coast

Guard, and many more were overseeing this barge and its removal. *None were helping, but all were overseeing.*

The company that owned the barge was being fined hundreds of thousands of dollars a day by almost all of the agencies. This had been going on for about two weeks when they finally did a Google search for local salvage companies, and because I was number one on Google, I got the call.

When they asked if I could remove all these boulders, cut up all this steel, and haul it all off this island that had a toll bridge at the entrance with a very low weight limit. *Meaning they would not allow large trucks or heavyweight to cross it.* Then they explained that I needed to do all of this without disturbing any of the natural plant life surrounding the area. All while every County, State, and Federal agency you could think of oversaw what I was doing and would inspect it with rigorous detail and issue heavy fines and penalties for any violation at all. I still said 'sure, no problem" as my heart beat out of my chest in excitement and intimidation.

Then they added that I was going to have to contract with professional plant people to uproot the sea oats, have them moved, and then hired to come and replant them again once the work was complete. I continued to exude confidence as again I replied, "no problem".

This job was a logistical nightmare.

Not only were there all the variables that I've mentioned above, but beach access was almost a mile away from the site of the barge. Meaning big machinery tracking up and down their beach carrying heavy chunks of the barge that had been cut off by torches would be required, but they could not leave a single drop of oil or grease behind.

Meaning whatever company got hired for this job was first going to have come out of pocket and purchase or lease brand new heavy equipment with no leaks, add all of this to the fact that when you did finally reach the beach access point. There was a seawall that was going to have to be crossed but not damaged, with all this machinery and weight. Jobs do not get more nightmarish, dangerous, or complicated than this. *I still said Yes.*

The guy I met with told me to draw him up a proposal detailing how I was going to handle everything, submit a proposed plan of action, along with a bid and copies of my liability insurance and workers' compensation certificates.

After that, he said he would try to get it approved as quickly as possible. I was in way over my head. Still, I remained confident. Why? Because I knew a guy…

I drove back to Fort Myers and straight to the scrap yard that I did the most business with. I walked into my buddy's office and told him about the job. After hearing the details, we set another meeting, and all met at the site of the barge to discuss a plan.

Once all was said and done, we put in a bid to remove the steel and to preserve the environment for more than a hundred thousand dollars. We were going to cut the barge up and transport the steel on another barge as opposed to having to deal with the issue of the weight limit on the toll bridge, the Sea Oats on the beach, or the crossing of the seawall that they were so worried about.

The decision-makers for the company that owned the barge nixed that idea though because they did not want another barge on or near the beach and wanted the metal and equipment driven on and off the Island instead, so they awarded the demolition contract to another company.

However, I had too much vested in this project to just walk away. I was not going to be defeated just like that. I wanted that metal. So, I went back to the foreman to see if I could haul the metal away for free on my gooseneck trailer 20,000 lbs. at a time after they cut it up and phased it. *Being as they could not drive big trucks across the island's toll bridge anyway.*

He agreed and I got what I wanted all along anyway. *Which was a hundred tons of steel given to me free and clear and without any risk of legal liability.*

The other company dealt with environmental concerns, and with the Government agencies. They hauled off the boulders, they cut up the steel, and they crossed the sea wall and piled the metal in a large open staging area. All I did was drive up and get loaded by a machine, and then drive to the scrap yard and get unloaded by another machine and get paid. I did that

three times a day for two weeks until I had hauled off and sold that entire barge.

This job profited me in more ways than with just money as well. It was when selling the metal from this job that I would come to realize some truths about doing business with the same person, all the time.

I remember this lesson as clear as day. Advertised price to the public = scale price. Scale price for Unprepared Steel was $9.50 per hundred lbs. *or 9.5 cents per lb.* and my deal with my buddy who owned the scrapyard was that I would always get 1.5 cents per pound higher than the scale price on Ferrous material (steel) and I would only sell my metal to him. Or at least give him the right to of 'first refusal.' We had had that deal in place for several years.

I should have got .11 cents a pound for the steel but instead, my buddy decided on this day, to exercise his leverage and lower my rate to 8.5 cents per pound on all this barge steel. Causing me a loss of 2.5 cents per pound times approximately 200,000 lbs. That move took almost $3,000 out of my pocket. That was the difference between that job paying me $17,000 and $20,000.

I had become complacent and comfortable only selling my metal to one person over the years. My buddy and I had done Millions of dollars worth of business together and mostly that has worked out ok and in my favor.

Except for this time.
I used to put a lot of effort into trying to come out on top of every deal. But sometimes, when I'd hit for a lick and had a lot of weight, my buddy would pull a slick move and dock my weight, lower my price, or do something not quite right. He would do this to even out the score between us a little bit.

It all served to teach me valuable lessons though. I called it Education, and 'Education is not free'. The best way to learn to play poker is with your own money, or so they say.

I learned that day, that when you do business with only one person, then that person can treat you any way they want to.

That next day I went and met with the owner of another scrap yard across town, we became friends too. He became the recipient of all the rest of the metal that would have otherwise gone to my other buddy. Today I maintain friendships with both, and both have taught me valuable lessons about business.

My first buddy taught me to listen more than I talk. He accomplished this feat one day when I was in his office and someone from the yard came in to see him and was asking for a special price for an unusual item that they had in their truck.

My buddy and I both walked out and looked in the back of the guy's truck, and we both knew immediately what we were looking at. If it had been my deal, I might have identified the material and negotiated a price, but my buddy did not do that. Instead of saying "Oh I see you have such and such" as I may have done. He instead asked the guy "Whatcha got here Bud?" the guy answered and when he did, he misidentified the technical term of what he had. Thereby downgrading his product and letting both of us know he did not know the true value of what he was trying to sell.

My buddy said ok and paid him what he asked for even though he knew it was worth more than the guy was asking for. Observing that exchange taught me to talk less and listen more. To ask more questions and make fewer statements.

My buddy explained to me that **Good business is "what happens when goods or services are exchanged, and everyone involved is happy with the outcome."**

It was not my buddy's job to educate the man.
The guy made a proposal, my buddy accepted. Each walked away happy. How is that not good business?

My other friend though taught me how to do better business. As his approach was completely different.

I remember one weekend bringing some metal into his facility. I weighed in, unloaded, weighed out, and went and got paid just like I always did. I had a special pricing arrangement worked out with this friend too and when I looked at my receipt, I saw the special pricing mark up and left happy.

My friend didn't work on the weekend, so he wasn't there, but the next Monday, My friend sent me a text informing me that the price on the metal I had sold him that weekend had gone up on Friday, and they didn't know about it yet in the scale house. So, he put a little extra money in an envelope and was texting to let me know it was there waiting on me. Wow! I Was Impressed.

It's one thing to offer a great deal from the start. It's another thing to even upgrade a friend and offer special pricing, but to go back and adjust the sale after it is complete and call a customer to come back to please pick up more money *when no one was ever unhappy or complaining in the first place.* That was something different. That was an example I wanted to follow.

I wanted to make my customers feel as good about doing business with me as my friend had just made me feel about doing business with him. It was only an adjustment of about $40 but paying me that forty made him another million for sure, as I began to sell a lot more of my metal to him after that.

One taught me to do good business.
The other taught me to do better business.
I learned from both.

One **wanted to pay as little as possible for the metal he bought** *and still* **keep your business.** For example, many times, my buddy would request to be the last one to bid on a job or a load of metal and then he'd bid a half a cent or one penny per pound higher than the highest bidder. Thereby paying as little as possible, but still enough to win the business.

The other one, however, **would pay you as much as possible for the metal bought,** *in order* **to keep your business**. He would just come right out of the gate with his top price and offer you as much as he was willing to pay, and it was generally higher than most others opening bid. In doing this, he created brand loyalty.

My buddy would get a lot of customers shopping prices and selling to the highest bidder. My friend, however, would develop a loyal tribe of customers who were happy to take less money (at times) from him, even when my buddy right down the street was paying more. That is brand loyalty.

My buddy has since sold his business and gotten out of the scrap metal industry entirely. While my friend continues right along. Their tag line is Honest Weight | Highest Prices Paid! They live up to that.

I am not downing my buddy in any way though.
He believed in me at a time when not many other people did, and I am grateful for the many opportunities for business that he and I shared.

He has moved on to bigger and better endeavors, but I often reflect on his sage advice when negotiating contracts and deals.

I used to like to try and squeeze every nickel out of a deal that I possibly could and try to arrange circumstances so that they always benefitted me the most.

I was a Pit-bull in negotiations and my buddy said to me one day during some tense negotiations, "Look man, you can't always win every deal. Sometimes other people have to walk away feeling like they have won too. Or else people will just stop doing business with you."

Those words ring in my ear every time I find myself negotiating a new deal. It must work for everybody, or else it is not a good deal. He told me that right after I had him, *pay me, to buy his trailer, with his own money.*

The deal went down like this. My buddy had an old trailer in need of a floor replacement, new tires, and lights but it was a fourteen-foot, double axel trailer with six-foot sides. A perfect trailer for hauling junk.

It would have been worth a couple of grand in good shape, but it was not in good shape, so he wanted $500 for it.

I didn't have the $500 cash to pay for it, but I did have a deal working later in the week for some underground steel tanks that I had already been contracted with to haul off and wanted to sell them to my buddy.

He was offering me .05 cents per pound for them graded as unprepared steel. I was arguing and trying to get him to pay me 6.5 cents per pound. He would not budge.

Then I said "if you pay me 6.5 cents per lb. instead of 5. I will buy your trailer from you the same day." He relented and said "ok."

The other 1.5 cents per pound that I got from him multiplied out over 35,000 pounds *the total weight of my 3 steel tanks*, equaled another $525. Just enough to buy the trailer and a new light kit too.

I say that I bought his trailer with the money I talked him into giving me to do so. Perhaps he sees it as putting a trailer in the hands of someone who would fill it and then bring all the metal it held to him day after day.

To this day, each of us thinks we won that deal.

On another day, I answered a long-distance call that came from Google. It was a Comcast representative wanting to know if I could come to haul off a bunch of their digital cable boxes. It was a long haul that I would end up making once a month for the next several years but the first time that I went, I broke down on Alligator Alley. Which is a 100 mile stretch of Florida highway that cuts right through the middle of the Everglades. Alligators and Panthers are known to frequently visit the roadways. It is not an ideal place to breakdown. Yet, here I was overloaded, weighed down, with a flat tire, no jack, a suspended license, and sixty miles from anywhere close with a flat trailer tire. I had a spare but no jack.

I made a sign that said I NEED A JACK and then tried to flag down traffic on the side of the road for thirty minutes and no one stopped. Dark was not far off, and I had many miles yet to cover. As well as a wife depending on me to make something happen. Once I realized that no one was going to stop and rescue me and that I must figure out how to get this load home by myself. I reexamined the situation and came up with a crazy idea.

The tire that had gone flat was my driver's side. It was my rear axle, trailer tire. So, I placed my good spare trailer tire in front of my front trailer tire. Then jumped back into the truck and eased forward and drove my front trailer tire up onto the top of my spare. Thereby raising the flat rear tire off the ground just enough to unbolt it and remove it. After which, I eased my truck backward, back off my spare. When I did, I noticed the rear axle was only about 1/16" away from dragging the asphalt due to the heavyweight of my load, but that was just enough to get me home.

Somewhere near the halfway mark on Alligator Alley is a side road called Hwy 29 and it was the back way from Alligator

Alley through a little migrant town called Immokalee and if I could get through Immokalee and past their Police station, *which I'd have to drive right past*. Then I had a chance to make it home. As there were a lot of backroads between Immokalee, and where I lived in Lehigh Acres.

I told Shannon, that she had to drive as we were very likely to get stopped driving with only three wheels on a trailer made for four. I further explained that I had a suspended license (*I use to get a lot of tickets back in the da*y) and that if we got stopped, they'd write her a ticket, but they'd send me to jail. So, she had to drive.

She threw a fit. No way did she want to be responsible for hauling that gigantic, catawampus load that I had piled on top of the trailer and were now trying to limp home. But she did, and we made it home just fine.

At which time I jacked up the trailer and mounted my spare tire, but that experience taught me to always carry a jack and to appreciate a woman with 'balls'.

She fought with me. We yelled at each other. She was scared, then she cried for the first twenty miles, but in the end she did it. She drove us home and saved us from catastrophe. She was a hero.

I would end up going back and making that run several more times. Each time making $1,200 to $1,500. Then one day they sent me to another one of their warehouses in Palm Beach Gardens and the manager there gave four

semi-truck loads of copper wire.

It was about the lowest grade of copper wire that you could recycle, so it was just a notch above garbage and I only got paid a few cents a pound for it, *but a whole lot of anything is still a lot* and the first check from that load of wire was more than $14,000 and I had three more loads waiting on me to go get. In the end, that warehouse full of wire, cables, and cords paid me almost $30,000 in just three days.

 All from a Google search that someone did and my efforts to place my name at the top of the page. I would wind up getting a lot more calls from Google as well. Calls to remove old broken-down semi-trailers that were being used for storage on many occasions.

I removed Mobile MRI machines, Stationary MRI machines, fuel tanks, Greyhound busses, City busses, bulldozers buried out in the Everglades, ware-houses filled with pigeon feces. Anything you can think of, I would get calls to come remove because I dominated my industry on Google. I became the hardest working Cracker on the planet.

City bus that I hauled off for a municipality, after receiving a call from being found on Google.

Mobile MRI machine that I bought and recycled after someone called from Google. The MRI machine itself has thousands of pounds of copper inside of them. I made about $3500 on this and only had to have a semi-truck come pull it.

Another MRI machine that I removed. This one was stationary though inside of a medical office and we had to remove the entirety of their front glass to do so. This one weighed about 30,000 pounds. This was from a Google call that came from about 300 miles away from where I lived. I was all the over the internet. This was worth several grand after all expenses were paid as well.

This was an old bread truck from the 40's, or 50's,. I can't remember which, but it was old, it was an eyesore, and the property owner did a Google search and called me to remove it. So, I did.

Another Greyhound bus project someone abandoned and called me from a Google listing to come remove.

This was I would get calls to haul off and remove tractor

trailers all the time. This is just one example. This job had three of them and was a result of a Google call as well.

Here we are improvising. I needed Charlie to cut the doors off, but we had no ladder. So upon my shoulders, he stood. I never let reasons 'why not' stop me. I always looked for ways around the reasons why I could not. This is just one example.

This was a 7,500-pound boat keel from a sailboat.

It was the most difficult thing I have ever moved. It took me all day, 3 men, a 10,000 lb. winch as well as 2 come-a-longs to 'barely' get this loaded on my car hauler.

5 miles down the road, it was so heavy its weight ripped my trailer right off the ball hitch and the keel and trailer both landed in the ditch. I had to then call a tow truck at that point. Then buy a new trailer axle.

All of that just to say the internet was working for me. It had leveled the playing field and allowed me to compete in an arena that I had no business in when I began, but still had come to dominate.

I was growing tired of it though. The sun was hot, the steel was heavy, and the repairs to my trucks and trailers were expensive. It was time for something new.

I was burnt out on metal. I ripped my pants and went home bleeding, or with a new scar, at least once a week. I felt like I had hit my ceiling. I needed a new challenge. I needed change. I was feeling burnt out with my business and my marriage both.

Reinventing Myself

People began to notice my success. People that remembered me when I was jumping in dumpsters had watched me rise and my success. They started asking me how I did it and if I would help them.

So, I began to help others. Mainly my metal clients at first. I would help them raise their internet profile. They would get more business in the front door and that would produce more metal for me out the back door.

Then I started college. I had taken some college courses while incarcerated and had earned the equivalent of an Associate's degree in Paralegal studies, but now I was out and felt like I wanted to learn more about Marketing.

I was on a quest to learn more about how to grow a business. So, I enrolled in Southwest Florida College and then later Hodges University.

The process of enrolling in college was not without its own set of hurdles. The Government requires men at the age of eighteen to register for Selective Service. However, they allow them up until they are twenty-seven to do so.

If you fail to register for Selective Service, you fail to qualify for any type of Federal Student Aid. Since I had been locked up shortly after turning eighteen and was not released until after I was twenty-nine. I have never registered for Selective Service and therefore did not qualify for Financial Aid. Unless I could prove I met one of the exemption criteria. Which I could. Incarceration was one of the exemptions.

Except for the girl who ran that department at the college was hell-bent on denying me and argued that I had been eighteen for two hundred and sixteen days and that I had two hundred and sixteen opportunities to register before my incarceration.

I could not deny that argument, but that argument was also taking an unnecessarily hard and stringent view of the statute. A view more restrictive than Congress had intended. I knew the law.

I went over her head and called the Department of Education in Washington D.C. myself, got the head person over these matters on the phone. I asked to record the call and received permission. Then explained that I had been incarcerated from age eighteen to age twenty-nine and that my incarceration prevented me from registering with Selective Service and did I qualify for the incarceration exemption? She replied Yes and agreed with me on all accounts.

This lady at the college still would not accept her answer. She refused to process my paperwork, even after listening to the recording that I emailed her. So, I called her immediate supervisor and explained it all again. I then emailed her the sound clips of the recording. After listening, her supervisor apologized to me and said she would have my application for financial aid processed immediately.

After that, I was asked to sit down and interview with the College Administrator and the Dean of the Business School. I had to explain my entire story up to that point once again. They asked for letters of recommendation and I provided them about fifty of them. My idea was to overwhelm them, and I did.

The U.S. Government backed my loan, and they allowed me to enroll. I owed it to myself and 'returning citizens' everywhere to stand out for good reasons and to be my best, and I did.

I was making A's. I was making friends. I was having a great time. I even made the Dean's List several times.

I was learning to write in APA Format. I was giving presentations and becoming comfortable with public speaking, but most of all I was falling in love with what I was doing. I enjoyed being in class much more than I enjoyed being in the field and I started thinking that maybe I should leave the world of scrap metal behind and pursue a career in Marketing.

It was with this idea in mind in my second Collegiate year, that I signed up to be an intern for a local marketing agency. The owner was a Facebook specialist.

I went down to her office and interviewed well. I felt like when I left that I would be accepted for the internship. Except I was not. I never heard back from that lady ever, and neither did the school.

I never did get an answer from her or the school as to why I was not accepted. Nor did the school ever send her anyone else. It was a very strange situation. I'm not sure if my incarceration history played any part in that or not. I may never know. About two months later though, on my own, I attended one of her 'Facebook for Business' workshops and was blown away at the wealth of knowledge I received from her.

It was worth every bit of the $40 per head she charged for the class. I got so much out of it, that I signed up for her next class – *even though it was no different than the first one that I attended*. I wanted to gobble up all of the information about Facebook and social media that I could. This was the wave of the future and I knew it *even way back then.*

A few months later, after I had cleaned out all the prisons, and traveled all over the State of Florida buying junk cars, dropping dumpsters, cutting up planes, and hauling underground tanks. I hit a slump and thought that hiring a marketing firm might be just what my metal business needed. So I called the Facebook specialist lady and requested an appointment.

On the day of my appointment. She could not make time to meet with me but sent her assistant to meet with me. Who never advised me of anything at all. She just asked me questions and took notes. After which she said she would have the owner get back in touch with me, and then charged me $40 for the 'consultation.'

Then came Marley!

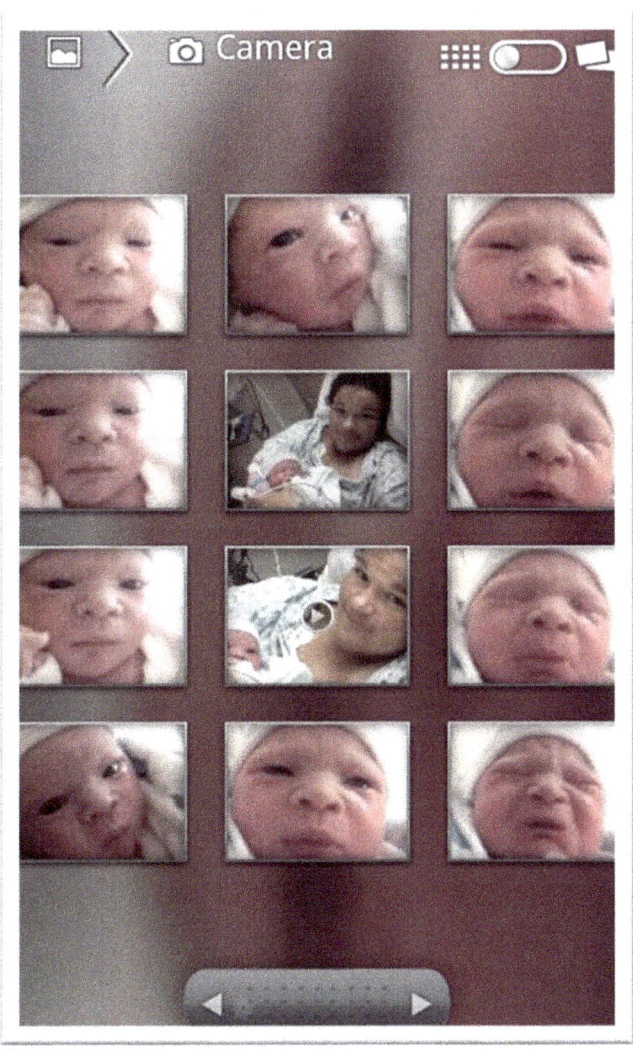

On the day of Marley's birth, I took so many pictures, this is what my phone gallery looked like when I opened it up. I had to catch the screen capture.

Marley

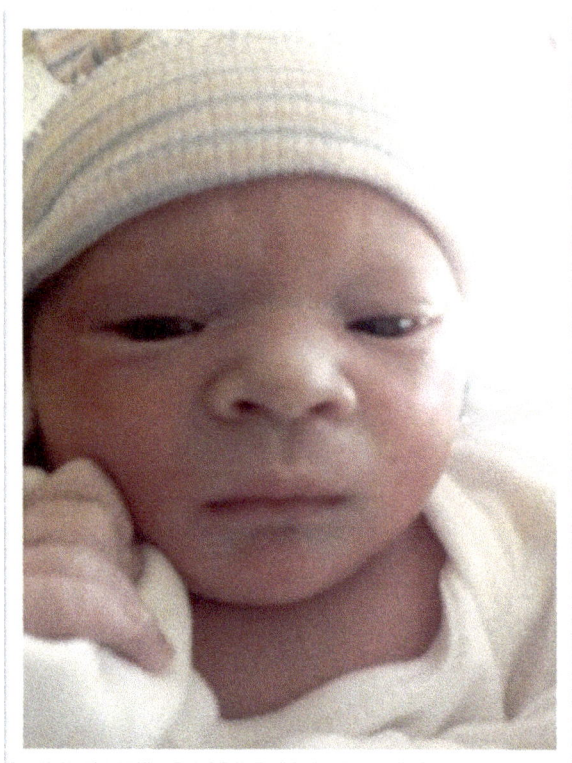

The circumstances of Marley's birth are quite a bit different than those of Mya's. Shannon and I had gotten to a point that we hardly showed much interest in or affection towards each other at all and had grown tired of living life together.

We had discovered that we each had conflicting sets of life goals. We were each weighing the ramifications of leaving each other against the benefit of staying together for the 'good of the baby'. When Marley came along and surprised us both.

I will just say that God works in mysterious ways because little Marley is the greatest blessing ever. I can remember wondering that as a dad of one beautiful child, who already owned the entirety of her daddy's heart. How would there be room enough to love another child?

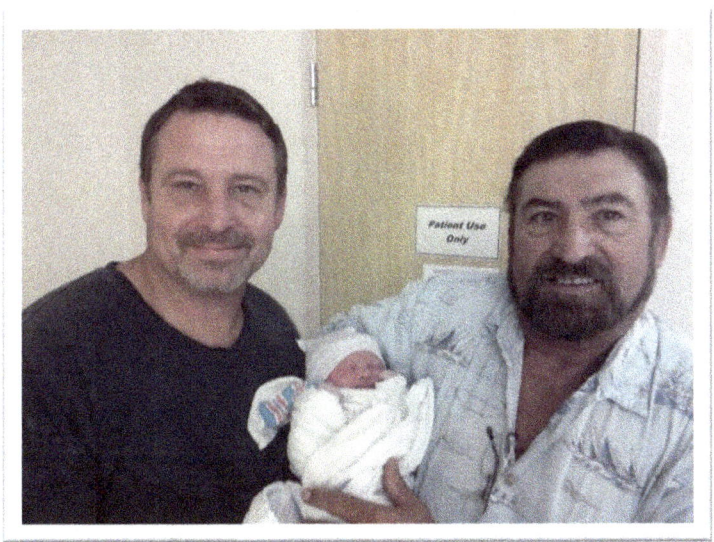

Me and my Dad minutes after Marley was born

That never surfaced as an actual problem though. As being present when she was born and the Doctor handing her to me and me holding her as she took her first breaths of air. I felt my heart double in size. I loved them both greatly, equally, and each with the full capacity of my newly enlarged heart.

I was there for the delivery of both of my children. I remain grateful today to both God and their mother for carrying them, delivering them, and helping me to raise them.

They are wonderful young ladies, and they make me want to be a better father, a better man, and a better human being.

Just like Mya, I took Marley with me everywhere as well. I had my kids around me as much as was possible. Later after Marley was born, Shannon and I separated for good. Then began a dance of juggling days, and freeing up schedules, and covering for each other as one would get called into work, etc. but my kids have always come first. My kids, and my dog. My kids, my dog, and my business, and that right there is probably why my marriage failed. Nowhere in that top three list of priorities was my wife. She would later say that I worked too much, and would roll over in bed, and cuddle with my dog.

I cannot deny any of those charges, but she cannot say that I cheated. She cannot say I hit her. She cannot say a whole lot of other things, and somehow, I thought that made me better. I took pride in my work ethic.

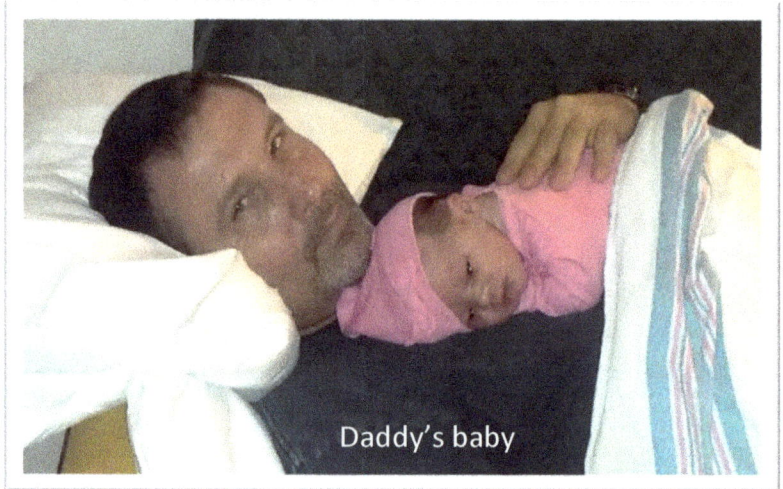

Daddy's baby

These were our conversations during her third trimester with Marley. Not what color we would paint the nursery. Not college funds. Not life insurance, not play dates, twin sister outfits, nothing like that. We were just discussing how unhappy we both were with our lives.

I wanted to make changes and so did she. So, we did.
I will detail that shortly but for now, here are some beautiful photos of my Princess Marley. Whom, I originally wanted to name 'Freedom Nicole'. I was talked out of that after a stop at a convenience store one night in Tampa. Her mother went in

and bought a Bob Marley Mellow Mood Iced Tea and after taking the first swig, she turned and asked me "Are you sure you won't reconsider the name, Marley?"

We had discussed that name earlier in the first month of her pregnancy, but I had just seen the movie 'Marley And Me' with Jennifer Anniston and there was no way I was naming my child after a dead dog. It was not even up for discussion. Fast forward eight months, and now I liked the ring of my children's names being Mya and Marley. The names fit them both so well.

It's an honor and a privilege to be her daddy and see those eyes look up at me, in wonder and amazement

Shannon and I have always agreed on keeping the girls together. They have an incredible bond.

Hanging out with Grandma Candee (my mom).

She is still 'Daddy's baby'

Changing Careers

July 10, 2012, the day after Marley was born. I was leaving the hospital and was on my way home to get a change of clothes for Shannon and to check on Mr. Smith. When my phone alerted me to an email that had just come in from the owner of that marketing agency that I had requested help from. This email was informing me that she was denying my request to take me on as a new client but would still be keeping the $40 consultation fee.

Folks, this email ticked me off and was just what I needed to motivate me into action. After reading the email, I called the Secretary of State, for the State of Florida and inquired as to what kind of license was needed to start a marketing business and was told that it was a completely unregulated industry and no professional licensing was required. That's all I needed to hear. I decided to start a marketing business before I even hung up the phone.

When I came back into the hospital room, I was full of excitement, and enthusiasm for my new business venture. I even had a business name already 'Effective Marketing Solutions'.

Shannon on the other hand thought I was crazy. She had just delivered our second child and wasn't even allowed to leave the hospital yet and here I was rambling on about this new business that I was going to start. She was focused on healing and recovering. While I was talking about flipping our entire world upside down and going in an entirely different direction. Away from everything we knew and were comfortable with. She thought I was crazy, but I wasn't. I knew change was in the air.

Shortly after we all came home from the hospital. My buddy who owned Allied Recycling sent me to Orlando to oversee a very complicated demolition job that his guys were having a lot of trouble with.

It involved the removal of an old printing press that took up two stories and four gigantic rooms inside of a warehouse. The biggest issue of all was the eighty thousand pound steel drum right in the center of it all. It was one of the most challenging jobs that I have ever been a part of.

His guys were having trouble and he needed me. So I left my wife and newborn child and spent two weeks in Orlando overseeing this job.

Marley cried all day and night too. She got a bad diaper rash. Her momma got sick, and I wasn't there. Not that I was off galavanting or doing wrong. I was working.

I had borrowed some money from my buddy earlier in the month, and I owed him this, but that didn't matter.

What mattered was, I wasn't there with Shannon and those two babies. Shannon had to deal with all of that herself. I'm not sure she has ever forgiven me.

When I returned, I got sick too, and there we were two very sick adults, with a toddler walking around getting into things and a newborn that wouldn't stop crying. We were one big happy family.

Effective Marketing Solutions

Once I recovered, I began to work feverishly on my new business venture. I wanted to come out the gate with a bang and just keep churning on the momentum. I had some cool business cards designed. They were flashy and different, and so was I.

By the end of 2012 things were winding down with my junk removal business as well as with our marriage. We both loved our girls truly, madly, deeply, but we did not talk to each other much at all. Not because anything was wrong, or because we were fighting. Not at all. We just were not really into each other anymore.

I had dreams to move up, reinvent myself, and live a life much different than the one I currently had. Shannon did not share these same aspirations, goals, or dreams.

This book is not written to slander my children's mother, but I did often feel as if she had a problem for every solution, and I, on the other hand, had a solution for every problem. We were two completely different people.

My Grandmother had said I was not ready to get married and that my doing so was a mistake. She apologized to Shannon on my behalf in advance. We fought about that then, but I have to admit now, that she was probably correct. Not correct in that it was a mistake. I do not think that at all. Just correct in the sense that there was no way I was ready for that kind of decision. But it wasn't a mistake. I got married to save my life!

Being married to Shannon made me a better man and gave me two beautiful daughters. Marriage and family life brought normalcy to my life. It replaced my chaos with order. It gave me something to care about besides myself and after having achieved a taste of success my self-esteem began to come back as well. I began to develop into who I should have been all along.

Effective Marketing Solutions only served to drive a deeper wedge between us. **We** had been Metal Recycling & Salvage, but **I** was Effective Marketing Solutions not because I did not offer for her to be a part of it with me. I did, but her time and energies were now in demand times three. As she had me and two little ones. She was not interested in business.

Starting a new business is hard. Especially when you are brand new in the industry. Me starting this new business had also caused the lady who taught the Facebook classes, to have a little bit of beef with me. As she later wrote me a nasty email and accused me of being sneaky and only taking her classes, to use the information to start my own business. Then used her influence and connections to try and blacklist me before I could even really get started.

The few connections I had made and the network I was beginning to build all turned their backs on me and would no longer return my calls. I was not even in business for thirty days and already had haters and people hoping to see me fail. Nevertheless, I persisted.

I landed my first big opportunity with a new business in town called Downtown Bronze Salon. The owner was a high school classmate of mine and we had recently reconnected and she was willing to give my new business its first opportunity. I remain grateful to her to this day. However, once that job was complete, I had nothing else coming in. I was brand new, so I had no established online presence as I had enjoyed with Metal Recycling and Salvage.

Late in November 2012. I went back to see my buddy at Allied Recycling and asked him for someday labor work just to help supplement my income until things picked up with my new business. The timing was perfect, as he had a large demolition project in the yard that he thought would be perfect for me.

He worked me liked a Hebrew slave. I spent several days shoveling, prying apart, and picking up heavy loads. December 3rd, 2012 was a particularly difficult day working for him. As he was in rare form, taking out his frustrations on everyone else around him, namely me. By the end of the day, we got into it with each other and he told me to go home and not come back.

I arrived home tired, hungry, stressed out about finances, and overwhelmed with life. When I walked through my front door Mr. Smith got up and came over to me wagging his tail, all happy to see me. Mya was two and she came waddling over to me, happy to see her daddy. Then I walked into the kitchen and little Miss Marley was on a play rug in the living room, laying on her belly and pushing herself up and cooing and cawing happy to see her daddy too, and there stood Shannon.

She had her back to me, as she was preparing dinner and cleaning chicken in the sink. She never turned around. She never said hello, how was your day? I am happy to see you. I am glad you are home. Nothing!

Nothing was wrong, we were not fighting, she was not ignoring me or giving me the silent treatment. That had just become normal. I was home and in the same room with her for about thirty minutes before she ever turned around and spoke. That was it for me. I swore to myself that I would not come home one more day to a woman that did not appreciate me. Period!

I took her to work the next day. After dropping her off, I went and made arrangements to sleep on a friend's couch. Then I went and applied at Waffle House near my friend's house because they were open 24 hours a day, 7 days a week.

I picked her up from work that evening and brought her home and then made dinner for everyone. After the girls ate, I put them in the bath and then got them dressed for bed. All without ever saying a word to Shannon.

After they were in bed and the lights were out. I walked into the kitchen where Shannon was and told her that I was leaving. She was free to date or carry on with her life in any way she desired. I would be there to help with the girls, I was not abandoning her or my responsibilities, but I was ending our relationship and I did.

The next twelve months were a very tumultuous ride. My plan was to move out, stay with a friend, and work at Waffle House during the midnight to 7 am shift during the week. Then clock out and work Effective Marketing Solutions from 8 am to 3 pm, then watch my girls while Shannon went to work from 4 pm to 11 pm. During which time, I would nap with the girls. Then shower, get dressed for Waffle House so that when she got off work, I could leave and go straight back to Waffle House.

If that schedule sounds hectic or unreasonable it is because it was both. This lasted about four months and by March 2013 I was rolling along pretty good, getting my groove back. Things had settled down with Shannon and I. We were co-parenting equally. We were both making progress at rebuilding our lives.

I lived on tips and what I could manage to earn with my new marketing business and gave her my weekly Waffle House paycheck to help with the girls and their needs. Emotions were settling. She was dating, and so was I.

In my transition, I had decided to do as many things differently as I possibly could. I wanted to be somebody completely different. I wanted a completely different life.

I was starting over, and you only get so many opportunities in life to start over from scratch and this was my third time. **I did not want to be anything that I used to be, ever again.**

Doing Things Differently

I moved back into my cousins' trailer and spent my weekends working on fixing it up. I was doing a lot of things differently. Including the clothes that I wore. As opposed to always wearing tank tops and 80's stonewashed jeans. I started trying to dress up and dress nicely on all occasions. I experimented with different looks. Some were better than others. I was trying to find myself.

If it was different, I did it. I put my left shoe on first instead of my right shoe in the mornings. I slept on the opposite side of the bed. I ate differently. I began to focus on eating healthy, shopping organically, reading food labels, going to restaurants that I had never tried before.

I started drinking coffee. Whereas before I was not a coffee drinker. I even traded in my truck for a Mustang.

I rebranded my business using the colors Green and Black and dropped my last name and just went by first and my middle name once again.

I did not want to be anyone that I ever was before.

I was doing a lot of different things with a lot of different people when I found a graphic design artist on Craigslist and went to meet him about creating some artwork for a new client.

Turns out this guy was not only a graphic design artist, but a web designer too. He just so happened to have an empty desk in his office downtown.

We struck a deal. He gave me the desk and I agreed to give him all my web and graphic design work.

So now I had a prestigious office downtown from which to work and launch my new operation.

This guy's name is Tom, and he remains a dear friend and mentor to this day.

Then came this one night that this chick came into the Waffle House somewhere about 2 am and was lit up and had been drinking. She went over to the jukebox and played some George Jones, Merle Haggard, and Hank Williams Jr. and then just started singing and dancing right there in the Waffle House and insisted that I come from behind the counter and dance with her. So, working for tips, I felt it my duty to oblige her.

In the middle of the Texas Two-Step that she was trying to teach me, I asked her name. She said "Tiffany" or "Texas Tiffany" depending on who's asking.

My jaw hit the floor as that last phrase rolled off her tongue with a bit of a Texas twang. This was the whitest black chick I had ever met. She was certainly different!

She moved into my place the next night.

We would get crazy stares from people all the time.

We had a good time hanging out with each other though. She had me dying my hair and my beard. She even talked me into getting Pedicures with her before it was all said and done. She was very high maintenance. I wanted different. She provided that for sure.

Shortly after this, I met an international mural artist and jewelry designer in Sarasota and took him on as a client. I created a Facebook page for him and would create social media posts for him daily. However, my life was one great big phase of transition at this time. I had no structure. As I was trying to learn to do business in a world of  professionals and that was something, I hadn't yet become acquainted with. Sometimes, I made mistakes.

The work I did for this guy was not my best. I was busy trying to please him, and everyone else but I cannot say that I was accomplishing much. When I happen to see a post of his come through my Facebook news feed.

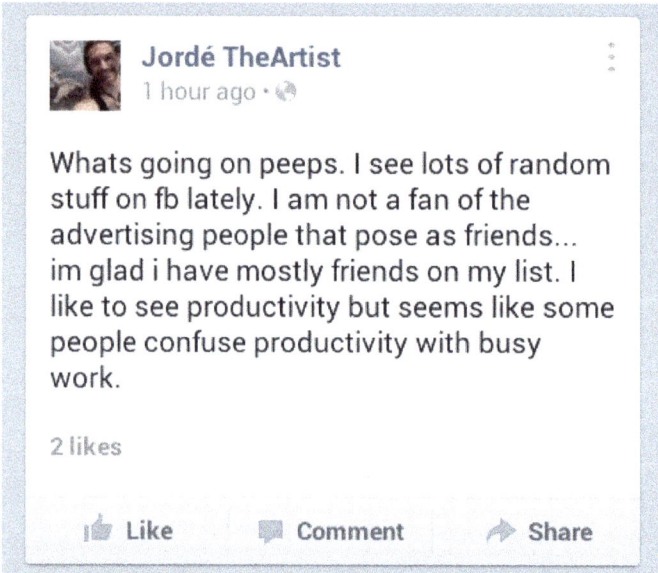

I knew this post was pointed directly at me. At first, I couldn't believe the nerve of this guy; but the more I read his post and played the events of the past month or two over and over in my mind. The more I realized that he was right! Busyness and Productivity are not the same things. I had never realized that before and this information served as a substantial building block to my future. **Do not become so occupied with 'busy work' that you become unproductive. Focus on being productive, not busy.**

The information came a little too late though as it was now Fall 2013 and I was barely holding on. I went back to scrapping on the weekends. My new Mustang became a scrap mobile.

It would be only a few months of this, and I would ruin the rear end and transmission in this vehicle. Before eventually trading it in for a 4-wheel drive Chevy Avalanche but right now, that was unforeseen and unknown.

My trailer was not a good place for me to be all alone, with only memories to fill the place. The water pump went out and there was no way I could afford to replace it. I just moved out.

In essence, I became homeless. Much of my stuff was stored in the trailer. I still had the key, but Tom was kind enough to provide me a key to his office. Mr. Smith and I slept there most nights in a sleeping bag, on the floor.

When Shannon worked, I would go over to her place and watch the girls, eat, and shower. I was always there for them but I was not much to speak of for anyone else. This period was an incredibly low point for me. I was bringing in a total of about

$500 a month at this time, and my Mustang payment alone was $600 per month. This was the time I mentioned way back in the first chapter about when I came home and would get a job and check No to the Felony question, got hired, and then fired.

Life was tough and I learned that I could not build a business alone in isolation. I did not want Shannon to know it, or anyone else for that matter, but I was failing. It was getting harder to conceal that though.

Everyone thought I was crazy to quit my junk removal business and venture out into something new. I had swan dived from a pinnacle of success into a very shallow pool of illusion. Now I had no family, no money, and no viable business, and nowhere to even live. **I was starting to miss being in prison!**

Tom was loaning me money and letting me live in his office. He was the only believer that I had at that time. Him and those two little girls that were always happy to see their daddy, and Mr. Smith of course. His loyalty and admiration for me never failed. That is how big the circle of people was that were not disappointed in me. I had to go back to work.

I called my friend who owned one of the scrap yards in town and asked for a job. He hired me on as a laborer in the yard and because of my prior experience he paid me $12.00 an hour and gave me 48 hours a week. That 8 hours of overtime certainly helped. It was a humble position. The work was hard, a lot of people were telling me what to do, but I was thankful, and it was consistent. That alone was progress.

Tom's lease eventually ended, and he moved out of his office and I moved in with a Christian lady named Ginny who had a rooming house. Her rooms were full, but she let me rent her screened-in front porch. I was starting all over again *for the fourth time.*

One day while working in the scrapyard, I began to think about all my connections from my scrapping day of the past. I then created a marketing plan that I could implement and sent a copy of the final draft *written in APA format of course* to the boss via email.

He looked it over and was impressed. Two weeks later he called me into his office and promoted me to Sales/Marketing and gave me a salary of almost a Thousand dollars a week. It was January 2014, and it was looking like a very happy New Year for me.

I WAS BACK! Life is like a slingshot and sometimes you must be pulled backward pretty far so that you can launch forward again.

Back to Scrapping

This new position would go on to last about nine months.

Everyone in the industry had begun to tighten their belts and I had a high-paid salary position. I was one of the first to be laid off, but I was also given three weeks' severance pay. Another example of my friend and his family, showing me an example of how to do 'better business.'

Immediately following this lay off was my divorce hearing. Shannon and I had been separated since December 4th of 2012 but were still very much involved. Not in a romantic sense, but in a parenting sense. We had long ago worked out a parenting plan and had gotten past all the hurt feelings and ugly words that were prevalent immediately after I moved out.

We both began to put forth an effort to get along. Not just for the sake of the kids, but because we were both decent human beings and there was no need to fight and to be ugly. How we treated each other would ultimately be our decision. We decided to get along. That continues to be the case today. We respect each other, trust each other, and we communicate about our lives and our kids. I think that is a healthy example to model for Mya and Marley.

I always felt like we could work things out civilly as I only ever wanted what was fair for each of us. 50/50 shared custody and 50/50 shared financial responsibility.

The thought of not being present, active, and involved in the lives of my children never once crossed my mind. They were mine and I loved them. I had wanted them for so long, there was no way I was giving up my rights or responsibilities. *Nor was I going to allow them to be taken from me either.*

Early in our separation, we worked out an amicable parenting plan. She had them Sunday, Monday, and Tuesday, and I had them Wednesday, Thursday, and Friday and we alternated Saturdays. We worked out shared expenses for all things necessary.

We still did fight with each other on occasion. Not every day was glorious, but I was still there for her when she needed me. For example, once while she and I were not getting along at all. Shannon's car broke down and she had no way to get to work. So, I asked my mom to loan Shannon her car for a week while I came up with enough money to get her car fixed by a friend of ours.

Why? Because she is my children's mother and if she is not ok, then my children are not ok. Making sure my children are ok is not only my pleasure, but it is also my job. Period. That is how I feel, and that is how I see things.

Once she realized that I wasn't abandoning her and I had proved that I was going to be there and do my part for our children, some of her panic subsided and we began to get along much better.

The day after our divorce hearing was a Friday, and I was hired on as Sales/Marketing Manager for Right Away Recycling. It was for less money, but I started the next Monday, so I agreed.

My opportunity at Right Away really didn't last very long though. Scrap prices were on a drastic decline and the owner was not one of the major players in town. That's part of why he hired me because I use to be. Nevertheless, scrap was on the decline.

When I reported to work on December 1, 2014. I was told that I was being laid off again, and very shortly after laying me off, the owner went out of business completely.

So I went to Allied Recycling and asked my buddy for a job, and he hired me in the same position Sales/Marketing/ and put me on salary.

My opportunity here was a little different. I would utilize my connections and experience to pursue not just new metal accounts for Allied but I would also be the job foreman over jobs I brought in as well.

My position here would last from Dec. 2014 to June 2015 but by then scrap prices would be so low that it was costing more money to process the scrap than it was even worth and I would end up being laid off again. Before any of that would occur though, there would be one more prison clean-up.

Remember Martin Correctional Institution and the Major who said that I would never get that metal?

I got to thinking about it and since all of that had happened five or six years prior. I figured I would call and see who was running the place these days and see if I could reintroduce myself to them.

Turns out that they did have a new Major and the old one was no longer even employed by the Dept. of Corrections anymore. One of the officers that I met, informed me that he had actually been demoted and then fired a short time later for some sort of corruptness and had then gone on to be hired by the County Sheriff's Department where his misdeeds continued, and he was fired from there too and was currently working a construction job. *I couldn't help but smile at the irony.*

The new Major that replaced him knew nothing of our history or anything about my company Metal Recycling and Salvage. Or how I had been blacklisted as this was all several years prior and old news.

So we struck a deal and I went in with a great big track hoe and ordered several semi-dump trailers from Allied Recycling and began what would be a clean up that would last several weeks. The completion of that job would also be the completion of my time at Allied Recycling as well. As two major events took place once the last truck was loaded with all of the metal from Martin C.I.

One, I was laid off again. As scrap metal had become almost worthless. Two, I got a referral from a friend/client of mine. Thus my third business, Blue Grey Marketing was conceived.

Even though I had shut down Effective Marketing Solutions. I still had managed to keep one client on the side. He referred me to a friend of his. This new guy that I was referred to owned two businesses and also referred me to a friend of his that owned a popular restaurant in town and all of a sudden, I had a new opportunity.

Anisity

Something else of significance had happened during this time as well that I haven't yet mentioned. Almost eighteen months earlier in late January 2014, I walked into a neighborhood deli near where I lived and seen this super hot chick working the deli counter. She was half my age and had the coolest name, Anisity (pronounced Honesty). She made these incredible heart-shaped brownies that she had wrapped in cellophane and was selling from a basket on top of the deli counter. I bought two and asked her for her phone number.

She later would say, that she thought about giving me a fake number as she correctly wrote down each digit of her number.

I would continue to stop by nearly every day and when the Fair came to town. She finally allowed me to take her out. It was our first date.

We had a great time as she had me riding all the scary rides much to my chagrin but there was no way I could wimp out, not on the first date. So I rode everything she wanted to, and at the end of the night, she rewarded my

bravery with a terrific kiss. One that tasted as sweet as the Carmel apple and the Cotton candy that she had been eating all night long. We became inseparable.

Fast forward to June 2015 after I had been laid off by Allied Recycling, and given the referrals for three new businesses. She would move on from that deli and begin a job as kitchen manager/ bartender at a popular establishment in town - *until the business sold* and she had then became a server at Applebees. She was not very happy with the opportunity that Applebees was offering. So I proposed that we go into business together.

She said yes. Since my favorite color is Blue and her favorite color is Grey. We named the business Blue Grey Marketing and as of this writing, BGM as we refer to it, continues to grow in strength and reputation almost daily, but it wasn't always that way.

Blue Grey Marketing

We had many hard days in the beginning as I had been out of the marketing game per se' for almost two years. Though we had a head start with the recent referrals, we were still far from viable. We were under the gun right from the start. She had given two weeks' notice at Applebees and our bills continued to be due. We had an incredible first month in August 2015. I had revived my old Effective Marketing Solutions Facebook page and changed its name. That page had barely 300 likes. She invited her friends to like it and we jumped up to 800.

I signed up four more new clients, and we rocked it out our first month, I even went and rented office space. This was going to work. I was excited! Then it became September, and all momentum gained the month before was lost.

A couple of the clients I had signed up in August were contacts and relationships I already had established. However, after the first month of service and with only a handshake agreement.

One guy said it was the end of summer and he was slow and couldn't afford it.

Another guy ended up going out of business, and one of the new clients that I signed up did not like the price increase when the 30-day introductory offer expired. A few leads that I had been optimistic about fell through. So here we were going into October, and we had no momentum. No money. No safety net. With three children between us needing to be fed, and rent on the new office space was already past due. We had $3.00 between us. Just enough for a gallon of gas or a roll of toilet paper. I remember we had to choose. We needed both.

I bought gas and Anisity went in and stuffed as much of the toilet paper from off the roll in the convenience store's bathroom as she could, inside her purse.

Why do I tell you that?

Because starting a business isn't easy. Raising a family brings about the need for more sacrifice than one could ever think to imagine. I also learned to come up from this too. Like we use to say in the Chain-gang. I had to "get it from the dirt.".

Meaning, you had to create what you want out of nothing. If you want it, you have to plant it, grow it, create it, and only then will you have it. No one's coming to your rescue.

So I did. *Correction*, we did. Let me just say unequivocally, Blue Grey Marketing could not have survived then, or now without Anisity. It was my vision, experience, and opportunity in the beginning; but she has come into her own and is counted on daily for our operation to be successful.

However, in October 2015 survival was on my shoulders. I was out of options and out of leads. I grabbed a box of my business cards and drove to downtown Fort Myers.

Downtown Fort Myers is a very happening and prestigious place in SWFL. I wanted to do business there. So, I got out of my car and began walking.

I walked into the door of every single business that had an unlocked door. I introduced myself, handed out a couple of cards, and told them I had reopened my agency and just wanted to introduce myself to all the businesses and was happy to schedule a meeting with them, in the event they had any questions or needed marketing services.

I met a lot of people, and have even remained friends with a few. That days effort led to several opportunities at a tattoo shop, a jewelry repair and Rolex dealer, several restaurants.

We worked downtown for the next year or so, but the greatest stop to come out of that afternoon was when I met the owner of a large restaurant conglomerate. Their family owned most all of the 'coolest' restaurants downtown.

I happened to walk into his office complex not even knowing it was his or understanding the significance of where I was. I was just walking and handing out business cards in every open door that I could. He happened to have recently ordered a new shipment of business cards and was waiting on their delivery when I walked into his office carrying mine.

The receptionist had let me back thinking I was delivering his cards, not knowing I was there passing out mine. Not one to waste an opportunity though. When I realized whose office I was in, I immediately began telling him how I could improve his online presence. This piqued his curiosity which led to a full-blown consultation and him hiring me to handle the social media accounts for all of his downtown Fort Myers establishments.

It was quite unusual as they all make decisions as a team and did not normally make decisions like that without having had at least two or three board meetings about any given topic. He was the owner's son though, so no one questioned him. I was ecstatic. I had just landed the hottest client in all of three counties.

This experience would go on to teach me many valuable lessons and served to make me a much better business person. Unfortunately, many of them wouldn't come until after they hired someone in house to do the job they were paying me to do.

I had a policy then that offered a discounted 30-day introductory pricing. After which the price was adjusted upward.

Also, I did not operate professionally in the sense of invoicing, and I accepted checks from each of their restaurants made out to me personally. As opposed to my business. Thereby, they were paying me as an employee, as opposed to a marketing agency.

That made it really easy to replace me with another new hire later on down the road. Which is exactly what happened to me on January 5th, 2016.

I remember that day well, what a horrible day that was. Anisity and I had started the day with such optimism and had a meeting in Tampa. *A big city two and half hours north of where we lived* and halfway there the transmission went out in the car she had just bought. We had to call and cancel the meeting and then call to be towed back to Fort Myers. Only to be told the repair would be about $2,400 which was $3,500 more than what we had. That was our morning.

In the afternoon, the phone rang and it was the office manager for the downtown restaurants and she informed me that they had hired a college intern to run all of their social media and would no longer be needing our services. I had just lost by far, the biggest client I could have ever dreamed of having. After a deep breath, I told myself, 'This Too, Shall Pass'. Then asked the Universe "What am I supposed to learn here?"

I had learned that bad times come, but they don't stay.
'All I really have to do was keep waking up in the morning'. There is a lesson here. There is something that I am missing. What's going on? Why were all these things happening to me? Why does everything I build crumble? I couldn't help but wonder, what I was doing wrong?

Networking

Feeling down and discouraged. I disengaged from my thoughts and started scrolling Facebook. When I seen an event posted for a local business networking meeting taking place the next day. In light of my recent client loss. I felt that I couldn't give up. I needed to press on and try something different and networking seemed like a great idea.

The next day was tomorrow, and tomorrow is a new day. I needed the benefit of a new day more than anyone I knew. So I went. I had a great time. It was the first real networking meeting that I had ever been to.

They had an agenda they followed, and then we mingled. People were genuinely interested in my services and my business. I remember the leader of the group came up to me and introduced herself and said "Is this your first time networking?" I replied, "Yes it is". She welcomed me and then offered me two pieces of advice that I have never forgotten.

First, she said *"don't tell anyone what you do. Instead, ask them what they do. They will tell you, and if they care what you do, they will ask, if they do not ask, then they do not care."*

That sounded like pretty sound advice, so I listened more intently when she offered up tidbit number two.

"Always make the appointment before you leave the room. Do not leave with an agreement to get in touch with each other. Schedule the appointment before you leave the room."

Again, it seemed like pretty sound advice to me. I was intrigued and left there with three leads and that was enough to fill me with optimism. I marked their next event on my calendar. That event is where I met my friend Tim Jacobs, who has become a friend, and a mentor as well.

They say '**you are only one relationship away from changing the rest of your life**'. Tim Jacobs was that relationship for me. He was involved in a group called Master Networks and was the President of a local chapter.

He invited me to attend, and to this day, I say he gave me the wrong time (he of course will disagree), but I walked into his meeting 15 minutes before it ended *thinking I was 15 minutes early* and quietly sat down. I observed as one person after another stood up and thanked someone in the room for passing them a referral that week. Or to pass a referral to someone else. Everyone in this room was doing business with each other. This was cool. I needed to join.

That group had exclusive seating and the Marketing seat was already taken. So I couldn't join that particular group but there was an opportunity to join a new chapter starting up in another part of town. So I started attending there. It was not anything like the one I had seen across town. As this one was just starting *but I was excited none the less*.

I had had a taste of what this group could become. I wanted in. I worked towards building that group with gusto. Every time I went, I learned something from the other Entrepreneurs in the room. I began to have face to face meetings. I would visit other chapters and would sit under the training being offered every week and I began to grow as a business person. I learned how Professionals do business.

Blue Grey Marketing evolved during this time. We met others that could help us provide better value and improve our services. Our reputation began to grow as was our brand.

Then came the day that the Regional Partner (the boss man) Brian Solt invited me to lunch and asked me if I'd like to be the Chapter President. Before I accepted, I told him about most everything that I have told you in this book. Certain that he would now want to 'reconsider his offer', or go in a 'different direction'. Much to my surprise, he thanked me for the disclosure. Exclaimed it was hard for him to believe, as I didn't carry myself in any sort of way that would lead one to believe that I had been through so much. However, his offer to me as Chapter President still stood if I wanted it. *Boy did I ever!*

I lead that group of businessmen and women with a team for almost two years before I moved to Texas!

Trusted With Leadership

Master Networks is a nationwide professional networking organization that operates in several states across the Nation but is headquartered near Dallas, Texas. They have an annual conference called Connect and I attended in 2017 with Tim Jacobs, Brian Solt, and a few others. That year I was also the recipient of their annual 'Culture Keeper' award. An award that is awarded annually to the individual that most consistently goes above and beyond what is asked, and who displays outstanding character both personally and professionally.

 I walked across the stage and shook hands with Chas Wilson, the Founder. What an incredible journey this had been from where I had begun to where I currently was.

The moment had only lasted about 45 seconds, but for that brief microcosm in time. I wasn't an ex-convict, I wasn't an ex-junkie, I wasn't an ex-husband, I wasn't an ex-anything.

I was simply Mark Cass, Master Networks Chapter President and winner of the prestigious Culture Keeper award, and was shaking hands with Chas Wilson.

I was standing on a stage in Dallas, Texas in proximity to some of the most brilliant and influential people in America. Being honored on a stage in front of hundreds of other very important and influential people from across the nation. The camera bulbs flashed and I was off the stage as the next award-winning recipient crossed it for their chance to be honored.

They had several speakers there that weekend and one of them that I remember spoke about how it is not honorable to work 18-hour days. I had been so proud of my work ethic before he explained that an Entrepreneur must allot time each week to attend not just to their business, but that it was equally important to allot time to tend to their family. As well as to their personal development. Growth needed to take place in all areas simultaneously. Business, family, self-development, spirituality, and physical health.

I had never heard anyone talk like this. It may seem so simple, but when you are grinding away eighteen hours a day, trying to get a business off the ground and grow it. I assure you there is rarely time for anything else. I was learning that you had to create that time. No one had ever told me that before.

I met another guy there at Connect that would go on to be a mentor and a treasured friend as well. His name is John Pesano. We had dinner one night, and after I got through telling him about Blue Grey Marketing and our work on social media he replied "It seems like you're very passionate about what you do, and you're probably very good, but you are trading hours for dollars and you have no way to scale that. You can only grow as big as you are. You can't possibly do more, there aren't enough hours in the day." Those words hit me like a hammer. No one had ever talked to me about scaling a business before.

I had not even considered that. I just knew I was working a lot for what still seemed to be very little. These people in Master Networks were pretty smart. I was definitely in the right room.

I would later fly back to Dallas and meet with my new friend John. He took me to work with him every day for a week. Showing me how he did things and introduced me to his business partners and taught me things I did not know about SEO. They allowed me plenty of time for questions and were thorough and patient in their answers. In short, John and his team took me to SEO school.

I flew back to Florida and changed my entire business model. Blue Grey Marketing became an SEO company first and social media second. Our focus became getting businesses ranked first on Google and we used Social Media to support those goals. Our gross revenue increased by a hundred grand in the next twelve months.

The next year I attended the Connect conference again and listened to Chas Wilson's keynote address. It was on business and how to 'Manifest Millions'.

He broke down top-line revenue numbers and how to increase them, by adding value to your service packages and increasing your prices. He talked about not dividing your time, and energies with business ventures that were not within three feet of your current business.

For example, in my marketing business, I could consider another venture in consulting, or teaching business principles, maybe putting on marketing workshops but opening a restaurant would be too far removed from marketing. Therefore, it was not within 'three feet' of what I was currently doing.

That made sense to me, as I had been dabbling with a few different MLM opportunities that were all the rage at the time and nothing was working as my time was being too severely divided. So, his words were hitting their mark with me.

He further explained that most businesses look to cut expenses as opposed to how to create more revenue. That perked my ears, as I already had a knack for seeing opportunities where others did not.

Man, this guy was good. He walked back and forth across the stage and the audience hung on his every word. He held my attention and the attention of hundreds of others because he was giving away his best information.

These were valuable words. *If one could find a way to make some changes and apply them.* I took notes. I bought his book. I had to get in this guy's circle. He was smarter than me.

Meeting Chas Wilson

That had become a thing with me, seeking out relationships with people that were smarter than me. I never wanted to be the smartest guy in any room. I hated it and felt uncomfortable when I was.

He was doing what I wanted to do. I had a story. I had a message. I had had many failures, yes, but I had learned lessons with each one of them. I had defied the odds of recidivism. I knew something about perseverance and not giving up. I knew about continuing after extreme disappointment. I knew about having to choose between toilet paper or gasoline. I had been there.

I had learned to create opportunities out of thin air. Going back to the days of running a lotto board at Desoto. To starting a business without even knowing that a business license was needed. I had been there. I also knew how to be better than that. I had grown so much.

I knew all about prejudices and people dismissing you before even giving you a chance. I had fought through that. I knew about having to be better than other applicants, to even be considered. I knew the world was full of people who had been mislabeled by society and were struggling to overcome it. **I knew how!**

I knew how to grow a business. I knew how to not just survive, but thrive. I know. I did it during the worst recession this country has had since the Great Depression.

I knew what I was going to do, *I was going to start another business*. I wanted to become a public speaker. I wanted to write books, I wanted to tell my story, and to use the lessons of my life to help and to encourage others. I just was not sure how to get started. I wanted to be an Author, a Speaker, and a Serial Entrepreneur. I wanted to help people grow, not just their businesses, but themselves too.

After Connect, I approached Chas and asked to schedule a face to face meeting. He agreed and we did. It was three weeks away.

I did not want to go see Chas and tell him about 'what I wanted to do' though. He appeared to be a man more impressed by action than words. I decided to write a book before flying back to Dallas to meet with him. I wanted him to take me seriously and writing a book in three weeks was a pretty serious endeavor. My idea was to walk into Chas's office and slide my book across his desk and tell him I had written that after being inspired by him at Connect.

It did not quite work out like that. It took me six weeks to write the book, have it edited, cover designed, and on June 18, 2018, I uploaded it to Amazon and made it available for purchase. It is called '3 Ways To Reach The Top Of Google – The Quick Way, The Right Way, and The Expensive Way'.

Three weeks before the release of my book though, while it was still being edited and the cover being designed. I flew to Texas for my meeting with Chas Wilson.
I was excited about this meeting and we had a great one. I remember Chas being impressed that I flew in to see him in person as opposed to opting for a live chat online. I replied that having his time and attention was worth much more to me than an online chat and thanked him for meeting with me.

I continued and told him my story, much as I have told you in this book, and asked him how I can press in and do more. He stated that he felt like I had a powerful platform to speak from and could help many people, but a story alone did not qualify me to get up on stage and tell it. I still had to 'earn it before I would deserve it'.

I thanked him for his time and walked out of his office, and down the street strolling my suitcase on wheels behind me. I am sure I was a sight. But I had just met Chas Wilson, told him my story and he did not reject me. Further, I had successfully opened lines of communication and began a friendship with another person much smarter than I was. I had upped my averages.

The next month, I upped my averages again, when I packed up and moved to Texas. This was more an issue of my lease being up though. Blue Grey Marketing had been growing in the SWFL area and we had a big two-story house with three offices downstairs and three bedrooms upstairs. It was more square footage in office space than we could have reasonably rented anywhere else in town. We were doing well, but Hurricane Irma hit our house in 2017 and by June 2018, when our lease was up, the landlord wanted to renovate. As our house had withstood some damage during that Hurricane and we were informed that we had to move and there was only one place on earth that I wanted to be. Texas.

Moving to Texas

Texas had seemed to be so full of opportunity. So full of people that genuinely cared about helping others grow their business. So full of Master Networks members. Something there was calling me.

I considered myself to be more of a dual resident though. As I continue to fly back and forth from Dallas to SWFL for business, family, little girls birthdays, and other special occasions at least once every six weeks or so. So now Blue Grey Marketing had become a national marketing company. *Aren't you considered National if you operate in more than one State?*

Up Your Averages

When I uploaded my book to Amazon, I had to create a new entity as Amazon needed to cover all the legalities of paying me for book sales. This led to me having to create another business entity.

So, I guess I am doing this huh? Creating another business. This is real. How many does this make now?
Counting to myself – There was the Hustle and Grind from all the early days. Then Metal Recycling & Salvage, Effective Marketing Solutions, Blue Grey Marketing, and now, what would I call this new one?

I fell in and out of love with many different names but in the end, I went with the one that had been in front of me all along. My saying. My motto. A term I had coined, 'Up Your Averages'. To me Up Your Averages simply means trying each day to be a better version of yourself.

It has been said that 'you are the average of the five people that you most closely associate with.' I looked around myself one day and decided that I did not want to be anyone that I knew. I began that day seeking out better friends. Having better friends, led to entertaining higher thoughts, and better opportunities came because of that.

As I began to have higher thoughts and to make better decisions, my life began to get better.

It started that day I turned twenty-one in that confinement cell at Desoto CI. Every day has not been a step forward. I will admit that. However, each day that was a step forward brought about an improved set of circumstances, and each day that wasn't, my circumstances worsened just a bit and I learned not to do whatever that was anymore. I have got three years in on a four-year college degree, but very little of my knowledge has come from the classroom. Most everything that I have learned, Life has taught me.

I learned what I know about business and life because I lived it. I have been thrown by every horse that I have ever broken. A few things I have learned along the way and know to be true are:

Who you choose as your inner circle of friends will be the most important decision that you will ever make. *Choose friends that behoove you.*

If you are the smartest person in the room, you are in the wrong room. *Make friends with people smarter than you. People that challenge you and have higher standards than you. They will inspire you to improve and then afford you opportunities to do so.*

Givers gain. *The more you give. The more you get.*
People will appreciate you when you provide value.

We all make mistakes, and we are all difficult to live with. *It is not just you, or your partner. It will be that way with another partner in the future too. Be slow to anger, and quick to forgive. We are all humans. We all fall, but the best of us get back up.*

A person is only as good as their word. *If your word is no good, then you're no good.* Period!

Eat food as medicine. Or you will eat medicine as food.

None of this means anything if you are not healthy enough to enjoy it. Your body is precious. Treat it well.

There is a God. He loves you.
The more time you spend with Him, the better your life will be.

Wet Money Spends Like Dry Money!
Money spent being earned in the rain, is just as valuable as money earned in dry and comfortable conditions.
When the competition stops working because of the rain, or because it is a holiday, or for any excuse at all, then that is your opportunity to lap them. Henry Ford said, "It has been my observation, that most people get ahead during the time that other people waste."

If you want to do it, you will find a way.
If you do not want to, then you will find an excuse.
Be the person who finds a way, not the one that finds an excuse.

The decisions you make today will have a direct impact on what kind of day you have tomorrow. *Govern yourself accordingly.*

No one will ever care about your business the way you do.

Be kind to people who cannot repay you.

There is beauty in tragedy. Look for it and embrace it. *Disappointment and heartbreak are often the fertilizer for the next beautiful bloom.* Through pain, we grow.

Storms come not so much to destroy our path as to clear the way for a new one. *Read that again.*

Man, I could go on and on and I have not even really got to business yet, or SEO, or Social Media. There is so much inside of me just waiting to come out to people that are open or in need. I have not had the life I have had and went through all that you read about in this book just to sell websites. That would be ridiculous. I have a higher purpose and that is to tell my story. To encourage people to be Encouragers. The world has plenty of critics. As have I, but those who encouraged me, those who believed in me when no one else did, those who saw value in me and invested their time, those are the people that I remember.

Those are the people that I credit for the success that I have tasted. I encourage you to be that person who believes in someone else today. Someone needs you to be, and you need to be too, for you. **Up Your Averages!**

It is not the large steps that we are necessarily aiming for. It is the small ones repeated daily that make the biggest difference. Up Your Averages is more than a brand. It is a movement whose mission is:

'To connect with people that are already where we want to be, to mentor those wanting to be where we are and to encourage those fighting discouragement everywhere.'

Clemency Hearing – 2019

Before we get all caught up holding hands and singing Kumbaya though. There was another storm that I had to weather to get to this point and it goes right along with this story. It's the other half of my inspiration. Going through it gave me the clarity that I needed to finish this book, provide it with an ending, and officially launch the 'Up Your Averages' brand.

__Clemency__ is an act of mercy that absolves the individual upon whom it is bestowed from all or any part of the punishment that the law imposes. This is the power to grant full or conditional pardons, or commute punishment. These powers are vested in the Governor only with the agreement of two Cabinet members who are also statewide elected officials.

When I was released from prison in 2003. The rules for Executive Clemency in Florida dictated that I wait 4 years to apply for the Restoration of Civil Rights. 8 Years for a Full Pardon w/out Firearm permissions, and 10 years for a Full Pardon w/ Firearm permission.

I applied for the Restoration of my Civil Rights as soon as I was eligible. This was in January of 2007. The people in Tallahassee told me after I applied, that there was a 10-year waiting period before my case would be considered. They were 100% correct.

In January of 2017, I got a letter in the mail, telling me it was my turn. They were now ready to hear my case, but before doing so I needed to fill out a packet of information updating the Office of Executive Clemency on all my activities and work history for the past 10 years. Make a formal statement about the incident that led to my incarceration and what my part in it was. Then another formal statement as to why I felt I should be granted Clemency. Along with any other information that I deemed relevant for them to know.

I had been out 14 years by this point and was able to upgrade my original Restoration of Rights request to a Full Pardon request. It had been so long since I had even thought about any of this stuff. Was it worth it to go back through it all again, digging it all back up, and rehashing it all? **Yes, It Absolutely Was!**

It was my best shot yet, at a chance to be exonerated and to finally set the record set straight. In some ways, I had been preparing for this hearing ever since the day I turned twenty-one. I got my hopes up again and grew more excited daily. I knew this was 'my time'. It finally all made sense. I needed to go through all of what you have read to have this glorious ending.

They said I could submit letters of recommendation and character references so I began to debate with myself as to how many I should submit. Having no point of reference at all. I just assumed most people had about 5-character letters. So, I wanted more, but not too many. How many were too many? How many was not enough? I did not know but I felt like 20 was a good number. Enough to impress, but not so many that they would not read them all. Or so I reasoned.

I wanted a good cross-section of people who knew my character from throughout my life. I asked 5 family members, 5 people, who knew me pre-incarceration, 5 people who knew me post-incarceration, and 5 clients.

I even had Shannon write me a letter of recommendation because I figured it would say a lot about a guy's character if even his ex-wife vouched for him and had positive things to say, *like how rare is that*?

They asked me to provide 10 years of work history and I went through running heavy equipment with my dad. To Metal Recycling and Salvage, Effective Marketing Solutions, Blue Grey Marketing, and later amended it to include Up Your Averages. *As I had published my first book in between submitting the application in April 2017 and finally being granted a hearing on March 13, 2019.*

I wanted to be sure they knew that I was an Author, a Speaker, and a Serial Entrepreneur, with offices in Florida as well as Dallas, Texas. I wrote about winning the Culture Keeper award, included a notarized copy of my co-defendant's confession. **Everything!**

My hearing was scheduled, for March 13, 2019. I had been out of prison for 16 years by the time the day finally arrived. It had been more than a quarter-century since this nightmare all began. Man, how I hoped it was now nearing the end.

I flew from Dallas, Texas into Tampa, Florida on March 12, 2019, and drove to Tallahassee, and spent the night at my cousin's house. To be there first thing in the morning as the hearings began at 8:00 am.

The Governor called the meeting to order and was seated in the middle of a giant podium sized desk and was flanked on either side by members of his cabinet.

I had 5 minutes to speak and Brian Solt had come with me to speak on my behalf as well. He was allotted 5 minutes too.

We both waited in anticipation as names were called, introductions were made, greetings good morning issued by all the applicants, as they each stood and approached the podium.

The Governor appeared to be in a good mood and not all, but most, of the twenty people whose names were called before me, were granted their request of the Governor.

Then they called my name. I was number twenty-one. I stood, and Brian and I both approached the podium. I looked each one of the board members in their eyes and read the following statement.

Good morning Governor DeSantis, Attorney General Mrs. Moody, CFO Mr. Patronis, and Commissioner Mrs. Fried. My name is Mark Cass, and I am an author, a speaker, and a serial entrepreneur, that's how I introduce myself when given

the opportunity to speak before people publicly, and that's how I wanted to introduce myself to you here today.

I am the current President and Co-Founder of Blue Grey Marketing. A digital media marketing company operating in both the States of Florida and Texas.

I am also currently a Training and Development Coordinator for Master Networks, a Nationwide group of business professionals and entrepreneurs that seek to maintain the highest level of ethical standards and strive to teach other business owners and leaders to operate each day with integrity as well.

I have previously served as a chapter President in this organization, as well as have won this organizations' Culture Keeper Award which is awarded annually to the individual that most consistently goes above and beyond what is asked and who also displays outstanding character both personally and professionally.

I was honored with that distinction at our annual convention in April of 2017. The man who nominated me for that award is named Brian Solt and he is here with me today and I have asked him to come and speak on my behalf as well.

I introduced myself this way because I wanted you to see a picture of who I am, and what my life is like today. It is not a picture you would think to see when you read my record in black and white.

I take responsibility for the mistakes of my past.
I was an adolescent with horrible judgment.
But I have never been a violent person, nor have I ever been someone with a criminal heart. I was not then, and I am not now. I have learned that I need pillars of positive influence in my life, and I actively seek out relationships with people that

can add value to my life as well as those, to whom I can add value to theirs.

That is the difference between the old me with poor judgment in the past and the me I have come to be. I have learned that who you choose to be around influences a lot of your behavior.

Today, my circle of friends includes other people of value, character, and integrity. Folks with goals and positive aspirations. I am happy to be counted as an equal among them. I am active in my church, in my community, and with my family.

I believe in this principle so soundly that I have recently opened a new business or brand called 'Up Your Averages' and under this brand I have recently written a book about my life and am starting to get opportunities to speak about my experiences and the importance of positive thoughts, positive behavior, and positive associations.

This is not a mindset that I had in 1992 when I was an adolescent. Life has come to teach me these things over time, and I now look for opportunities to share them with others.

It is my intention to be viewed as an individual who has risen up, and above, from a tragic set of circumstances, a person who has not leaned on an excuse, and as a person who has persevered, and learned to make the right choices.

My life before I went to prison, or since I have gotten out, has not been one where I have not made mistakes. I have made plenty, but I have also learned from them, and have moved on from the things that influenced me to think in ways that were not my best, and the man that I am today, is one who stands before you with pride.

I am proud of the effort that I began putting forward towards earning your favor on this day, more than 25 years ago, when I turned 21 inside a confinement cell.

It was those efforts that led me to steer clear of any more trouble while incarcerated, and to complete every educational, vocational, and college course that I could while I was in, to continue college once I got out, and to strive for the highest of ethical and professional standards, that I both now live, as well as teach.

I would very much like to participate as a parent volunteer in my children's school. I would very much appreciate not having to be denied housing any longer due to a felony conviction. I would very much appreciate the opportunity to vote in next year's election.

I would very much appreciate the opportunity to tell my children that their daddy was Pardoned by Gov. DeSantis and the esteemed members of this board. Achieving a Full Pardon, with Firearm Rights, while there is still enough left of my life for it to be beneficial, remains my highest goal. It is for these reasons that I am requesting an act of your mercy today.

I was only allotted 5 minutes to speak and I made the most of it, utilizing 4 minutes and 58 seconds. I had been practicing for weeks, reading that statement, rewriting portions of it, making eye contact, pausing for emphasis, I had it down.

I had heard Chas Wilson say once before, "Never Wing It" "Always Practice". So, I did. Again, and again. He was speaking more regarding presentations in a business setting, and never going in unprepared; but certainly, it applied here too. If my request was not granted, then it was not going to be because I went in there unprepared.

After I spoke, Brian took the podium. He spoke highly of me, of our relationship, and the position that he put me in as a Chapter President in his organization. He further elaborated about how I was a leader, and an asset to not just the Master Networks organization, but to the community as a whole. I was humbled at his words and thankful for his friendship. Once he finished speaking, I stepped back up to the podium, waiting to answer any question they had, a slight tremble in my leg and hand as I stood there waiting for the Governor's next words.

In reality, it took me longer to write the paragraph above than it took the Governor to respond. He seemed to have given something else his attention halfway through my remarks, and Brian would later confide that he never felt like he made a connection with the Governor or any of the board members as he was speaking either. Almost like their minds were made up before we ever spoke.

Immediately, upon the completion of Brian's last utterance. Governor DeSantis looked up at me and stated "Thank you, we will take it under advisement. Next." I froze!

I had imagined a million different scenarios and ways this hearing could play out and not a single one ended like this. I had put twenty-five years into preparing for this hearing. All this time, all this effort, all this preparation, and the best I could get was a flippant dismissal?

Not a single question about what happened, or why. Not one inquiry as to what have I learned or how had I changed. Not a single comment regarding my co-defendants signed, and legally notarized confession, Nothing!

Not even the closure and the dignity of a Denial. Just an answer to keep me hanging on, and full of anxiety. An answer that said, I had not done enough time, so here is one last opportunity to do a little more.

All these thoughts flashed through my mind in less than a second. I gripped the sides of the podium. I could not walk away. If I did, the Governor's response would be final.

They would be on to the next applicant and my chance would be gone, just like a vapor of steam. I could not let that happen. I had to fight, I had to argue, I had to scream out and stop this injustice. I needed to make them listen. Though my voice trembled, I finally found words to say, "What does that mean, you will take it under advisement?" "Will there be another hearing?"

The Governor looked up at me and replied, "They will let you know" and I was escorted out. That was it, it was over! Another denial and it felt like a very calloused one at that.

If you are reading this electronically, you can watch the entire thing by clicking here. If not, then then you can view the hearing and my part in it by searching for the term 'Clemency Hearings March 13, 2019,' on the Florida channel website. Mine begins at the 1 hour and 37-minute time mark exactly. I did not realize this until a friend of mine watched it and pointed it out to me.

When I asked him why 1:37 was significant? He referred me to the Gospel of Luke chapter 1 verse 37 which states "with God nothing shall be impossible."

This would bring me a small amount of comfort when pointed out to me later, but right now I was just numb. I was hurting. I was confused. I was in shock. I never expected to be dismissed without so much as a single question.

Brian and I walked outside, and I thanked him for making the journey, and for being willing to come speak for me. Then I

apologized that his trip was wasted and his efforts in vain. He shook my hand, hugged me, and told me his time wasn't wasted at all, and that he'd have happily come and made the seven hour drive all over again. *Even if he knew the results beforehand.* He did it for me because he believed in me.

Man, where were friends like this guy when I first came home? Brian has certainly helped me to 'Up My Averages'.
I remain grateful to him for this and many other things as well.

Next, I went to lunch with another friend of mine, who happened to be at the State Capital on business. *Think about what I just said.* I had another friend who was at the State Capital doing business on a separate and unrelated matter.

How many of this book's readers will have friends that routinely do business at the State Capital? I do not say that with arrogance. I say that humbly and in awe of how far I have come.

From once not even having a name, and just being identified by a number. I still remember it, 140414. I used to say it every night at 8 pm during Master Count. For a long time, I used it as a PIN for Debit cards, and anything else that required a PIN. It was my number. It had been assigned to me. I identified with it. No one else had it. At one time, that number was the only thing in life that I owned. I will never forget it.

Then one day, not too terribly long ago. I quit using it. Every time I used it, I felt like I was looking backward, and I was not going that way anymore. I will not tell you what number I use now for personal PINs, but it is not that one.

I quit using 140414 or any derivative of it for anything. I do not need it. That is not who I am anymore. I had that number for a decade, but that was it. Only a decade. Now I have friends who lead Civil Rights Political Advocacy Committees. I have friends that run businesses, I have friends that point me towards the Lord. I have friends that are Millionaires and are highly successful. I have friends that I aspire to model my life after. That's 'Upping Your Averages'.

There was a time when I did not want to be like anyone I knew. That was not this day though. On this day, I had close friends offering me strength and support in my weakest moments. One was Brian Solt. Another one was Neil Volz. Neil is a guy I am proud to be friends with. He has his own story, and it is not mine to tell. So, I will only say that he was once caught on the wrong side of the law while working as a staffer for a politician. He did what the courts required and has now dedicated his life to helping others and has been heavily involved with helping local homeless people in our hometown but has also recently found a new purpose as the Deputy Director of Florida Rights Restoration Coalition (FRRC). He was one of the driving forces behind the Amendment 4 vote in Florida in November 2018.

For those of you unfamiliar with Amendment 4. Before November 2018. Florida's Constitution banned convicted Felons from ever having their civil rights restored and as such was banned from voting, serving on a jury, or holding public office forever. *Without jumping through many hoops, waiting many years, and then only based on the whim of whatever Governor happened to be sitting in the office when their case was finally heard. If they ever even applied.*

Amendment 4 abolished that. It was added to the Governor's election year ballot and the people of Florida voted overwhelmingly to pass the Amendment allowing 'returning citizens' to have their rights restored upon completion of their sentences (Murder charges and sex crimes excluded). My buddy Neil Volz was one of the main guys responsible for that.

He was at the Capitol that day and we had lunch after my Clemency hearing. He did not talk a lot. He mostly just listened to me. As I fought back emotion and expressed my disbelief.

When he did speak, he said "You know, if the Governor had a chance to sit and have lunch with you. I have no doubt he would grant you the Full Pardon you have requested. He just does not know you. That's the problem." So **many of us are**

judged by what a piece of paper says and not for who we really are, or for all that we have done, only the worst of it.

I agreed, it made sense, but his words were of little comfort. How do I go about getting a lunch date with the Governor of Florida, I wondered? Had it ever been done before? I mean he does eat lunch, right? Certainly, members of the public could not just invite him to lunch, or could they? And if they could, would he even accept a lunch meeting with me? Probably not, nor would it matter. Once they officially denied me. It would be two more years before I could reapply, and then it would likely be another twelve years standing in line before I could be heard again. So, fourteen years at least. No telling who would be Governor then. One thing is for sure though, it would not be me. *Or anyone that I could vote for.*

Neil and I shook hands, then he hugged me tightly. Afterward, I got in my car to drive to my sisters in Atlanta, Ga. As were my plans before the hearing anyway.

So many people would want to know what happened. I had so many supporters, how could I tell them all, that nothing had happened at all?

Once I got into my car, the dam holding back my emotions burst and I just cried and cried and cried as I drove. I felt pain. I hurt. I was confused. I wondered where I was going to go from here, and how was I going to now end this book?

I rejected all phone calls, as I was unable to speak or even form words. Coincidently, you may recall that March 13, 2019, was also the day that Facebook had a worldwide outage. No one could post across their family of apps. I was without the means to communicate with anyone. All I could do was drive, feel hurt, think, question everything, feel more hurt, and then drive some more.

I was not sure if I should just give up and drive my car off the road and kill myself or continue driving on through the pain. I was still debating which was the better of the two ideas when I crossed the Georgia Line. I was on some little country road, and passed a church with a sign that I believe was put there just for me to see. "God's Delays Are Not God's Denials."
Now, what in the hell did that mean?

The thought of another delay from God in the answer to my prayer for relief and exoneration regarding this situation was maddening and more than I could bear. It just seemed cruel and unnecessary. It angered me. How dare He? How dare anyone that thought I had not served enough time or done enough penance.

My mind drifted back to the famous photograph taken at Auschwitz. A prisoner had infamously scrawled on the wall "If there is a God, He will have to beg me for forgiveness".

Can you imagine feeling that way? I did not say those words out of my mouth. Nor would I dare, but I could certainly relate to how the guy felt that scrawled those words on those walls.

WHY? WHY? WHY? WHY God? Explain Yourself!
I screamed out inside my head as I was still too overcome with emotion to speak, and my eyes were watering much too bad to drive. I was balling in my car, chest heaving with sorrow. No one knew my pain, there was no one to share it with me. There was no one that it would matter more to. There was no one to remove it. No one was there to witness as I fell apart, grabbed my steering wheel, and just shook it and screamed with angst from deep inside my soul AAAARRRGGGHHH!!!!!!!!!

Finally, out of fear of tearing off my steering wheel. I pulled over, got gas, and then just sat and stared ahead blankly. I tried to call Anisity, but I could not speak. She held the line and hurt with me, as I just cried on the phone. I was not capable of anything else. We hung up and I wondered what to do now?

I wondered what good was my life. I wondered how I was going to end this book. During all this wondering, I text Chas Wilson and told him what happened. *They had not expressly denied me. However, their dismissal amounted to as much. The official letter of denial came about 3 weeks later in the mail.*

I expressed disbelief and bewilderment and he responded with the most profound statement and the wisest set of words that I have ever heard or read. His message to me was this. Verbatim.

"I can't even imagine what you are feeling and how disappointing it must feel. The story of the last 25 years has been written. The next 25 has not! You have such a unique journey and story that very few have experienced. Feel the pain and disappointing resolutions but then get clear about where to go from here. How can you take this and make a win of epic proportions!? Continue to prove them all wrong! Make the mess your message! How to rise when all the cards are against you. Think of the legacy you will build.... that's what you'll be known for my friend!"

I started my car back up and began to drive the rest of the way towards Atlanta and changed the focus of my thoughts. Instead of 'poor me', and 'why God why'? I began to think about Chas's words and then really chew on them. I read and reread his message. There was value there. I just had to mine it and figure out how to apply it.

'Where do I go from here?' 'How do I salvage this? How do I turn this into a win? How do I then take it further and make it Epic? Man, I do not know! I was the smartest person in my car, and I did not like that. I did not know how to process this information. Or what to do with it.

'Make the mess your message' 'How to rise when all the cards are against you.' How do I do that? What does that even mean? For the next four or five hours of my drive, I pondered those thoughts. By the time I arrived in Atlanta, I was no closer to a resolution. I was still struggling with how to apply Chas's words.

I hugged my sister when she opened the door and went to bed as it was late in the evening and my energy was spent.
The next morning brought no further clarity though. I was just numb. This was the first morning in twenty-five years that I had not woken up without some type of hope for the future.

Now what? Live with it? Accept the brand, as a Scarlett letter and spend the rest of my life doing penance for a crime I did not commit? Yeah, that was going to be a big No from me. I have never been one to give up and give in to self-pity. Whatever happened and whatever would come of all this, it would not be that.

So, what then? I was not sure but the one thing I had managed to get clarity on was the fact that '**my attitude was going to determine my outcome.**' And with that thought, I went to my Facebook group 'Up Your Averages' and did a live video. Since no one had heard from me since yesterday really, no one else knew what happened. I did not want to entertain a hundred phone calls or individual messages.

Instead, I opted for a live stream video and titled it. 'Your Attitude Determines Your Outcome'. I knew this news wasn't going to defeat me. It wasn't going to make me stop. The whole ordeal had ignited a spark within me. Chas's words had fanned the flame, and I was burning with passion. Something was being birthed within me. That something had not yet revealed itself, but I knew my attitude at this juncture was crucial.

That is the message I shared with the members of my Facebook group. If I accept a defeatist attitude, then the Governor's words are final and that is the end of the story. 'Mark tried so hard but was denied. The end'. It is a shame.

However, if I allowed the Governor's response to give birth to something within me or viewed this as a metaphorical fork in the road and then began a new direction. There is no telling what kind of beauty this could lead to. I began to get excited.

Could the Governor's denial, really be a 'good thing'?
- *How dare you entertain that thought, that is blasphemous to even consider I told myself*, but Chas's words

came through anyway. "Make the Mess Your Message, how to rise when all the cards are against you". Maybe those thoughts were not traitorous at all.

Maybe the no was worth more than the yes?
- *There you go talking crazy again.*
But how? How could the Governors 'No' possibly be more valuable than his Yes would have been?
- *It is not, you are crazy, shut up.*
No, no, no, just hear me out, I told myself." Your attitude determines your outcome". I had gotten clear on that.

I worked hard to shut down the negative thoughts from my mind and just focused on using what I had as building material. It looked like a whole lot of nothing. I only had my story and that didn't even have a happy ending at this point; but I had learned from my junk removal business many years ago, that there was value in garbage.

People overlook and dismiss opportunities all the time.
I did not want to do that here. From the surface, the Governor's denial appeared to be a continued liability; but once I began to dig down deep, I saw a treasure trove of experience in my life.

I realized; I had a story that would hold people's attention. I saw that I was able to help others. I was meeting lots of new, powerful, and well-connected people. I had the materials needed to build a platform. I began to feel as if I had received the greater gift. *Though I was unable to say that out loud just yet.*

I turned it over and over in my mind. There was something there. I still could not quite identify it, but I knew something big was coming. I still had more questions than answers, and on the drive back from Atlanta to Florida, further clarity came.

A Hundred Thousand Dollar Yes,
Or A Million Dollar No

Just in real quick calculations, not based on anything specific, but just to organize my thoughts. I placed a monetary value on what would have happened had the Governor and the board granted my Request for a Full Pardon, at about 100 Grand.

I reasoned that the scarlet letter being removed was most of that value, as that would open doors of opportunity otherwise denied to ex-felons. That was valuable. I would have a happy ending for this book, and that would help sell a few copies. I would undoubtedly get opportunities to speak, and share my story: but then what? It would be over. I valued all that like I said, at about 100 Grand *give or take*.

But the No, the Governor's denial, I was beginning to see as much more valuable. Using the same line of reasoning as I calculated the Yes with. I calculated the No to be worth a Million dollars or more.

See, the No keeps the story alive. The No keeps my passion fueled, and the No keeps me working toward the goal of refiling, when eligible again. The No filled me with emotional energy that I now want to channel back into helping others.

The No brought about Chas Wilson and Neil Volz's words. Words I would not have heard had the Governor said yes. It was these words that were now fueling my thoughts.

My live stream video had received more views in 24 hours than any other video I had ever done before. Seeing that got me to thinking that maybe I should be making more of them. I could use them to build a following or a tribe. Made up of people who were interested in hearing a positive word, about business and life. Something encouraging and inspirational for people like me.

People who had struggled to overcome something in their life whether that be incarceration, addiction, a lack of business growth, a devastating heartbreak, disappointment, or loss. I had something to say to those people. I can relate. I have overcome and am happy to share how.

People were out there making Millions doing the same thing. Why couldn't I? They had YouTube channels. They authored books. They sold out arenas with crowds of people paying to come hear them speak. Their names had become national brands. Why not me? Why not 'Up Your Averages'?

What had my friend Neil said, "They don't know you, if they did, they'd certainly exonerate you." Could it really be that by helping others, I would help my own cause? I became convinced of it. Then I started thinking about starting a Non-Profit organization.

As of this writing, I have many ideas in the works that have stemmed from this line of thinking and perhaps I will write about where this new journey takes me in book Three. That is so far unwritten though because the future is ours to create new each day. I have been working on closing out this book so that I can get my story out there.

So far, I have made tremendous progress in creating an Up Your Averages Facebook group.

There are podcast plans in the works, where I will be part of a show that highlights other 'Returning Citizens' that have success stories; and doing my part to help change the narrative about those who've once been incarcerated.

There are further plans to film and create a YouTube series with me retelling each of these stories I have shared with you here and many other big things. **The list of opportunities the Governors Denial has provided me is endless.**

Will all of this ever lead to my exoneration? I do not know the answer to that. I will continue to try and use every legal means available to me to clear my name for as long as I have breath. I did not do what they accused me of, and a Full Pardon remains my highest goal. This is true, but at this point, my official exoneration is not what drives me.

I see now that my entire story is a gift. I see it as a platform that is unique to me, and I see it as a way and a means to help others.

My journey has had extreme highs as well as extreme lows both, but it's been one that has taught me to depend on God first and foremost. It has taught me that **storms do not come to block our path, but instead to clear it.**

I have learned to see the beauty in tragedy and to appreciate each day that I wake up a free man in America. I have learned that God recycles garbage, and he can take the broken mess we have made of our lives and put all the pieces back together in the most beautiful of Mosaic Fashions.

Choose better friends. Be a better friend. Eat a healthier diet. Focus on solutions. Be an encourager. Keep your word. Build good credit. Get yourself a good dog. Up Your Averages!

With that, I will end this book here with a semi-colon because my story is far from over. There is so much more to come;

Mr. Smith
June 28, 2006 – May 11, 2019

Afterward

I have traveled many miles and had many more adventures and plot twists take place in my story since the time I finished this rough draft nearly eighteen months ago. Today, as I write this Afterward - I have moved to Denver, and am now making plans to start a new business. Lots of changes have taken place in my life and I will be happy to catch you all up to date in Book Three.

In the time that has passed between then and now, I have completed two more books that I will feature on the following pages and will be published in short order after this is. I have also performed a surgery of sorts on this book based on the various forms of feedback that I have received from many people gracious enough to spend their time reading my various rough drafts.

People have reported feeling a myriad of emotions as they read. Most have enjoyed it. A few have advised me against publishing, and I held onto that advice for quite some time.

Not long ago, however, I had a conversation with someone about the various forms of feedback that I had received and explained how I was going to wait ten years or so before I published this book and they replied **"It sounds to me like you just let them people put a ten-year gap between you and fulfilling your dream. Don't wait, publish now."** I agreed. So, I am. Thanks, Cari.

Other Titles Available from The Author

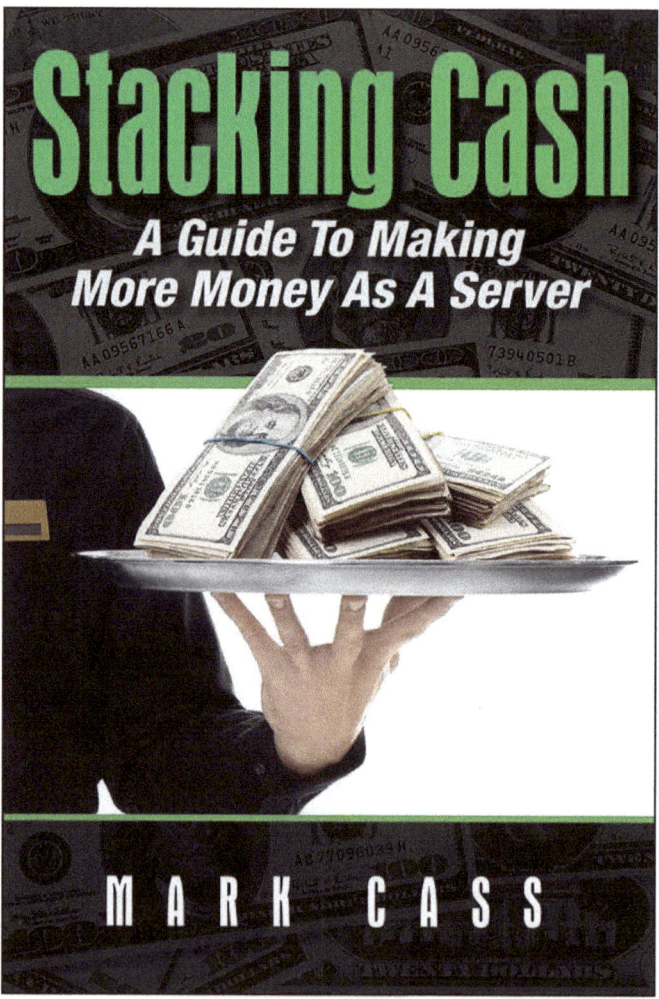

This book is a comprehensive sales and training manual for anyone working for tips in a restaurant, training servers, in positions of restaurant management.

If you are in the restaurant industry and would like to see your tips as well as your sales increase, then this book is for you. Training workshops also available. – *Available Now.*

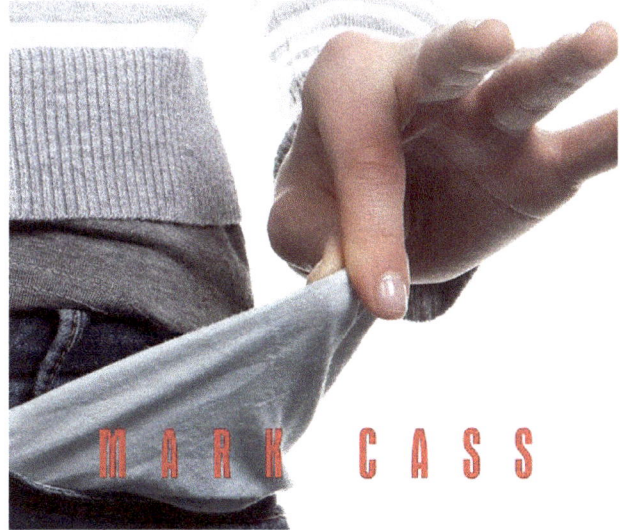

This book serves as a survival guide for those who are trying to survive paycheck to paycheck. Or find themselves running out of money before they do the month.

This book is as entertaining as it is informative. Topics include – How to fill up your gas tank for $1.00. How to buy a car with no money. How to raise your credit score by 200 points in 30 days. How to make money with your phone, and many other great money-saving ideas. *Available Next*.

This book will be my best book of all I believe. Fashioned as a daily devotional. It serves as a guide for improving the quality of your thoughts, health, business, and life.

Each day starts with an inspirational image with thought provoking commentary. Questions to ponder and goals to accomplish each day and week.

So excited to finish this one and get it to you. ***Coming Soon.***